By the same author

My Mother Told Me

Portrait of a Patriot

The Desert's Dusty Face

The Royal Malady

The Poacher and the Squire

The Western Rising

A History of Horsemanship

A History of Marksmanship

CHARLES
CHENEVIX TRENCH

GEORGE II

HISTORY BOOK CLUB

This edition published by
The History Book Club,
St Giles House, 49/50 Poland St, London W1A 2LG
By arrangement with Allen Lane, A Division of Penguin Books Ltd

Printed in Great Britain by
Butler & Tanner Ltd, Frome and London

CONTENTS

ILLUSTRATIONS

Illustration Acknowledgements

The author and publishers are grateful to the following for permission to reproduce photographs: Her Majesty The Queen for Nos 4, 14, 26; The Trustees of the British Museum for Nos 3, 8, 9, 10, 11, 13, 15, 16, 17, 18, 24, 25; The Victoria and Albert Museum for No 1; The London Museum, Kensington Palace for No 12; National Portrait Gallery for Nos 5, 6, 7, 20, 21, 22, 27; National Army Museum for No 23; The Mansell Collection for Nos 2, 19

ACKNOWLEDGEMENTS

I must first acknowledge with thanks the gracious permission of Her Majesty the Queen to use material from the Royal Archives in Windsor Castle. I am also most grateful to the late Mr Romney Sedgwick for permission to make full use of his edition of Lord Hervey's *Some Materials towards Memoirs of the Reign of George II* (1931). Mr Aubrey Newman most generously gave me hints on research into this subject. To Mrs St George Saunders of Writers' and Speakers' Research, to the staff of the London Library, and to Mrs Guy, who by now has become very expert at deciphering my handwriting, I hereby express my gratitude.

In the winter of 1680–1 Ernest Augustus, Duke of Kalenberg, sent his son, George Lewis, from Hanover to his Stuart cousins in London to try his matrimonial luck with Princess Anne. He arrived just in time for the execution of Lord Stafford, an innocent victim of Titus Oates's mendacity, and the event formed the basis of his assessment of the islanders' character. 'They cut off the head of Lord Stafford yesterday,' he wrote to his father, 'and made no more ado about it than if they had chopped off the head of a pullet.'[1] The King was affable, his uncle, the famous Prince Rupert of the Rhine, was well disposed, but the Princess was not. George Lewis and she failed to 'hit it off'. Neither spoke the other's language. He was a lout and a bore: she was a big girl, and perhaps rather sensitive about it. Someone kindly hinted to the Princess that her cousin's awkwardness was due to the repulsion which he felt for her person, and she retained a lifelong dislike for him. George Lewis returned home in the spring, in the inglorious role of an unsuccessful suitor, much to his mother's disappointment.

It was his father's formally acknowledged mistress, the Countess von Platen, who then suggested that George Lewis's other cousin, Sophia Dorothea, would do very well as a consolation prize. His mother, who disliked the Countess, thought it would be a lamentable mésalliance, but was overruled. At any rate such a marriage would follow the most approved dynastic principles. The territories of the Guelf family had been divided and reunited with bewildering frequency for the past four hundred years; but by the mid-seventeenth century they comprised, in the main, the adjoining duchies of Lüneburg with its capital of Celle, and Kalenberg with its capital of Hanover. By a fraternal arrangement between George Lewis's grandfather, Ernest Augustus of Kalenberg, and his great-uncle, George William of Lüneburg, the latter abstained from full matrimony, in order that on his death the duchies might be united. Instead, he married 'with the left hand' a Frenchwoman, Eleanor d'Olbreuse, who produced a daughter, Sophia Dorothea. What could be more sensible than to cement the Brothers' agreement by a marriage between their offspring?

It was, perhaps, a trifle unfortunate that Sophia Dorothea was selected only after more dazzling matrimonial prospects had faded. She protested vainly against the marriage, swore she would have to be dragged to the altar, and in a fit of temper hurled her betrothed's diamond-studded miniature against the wall. The couple had nothing in common. The best that can be said of George Lewis is that he was truthful and had some military aptitude. Socially he had neither graces nor aspirations: his manners were those of the army camp, his idea of a pleasant evening was a quiet game of cards, for low stakes, after a heavy supper. Although he spoke and wrote French easily, he had a very poor opinion of the French as a nation and distrusted French policies. His unprepossessing nature – in later life he was known to be cold, parsimonious, hard-hearted and selfish – may to some extent have been the result, as well as the cause, of an unhappy marriage. But clearly he was not the man to attract a young girl who was half-French in blood, wholly French in sympathy. Sophia was a brunette with large velvety eyes, a fine figure, delicate hands and feet. Emotional, mercurial, gay and shallow, she was bored by life in a petty German duchy. Her marriage to George Lewis was made easier by his frequent absences fighting the Turks or other enemies of the Empire. His periodic returns to Hanover resulted in the birth of George Augustus on 10 November 1683, and a sister, called after her mother Sophia Dorothea, two years later.

It was probably boredom rather than an amorous nature which first attracted Princess Sophia to Count Philip von Königsmarck, a Swede in the Hanoverian service, a bold, attractive scamp, a 'loose fish' who was in some disrepute because he not merely took his pleasures where he found them, which was excusable, but boasted of his conquests, which was not. They exchanged scores of letters which testify alike to their warm passion and startling indiscretion.

Why [he wrote from camp in the Netherlands] cannot I take wings like my desire? I should this moment be in your lovely arms, tasting the sweet delights of your lips . . . I am away with my thoughts, far away from the earth. If by chance an officer wants to speak to me concerning the regiment, I am furious at losing so much time without thinking of you. I hope after all these assurances that you will not ask me again whether I love you. If you still doubt it will kill me. But I must tell you that I have a consolation here, close to me; not a pretty girl but a bear, which I feed. If you should fail me I will bare my chest and let him tear my heart out. I am teaching him that trick with sheep and calves and he doesn't manage it badly. If ever I have need of him – God help me! I shall not suffer long.[2]

The need for the bear's attentions did not, in fact, arise, for Sophia Dorothea soon yielded to a wooing which must have presented a piquant contrast to the dutiful attentions of her husband. 'I slept like a king, and I hope you did the same. What joy! what rapture! what enchantment have I not tasted in your sweet arms! Ye gods! what a night I spent!'[3] Certainly George Lewis had never, on the morning after, expressed himself with such elegant fervour, nor signed his letters to her in his blood.

Unfortunately, Königsmarck was not insensitive to other charms, notably the ample attractions of the middle-aged Countess von Platen. He disengaged himself from her clumsily, and seems afterwards to have spoken of the liaison in his cups. He realized he had made an enemy of her, but was careful to make his peace with Sophia.

My greatest grudge is against La Platen, and on her I will avenge myself, for to her I attribute all my misfortunes. If I were lord of creation I would offer a sacrifice of her, and give her to the bears to eat; the lions should suck her devil's blood, the tigers tear her cowardly heart out. I would spend day and night seeking new torments to punish her for her black infamy in separating a man, who loves to distraction, from the object of his love.[4]

Madame von Platen never forgave him. She may or may not have forged the *billet doux* which brought him, inadequately disguised, to the Princess's bedroom in Leine Palace on the night of 1 July 1694. She certainly informed Duke Ernest Augustus, the father of the injured husband, of his presence there, and persuaded him to have Königsmarck arrested as he came out. He was never seen again.

Exactly what happened is not known. The Court of Hanover always professed complete ignorance. Local legend is that he was stabbed, fighting desperately, by four halberdiers while Madame von Platen stood by, and stamped on his mouth as he died.[5] Horace Walpole, however, asserts in his memoirs that Königsmarck was strangled immediately on leaving the Princess's room, and buried under the floor of the room next to hers. What is certain is that many years later some workmen renovating the palace found under the floor a skeleton almost destroyed by quicklime, but identifiable by a ring as that of Philip von Königsmarck.[6]

George Lewis neither relished nor acknowledged the role of a cuckold. Salvaging the remnants of his dignity, he arranged for a special Hanoverian Consistorial Tribunal to declare his marriage with 'the illustrious Princess' dissolved because her 'continued denial of matrimonial duty and cohabitation' was to be considered an intentional desertion. He, as the innocent party, was allowed to remarry: she was not.[7] Then, implacable, he consigned her to house arrest at the Castle of Ahlden until her death thirty-two years later.

He did not, in fact, remarry, but consoled himself with a seraglio of mistresses who solaced his middle and old age. Doyenne of these was a tall, skinny, wellborn lady named Ermengarda Melusina, Countess of Schulenberg. The picture we have of her was painted by hostile English diarists twenty years later when she had lost her hair through smallpox and wore an ugly wig and dowdy clothes. She was, wrote Lady Mary Wortley Montagu, 'duller than himself, and consequently did not find him so'.[8] But perhaps in 1694 she had been more attractive.

Next in precedence was the Countess von Platen's daughter, wife of a Hamburg merchant named Kielmansegge. She was fat, witty, well read, extravagant and oversexed. Her legal father had been chief minister to Ernest Augustus, but as her mother had been the Elector's mistress, it was sometimes suggested that her relations with George Lewis were pure and semifraternal.[9] Few believed this, though the patent of her Irish peerage later described her as *consanguinea nostra*. To confuse the issue – in a metaphorical sense – he later acquired another mistress, also called the Countess von Platen, a sister-in-law of the Kielmansegge.[10]

It was not, perhaps, the most edifying family circle for the young prince George Augustus. He loved his mother. At the time of her disgrace he was eleven years old. He never saw her again, but cherished her memory. His grandmother, Eleanor d'Olbreuse, whom he was allowed to visit at Celle, warmly resented her daughter's treatment and kept stoked up the fires of his resentment. His mother's imprisonment was no doubt the principal and underlying cause of his lifelong hatred for his father.

Compared to, say, Berlin or Dresden, Hanover was a small provincial town, hardly bursting out of its mediaeval walls, with gates that closed every night and narrow, rough streets. The palace of Herrenhausen, two miles outside the town, lay at the end of a double avenue of lime trees. It was surrounded by 120 acres of formal gardens, orangeries, terraces, fountains, statues and hornbeam mazes. Nearby were forests where deer, wild boar, hares, foxes and pheasants fell in thousands to princely guns in great drives organized with military precision.[11] He must often have seen his Stuart grandmother, Princess Sophia, striding round these grounds. She was aggressively English, tall, erect and formidable. A hearty eater and drinker, she kept her health and her figure by spending hours each day in the open, walking at a great pace, and 'perfectly tiring all those of her Court who attend in that exercise'.[12] She naturally took her son's side against her erring daughter-in-law, but got on quite well with the little boy.

George Lewis succeeded to the duchy of Kalenberg on his father's death in 1698, and to the Electorate of Brunswick–Lüneburg when his uncle George William died in 1705. He then became known as the Elector of Hanover, his capital, though he was not formally admitted to the Electoral College until 1708.

Nor was this all. In 1701, on the death of Princess Anne's last surviving child, the Duke of Gloucester, the English Parliament decided to safeguard the Protestant Succession by the Act of Settlement which declared that on the death of William of Orange the crown should pass to Princess Anne; and on her death, to the Electress Sophia, her heirs and successors.

The old lady had Jacobite inclinations, and when English envoys arrived bearing the Garter for George Lewis, and to inform her that her long-standing hopes had at last been realized by Act of Parliament, she is said to have run to the wall and stood rigidly against it to conceal a portrait of the Pretender.[13] She greatly relished the prospect of being Queen of England, and a very good queen she would have made.

Her son was more divided in his views. On the one hand he was conscoius that the ancient glories of the Guelfs were much diminished; the wealth and power of England might restore them. But he spoke no word of English and had never been there since his unsuccessful courtship of Princess Anne. There was, indeed, an insuperable obstacle to another visit. English court etiquette decreed that only the King could sit in an armchair; but by German usage an Elector could sit in one, even in the presence of the Emperor. He could not see his way round this fundamental difficulty in visiting William of Orange or, later, Queen Anne, and neither had any inclination to visit him. Besides, the Act of Settlement had imposed many niggling, not to say insulting, restrictions on the power of a sovereign of foreign birth. It dictated his religion, as though the Lutheran Church was not good enough for anyone. It forbad him to reward with an English peerage the services of any good Germans whom he might see fit to take with him to England. He might not declare war, nor even go home to Hanover for a few months without Parliament's consent. And if ever Parliament decided to impeach one of his own Ministers – a monstrous suggestion! – the poor fellow could not even be given the King's pardon for obeying the King's orders.[14] How different, how very different, from his own dear Hanover, with its *gemütlich* populace who had never cut off their king's head, who harboured no impertinent ideas about governing themselves but were placidly content, generation after generation, under the benign rule of a Guelf!

His son, George Augustus, now known as the Electoral Prince, grew up into a dapper little man, erect and well built, with prominent blue eyes, a masterful nose and jaw and a ruddy complexion. The descriptions we have of him come mainly from those who knew him in middle age, moulded by marriage, experience, and the pleasures, responsibilities and frustrations of power. It would be unwise to assume that in his early twenties he was as Hervey, Horace Walpole and Chesterfield saw him. But it is reasonable to suppose that then, as later, his 'first movements', as Chesterfield noted, 'were always on the side of justice and truth'. Horace Walpole contented himself with admitting that he did not lie often. His formal manners were excellent. 'No one', said Chesterfield, who regarded himself as the greatest living expert on such matters, 'is more exact in all points of good breeding, and it is the part of every man's character that he informs himself of first.'[15] He had, on the other hand, an irascible temper, and often said very wounding things. Perhaps this was a characteristic developed in later life. But a man who in middle age was vain and self-centred was probably not entirely free of these defects in youth.

He had the usual training of a German princeling in languages, history, military affairs and court etiquette. He had a good grounding in the classics and spoke, in addition to his native tongue, French, Italian and English. He had a retentive memory for those facts which interested him, such as genealogy, dates and the minutiae of military history and administration. But his mind had no originality, no intellectual curiosity, and was nourished neither by deep thought nor intelligent reading. 'Boetry and bainting' he declared a dead bore, belles lettres he despised as trifling. As for religion, he 'jogged on quietly in that in which he had been bred, without scruples, zeal or inquiry'.[16] His narrow intellectual interests limited his conversation to military and genealogical matters, pleasantries and badinage. He was, however, or at least made himself, interested in England, talking much with his grandmother, the Electress Sophia, and learning to speak the language loudly, fluently and with an execrable accent.

His military interests embraced a passion for uniforms, tactics, weapons and armies. He was now exhilarated by the whirr of musket-balls, the acrid smell of powder, the thunder of artillery. He longed for an opportunity to display the courage and martial genius which he felt sure he possessed.

When he reached the age of twenty-two, his marriage had to be considered. After some abortive negotiations with the Court of Sweden the electoral choice fell on Caroline, daughter of the late Margrave of Anspach. Since she was orphaned at the age of thirteen she had been brought up in Berlin by her guardians, the King and Queen of Prussia. The Queen of Prussia, George Augustus's sister, was a lively intellectual woman on whom her ward had consciously modelled herself. Caroline had shown her independence of mind by refusing a brilliant match with the Archduke Charles of Austria, allegedly on the grounds that he was a Roman Catholic. The death of the Queen of Prussia in January 1705 was a sad blow to Caroline, who had to return disconsolate to Anspach.[17]

Thither in June 1705 came the Electoral Prince, incognito, in the guise of a Hanoverian visiting Nuremberg and Anspach for pleasure. Presumably his father did not wish the Guelf family to suffer another public rebuff, and perhaps he wished to keep the whole thing from the King of Prussia, who still hoped for the Austrian match for his ward. But the secret was not well kept. Poley, the English envoy at Hanover, reported the departure of the young man, adding: 'In what concerns the Prince's own inclination in this business, His Highness hath not hitherto appeared so much concerned for the character and beauty of any young lady he hath account of as the Princess of Anspach.'[18]

The 'Hanoverian gentleman' was duly invited to cards at the Anspach court. It is impossible to believe that his disguise was not penetrated, but formally at least it was preserved. He even had a few minutes' talk alone with the young lady and found that rumour had not exaggerated her beauty, charm and accomplishments. Stricken, we are told, with love at first sight, he returned to Hanover. He was closeted with his father for two full hours, reported the diligent Poley, 'the Elector appearing afterwards in good humour'.[19] His envoy, Baron von Eltz, was then sent on a delicate mission to Anspach.

Whereas it is already known by our trusted envoy that our son, the Electoral Prince, has seen the Princess of Anspach, and is seized with such an affection and desire for her that he is most eager to marry her without delay . . . It is necessary, however, that her inclinations be assured first of all . . . Our envoy [von Eltz] must sound her as to whether she is free of all other engagements, and if so much discover if her heart be inclined towards our son.

There were two awkward points on which he relied on von Eltz's *savoir faire*.

Our envoy must mention, but not in such a manner as to suggest that the Princess of Anspach is a *pis aller* for our son, that this matter would have been broached sooner on our side if negotiations for our son's marriage had not been going on in Sweden, as was perhaps known in Anspach, the result of which had necessarily to be awaited . . . Should the Princess delay in coming to a decision, our envoy, in the most polite and delicate way possible, will remind her that he must guard in every way against the Princess having any kind of communication with the Court of Berlin until such time as this project of marriage is so far established as to prevent any possibilities of its being upset . . . Our envoy knows full well that the sooner our son is married, the better.[20]

Von Eltz was graciously received. 'Her Highness seemed at first surprised and agitated, but she soon composed herself and said that I could rest assured that she was entirely free from any engagements.'

The Electoral Prince was not exactly a Prince Charming, but Caroline was a sensible young woman, now a mature twenty-two, who knew her duty and also knew that, situated as she was, a Prince Charming was unlikely to come her way. After all, it might have been his ogreish cousin, Frederick William of Prussia. It is possible that ambition was already stirring within her. Hanover, in the scales of German states, was on the way up, and she must have known all about the Act of Settlement. With maidenly modesty she declared that she had never flattered herself that anyone in Hanover so much as thought about her. Nevertheless, she would 'infinitely prefer an alliance with your Electoral house than with any other'. She concluded, with a prudence rare in a young lady, in counselling absolute secrecy, 'as the King of Prussia took it upon himself to such an extent to command her to do this, that or the other'.

So that was that. The Margrave, her brother, agreed, and the Electress Sophia was delighted, though surprised that the matter had been kept secret from her. (She was the greatest gossip in Europe.)

In Paris, the enemy capital, Sophia's ~~sister~~ niece, 'Liselotte', Duchess of Orleans, married to a notorious homosexual, expressed approval. 'I hope the marriage will be a happy one, it started off so gaily . . . It is very lucky when such a marriage gives everyone pleasure; it is not often the case, as I know too well.'[21]

They were married on 2 September 1705.

Caroline was a remarkable young woman. At the age of twenty-two she was already known as a blue-stocking who engaged in learned discourse with the philosopher, Leibnitz. She had a royal memory, and was a shrewd judge of character. She sounds rather formidable, but in her husband's view the disadvantage of a lively mind and a gift for repartee were balanced by qualities more desirable in a wife. She was a high-coloured blonde nordic beauty and like many big women, she danced very well. (So did he.) There was nothing modest or delicate in her approach to sex, which she discussed with a freedom remarkable even in those permissive days; but if she ever erred, she was far too discreet for it even to be whispered. Poles apart intellectually, in other respects they were well suited. In course of time she was to develop a complete, if tactful, ascendancy over him. But for the time being her desire for power had no means of fulfilment. Instead she applied herself to an agreeable social life, to learned discussions with Leibnitz, to pleasing her husband and to producing a family.[22]

In this she was not as prompt as she might have been. But seventeen months after their marriage, Poley's successor, Howe, reported,

The Court having for some time past almost despaired of the Princess Electress being brought to bed, and most people apprehensive that her bigness, which had continued so long, was rather the effect of distemper than that she was with child, Her Highness was taken ill last Friday at dinner . . . and last night was delivered of a son.[23]

Although the baby was in the direct line of descent for the thrones of England, Scotland and Ireland, no representative of Queen Anne was present. Howe himself was only allowed to see the child ten days later, which he found 'unaccountable'. The father apologized: '*He* was not the cause that matters were arranged . . .

with so little respect to the Queen and so little regard to England. I think the whole thing to be very extraordinary.'[24]

The baby, christened Frederick, was to go down in English history as 'Poor Fred'. Rarely has any son been so abominated by his parents, and nobody really knows why: it is one of the mysteries of history, which politics and family characteristics are not enough to explain. Years later Lord Chancellor Hardwicke was told by Sir Robert Walpole

of certain passages between the King [George II] and himself and between the Queen [Caroline] and the Prince [Frederick] of too high and secret a nature even to be entrusted to this narrative. From thence I found good reason to think that this unhappy difference between the King, the Queen and His Royal Highness turns upon some points of a more interesting and important nature than have hitherto appeared.[25]

Frederick's only contemporary biography, written by a creature of Walpole, was destroyed unpublished. There is here the smell of a mystery, which has given rise to endless speculation, some of it turning on the circumstances of Prince Frederick's birth.

There were no official witnesses to the birth. George Augustus habitually referred to Frederick by the offensive nickname of *Wechselbalg* (changeling) or the Griffe, which is a Creole term for a half-caste. Frederick grew up yellowish in complexion, with a curved semitic nose, and the Elector had two favoured Turkish servants, Mohammed and Mustapha. The Prince's enemies – and they were many – recalled the Whig *canard* that James II's 'son' had in fact been introduced into St James's Palace in a warming-pan, and asked if Poor Fred could be a changeling, introduced because Caroline failed to bear a child or because her child was stillborn.[26] The theory has been mentioned because it would account for the extraordinary and unnatural detestation which George Augustus and Caroline felt and freely expressed for Prince Frederick. But that he was a changeling is in the highest degree improbable. Caroline was far too prudent, George Augustus far too vain, impetuous, truthful and irascible to embark on such a complicated scheme of deception for no obvious advantage. Many passages of conversation between Caroline, Sir Robert Walpole and Lord Hervey indicate that, much as she detested 'Fretz', he was indeed her son. It is even less likely that he was a bastard, for in a small German court it would have been an easy matter to dispose of a royal indiscretion; and, in any case, seventeen months after their marriage George Augustus and Caroline were still infatuated, or at least perfectly satisfied with one another. It is as certain as anything can be without independent witnesses that Frederick was the eldest son and heir of the Electoral Prince of Hanover and his wife. There is no rational explanation for his parents' consuming hatred.

As a reward for his thus securing the English succession, George Augustus was then created Baron Tewkesbury, Viscount North-allerton, Earl of Milford Haven, Marquis and Duke of Cambridge. His father would not countenance a formal presentation of the patents of nobility, but suggested that a footman bring them to the Palace. This Howe indignantly refused, and eventually they compromised on a private ceremony. Queen Anne was much dis-pleased.

Presumably the young couple were, for the first few months of his life, happy with their baby son. At all events, his marital duties accomplished, George Augustus turned to martial pleasures. For the Grand Alliance of Britain, the Empire and the Netherlands was engaged in a long war against France, the War of the Spanish Succession; and every spring the Elector of Hanover took the field. In the spring of 1708, the sixth year of the war, he was commanding the allied troops on the Rhine. By anyone unfamiliar with the House of Hanover it might be supposed that the Electoral Prince would serve his apprenticeship under his father who, though no genius, was a perfectly competent field commander and a military administrator well above the average. He determined, however, to serve as far from his father as possible and joined instead the army on the Moselle, commanded by Prince Eugene of Savoy with whom his father was at variance, at the head of twenty squadrons of Hanoverian cavalry and under the professional guidance of General Rantzau.[27]

The allied cause was at the time in a bad way. Two years after his great victory at Ramillies, Marlborough was harassed by party intrigues and antiwar agitation at home, while in the Netherlands

the French, in June 1708, secured by bribery the fortresses of
Bruges and Ghent, thus depriving the allies of their use of the
Scheldt, an important line of communication in days when roads
were so bad. But so long as the fortress at Oudenarde remained in

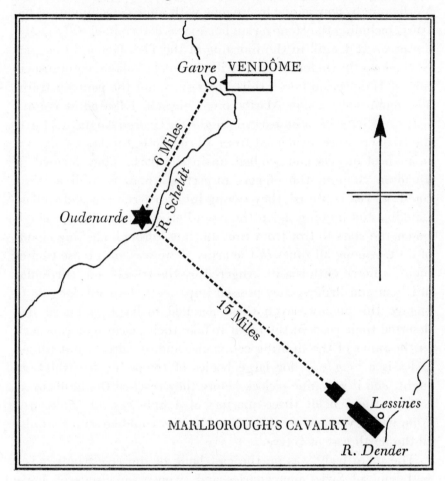

allied hands at least the French would not enjoy control of this
vital river.

On 9 July the French commander, Marshal Vendôme, a rough
and tough fighting soldier, sent forward detachments to invest
Oudenarde, and with his main army moved on Lessines, fifteen
miles south-east of it, where he intended to cover the siege. He was
disconcerted to find Marlborough already in possession of Lessines,
so he moved instead to Gavre, some eighteen miles north-west of

13

Lessines and six miles north-east of Oudenarde, to bar any movement of the allies towards Bruges. There he waited to see what Marlborough would do: already he had lost the initiative.

Although his army had two days' hard marching behind them, Marlborough (now joined by Eugene with some detachments of his army, including the Hanoverian horse) was determined still to force the pace. At 1 a.m. in the morning of the 11th General Cadogan set off along the Oudenarde road with sixteen battalions, eight squadrons of Hanoverian horse, thirty-two guns and the pontoon train. The main body, under Marlborough himself, followed at 7 a.m.

It must have been an exciting night for George Augustus. First, the troopers were awakened from a brief doze, the horses given a small feed of oats and saddled up in the dark. They formed in squadron column, the officers inspecting them as well as they could; at last mounted, they swung into troop column and walked clanking and jingling down the road. Perhaps it was light enough under the stars to trot from time to time, through choking clouds of dust. Among all ranks of the army there was an intense excitement, a fierce enthusiasm. Angered by the treacherous surrender of Ghent and Bruges, they pressed impatiently forward, longing to engage the enemy; even those detailed to baggage guard had deserted their posts in the night to take their place, against orders, in the ranks of the fighting companies and squadrons. But fifteen miles is a long way for large bodies of troops, even cavalry, at night, and it was nine o'clock before they reached the bluffs overlooking the Scheldt three-quarters of a mile east of Oudenarde from which vantage point the French army could be seen six miles to the north-east at Gavre.

The main body was on the east bank of the river: only seven battalions of Swiss mercenaries and twenty squadrons of horse under Lieutenant-General Biron had crossed to the west. Of these, four battalions had entered the village of Eyne, while the cavalry was at ease, watering, feeding and foraging – occupations which, in the opinion of other arms, always seem to take up a great deal of the cavalry's time.

His pontoon train arriving at 10.30, Cadogan lost no time in throwing five bridges across the river to supplement the two stone bridges within Oudenarde itself. Meanwhile Marlborough and

Eugene had arrived at a gallop with twenty more squadrons of horse. In an age when the accepted military practice was to plan and fight battles in exact formations and with stately deliberation, Marlborough was to force a confused encounter battle, in which all would depend on quick decision, rapid movement and seizing the fleeting opportunity.

Meanwhile the Electoral Prince was eagerly awaiting the completion of the bridges. Some of the cavalry had crossed by the stone bridges in Oudenarde, but they could not go far, in the presence of the whole French army, without infantry support. Barely a mile away were four Swiss battalions hurriedly preparing to defend the crossing of the Diepenbeck tributary stream at Eyne, and beyond them Biron's squadrons forming up in support. No doubt George Augustus viewed the scene before him with the cavalry officer's customary impatience at the costive movements of infantry, the leisurely activities of pioneers. Why could they not hurry up with those *verdamt* pontoons? Soon the opportunity would be lost.

The sweating, cursing pioneers hauled the last pontoons into position and completed the roadway over them just before noon. Cadogan led twelve battalions over, and with Rantzau's squadrons to guard their exposed left flank, wheeled to the right, deployed and moved towards Eyne. Behind them the main body of the army was passing down the road from Lessines. 'It was no longer a march,' wrote a Dutch observer, 'but a run.' In their eagerness to engage, the soldiers brusquely shoved off the track the coaches and wagons of important personages which impeded their advance.

The Hanoverian points soon clashed with Biron's patrols; there was some skirmishing, and word was carried back to Biron that an enemy raiding party was across the river. He moved up with twelve squadrons, and saw to his dismay that it was far more than a raid. Red-coated infantry was advancing against Eyne, and on the heights across the river he saw the rolling dust clouds of an approaching army. He sent back gallopers to Vendôme and prepared to fight for time. The Marshal at first could not believe that the army which, only two days ago, had been located fifty miles away was now bearing down on him. 'If they are here,' he exclaimed, getting up furiously from his picnic luncheon, 'the devil must have carried them. Such marching is impossible!'

Cadogan meanwhile had completed his preparations for storming Eyne, filling the Diepenbeck at many points with fascines so that he could cross on a wide front, and calling up four more battalions. He now, at 3 p.m., ordered Sabine's brigade to open the attack. In perfect order they crossed the brook and moved slowly forward, their

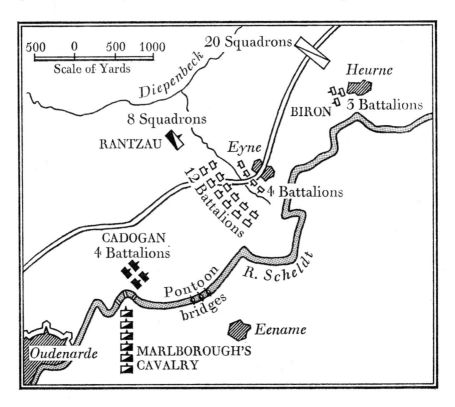

firelocks shouldered until they were within twenty yards of the Swiss. With the defenders' first rolling volleys of musketry, the battle of Oudenarde began.

The four Swiss battalions did not for long hold up sixteen British. Soon three had surrendered, and the fourth was in disorderly retreat. Rantzau's squadrons seized the village and rode in amongst them, breaking up their formations, cutting them down. At this alarming spectacle three more Swiss battalions, in support at Heurne, also fled.

Rantzau's eight squadrons, still well in hand, were now confronted in the open plain by Biron's twelve. Without hesitation,

Rantzau charged, and the French, their courage and resolution shaken by a succession of surprises and setbacks, were broken and scattered. Beyond them, and actually crossing his front, Rantzau

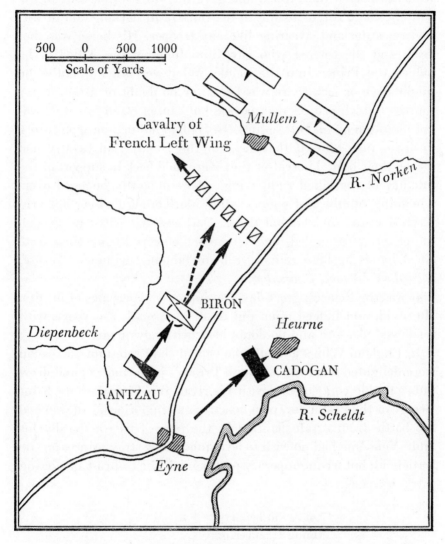

saw the whole cavalry of the French left wing. The Hanoverians' blood was up: they were elated by victory. Although heavily out-numbered by at least three to one, Rantzau charged into the French flank. There was a furious mêlée, but when twelve more enemy squadrons arrived, with a battery of guns, he had to withdraw in good order, with numerous officer prisoners, ten standards and other trophies.

It was a brilliant exploit, carried out in full view of both armies, which dismayed the French and gave the allies a fine start to the battle. George Augustus was in the thick of it, hacking and thrusting, sweating and swearing like any trooper. His horse was shot dead, and the colonel who gave him his own was killed as he helped the Prince into the saddle. Whatever other qualities he might have or lack there was hereafter no doubt of a hot, angry courage, which princes may possess but cannot often prove. It was not forgotten by his future subjects. He had no further opportunity to distinguish himself that day, for the Hanoverian cavalry had played their part. Thereafter they were held back in support of the infantry of the allied right wing, who stubbornly engaged overwhelming numbers of enemy while Marlborough's long left arm reached round and behind them. Darkness fell with the French completely surrounded, and Huguenot officers luring them into allied hands by false rallying calls of famous regiments, '*À moi, Picardie!*' '*À moi, Roussillon!*'

It was the Prince's great day, the supreme experience of his life. He could, and indeed often did recall it through the years, with unalloyed pleasure and no doubt also 'with advantages'.

In England Whigs and all who valued the Protestant succession were delighted with the Electoral Prince's performance, and drew unfavourable comparisons with his rival, the Chévalier de Saint George or the Pretender, who, inactive and inglorious, had watched the battle from a safe position in the rear. This was hardly his fault: Vendôme had no wish to be cumbered by stray princes on the battlefield; but a contemporary poet pointed the contrast in stirring patriotic verse.

> Not so did behave
> Young Hanover brave
> In this bloody field, I assure ye.
> When his war-horse was shot,
> He valued it not,
> But fought it on foot like a fury.[28]

As for the Elector, if he was proud of his son's triumph, he did not show it. He gave George Augustus neither a regiment nor any other opportunity to distinguish himself.

So the Electoral Prince returned to the bosom of his family to which was added one daughter, Amelia, in 1710 and another, Caroline, in 1713. Ever a conformist in social usage, he also took a formally acknowledged mistress – or reputed mistress, for there was some doubt, even among the cognoscenti, of whether she really qualified for this title: they may have remained platonic friends.[29] The lady he so honoured was Henrietta Howard who had, like many English people, travelled to Hanover to reserve a place on the bandwagon. Her husband was a well-born ruffian. She was an attractive, witty, sensible and kindly woman, about thirty years old, with an abundance of light brown hair, fine as silk, which she sold to defray the expenses of her entertaining in Hanover. Caroline, thinking she might be saddled with someone much worse, shrugged her shoulders and gave Mrs Howard a job in her Bedchamber. After all, for an eighteenth-century prince to keep a mistress was no more reprehensible than for a twentieth-century prince to keep a polo pony. It was the first of many occasions which were to show that, however often George Augustus was to stray from the straight path of marital rectitude, he still loved his wife, far, far better than anyone in the whole world but himself.

As for grandmother Sophia, she thoroughly approved. Mrs Howard would, she said, improve his English.[30]

If the Elector and his son had been asked their impressions of the kingdom they were soon to be called upon to rule, they would probably have agreed (for once) that it was opulent and power-ful, but rent by faction and stained by recent perfidy.

The population of England, Wales and Scotland – that of Ireland they could hardly consider an asset – amounted to about seven and a half million: Hanover's to three-quarters of a million. At the height of the recent war Queen Anne had in commission over 200 ships of war, manned by 50,000 seamen; 70,000 redcoats were serving under Marlborough in the Low Countries, and substantial forces in Spain. English merchant ships sailed the seas from Boston to Canton, and England was shortly to acquire a monopoly of the immensely profitable slave trade between West Africa and the Spanish Empire. With the wealth they accumulated, British Governments had sustained their Dutch and Imperial allies, and hired substantial forces from the smaller German states. The Elector of Hanover counted for very little in the affairs of Europe: but the moment he became King of England, he would count for a great deal.

The opulence of England was brilliantly reflected in the lives of its aristocracy, in whom George Lewis and his son would naturally be most interested, since they effectively ruled the country. The English aristocracy, old and new, did not despise trade: indeed the fortunes of many noble houses were derived directly, or by judicious marriages, from it. The grand Palladian mansions they built; their collections of paintings by Van Dyck, Rembrandt and Rubens; their great libraries crammed with classical and Renaissance learning, as well as the indelicacies of Restoration drama; the estates they neglected or improved; their formal gardens, mazes, statues and fountains; their mansions in Soho or Westminster; their coaches and hunters and gamekeepers and foxhounds, their Grand Tours and their gambling debts, their blackamoors and their Dulcineas – on all these they poured out the wealth that came, ultimately, from commerce and from rents which rose with the country's increasing prosperity. Where these proved insufficient, they must have recourse to places and pensions – to sinecures at Court or to the laborious drudgery of government. The acceptance of royal bounty they did not regard as in any way discreditable. Indeed it was, in the words of Lord Chancellor Hardwicke, 'a kind of obligation on the Crown for the support of ancient noble families, whose peerages happen to continue after their estates are worn out'.

A general election plunged most of them into a few weeks' feverish activity, animating friends, applying appropriate pressures to the freeholders in their shires, directing the choice of their pocket boroughs or bargaining with rivals for a fair share of county or borough representation. Others were heavily involved in 'business', that is to say in central or local government, working long hours at their desks or sitting up through night after night of parliamentary debate. For they ran the country. They almost monopolized the Privy Council, and the Queen hardly ever chose her Ministers from outside their charmed circle. (If she did, they were very soon ennobled.) Their parliamentary representation was not limited to the Upper House. The sons of peers, whether or not they had courtesy titles, were in law commoners, and many sat as such. Many peers were borough mongers, nearly all had great influence on county elections and accepted it as a family obligation to forward the political ambitions of their relatives. It was hardly an exaggeration for Pitt, a generation later, to describe the Commons as a 'parcel of younger brothers'. They acquired far more than their fair share of high appointments in the Church and Army, rather less in the Navy.

Yet it remains true to say that they were not, as a class, overburdened with work. They were far from being, like French nobles, drones buzzing round Versailles; but their public duties (unless they were Ministers of the Crown) seldom amounted to more than part-time work. Time, said Fielding, was their enemy; their first labour was to kill it.[1] They did so with style, setting their less fortunate countrymen an illustrious example of good taste and civilized conduct, and displaying public spirit on the comparatively rare occasions when this was required of them.

They formed a small circle. Whether as friends or enemies, they all knew one another. But theirs was not a closed circle: their sons were not peers, their grandsons were plain 'mister'. So they had family and social connections with the untitled gentry whose elevation to power in the counties had been a deliberate act of policy by the Tudors, bitterly regretted by the Stuarts. These did most of the drudgery of local government: if the Lord Lieutenant was a great noble, his deputies were probably not. Certainly the sheriffs, justices of the peace and officers of the militia, appointed by the Crown on the Lord Lieutenant's recommendation, were generally ordinary, untitled gentry. The great bond uniting them with the nobility, and dividing both classes from all others, was the ownership of land which they did not actually farm with their own hands. In the counties landownership was the touchstone of power: quite a modest freeholder had the vote, but a large tenant farmer had not. It would be inconceivable for anyone but a landowner to be a county justice. In 1711 Parliament passed a law which (though often circumvented by bogus conveyances) was intended to make it impossible for anyone but a landowner to be elected to Parliament. Even the game laws – a widespread grievance – made it a crime for anyone who did not own land worth £100 a year to shoot a pheasant, partridge or hare. For this very reason there was a constant infiltration of prosperous merchants into the ranks of landed gentry: as soon as a banker, shipbuilder or trader had made enough money, he bought land. He probably, and his sons certainly, would be accepted in county society.

The country squire of the early eighteenth century is a character well-known in fiction, admirably described by a French visitor in a work which purports to be factual:

He is naturally a very dull animal; perhaps his food is the cause of it. He eats nothing but salt beef, cold mutton, cabbage, carrots and pudding;

which last is his favourite dish and that which he likes best. His drink is ale, coarse Portugal wines and now and then a little of the strongest brandy. He drinks two favourite healths at his meals; the first is to all honest foxhunters in Great Britain, Protestant or Catholic without exception, the title of hunter reconciles them all. The second bumper is confusion to the Minister.[2]

This was no closer to the truth than the British generalization of all Frenchmen as subsisting on frogs. Squire Western was a caricature, not a portrait. No doubt some squires were very dull animals, just as were some French travellers. But there were innumerable untitled country gentlemen who led lives every bit as cultivated and civilized as their aristocratic neighbours. None the less they were, on the whole, less sophisticated, less urban, largely because they were less rich. A country squire might have learned Latin at the local grammar school rather than at Eton or Winchester, or from a private tutor; he probably spoke with a provincial accent and his clothes were made by a tailor in the nearest county town. Unless he had parliamentary ambitions, he sought urban delights in York, Bath or Tunbridge Wells rather than in London. He went to Court only once or twice in his lifetime and probably never crossed the Channel except to fight the French. But within his county he led a varied, busy and useful life. If he were a justice of the peace he would find himself trying minor offenders in his own parlour and more serious criminals in Petty or Quarter Sessions. It was up to him to see that the highways were kept in a reasonable state, and to fine villagers who shirked their four days a year of compulsory road maintenance. He fixed the rate for the support of those on poor relief, and must see that the overseers provided useful work for them to do and tools with which to do it. He supervised the village constables and kept an eye on local gaols and workhouses. He licensed alehouses, saw that orphans were cared for and issued affiliation orders. All this, with some electioneering every two or three years, occasional exercise with the militia, duties connected with the Parish Church, and improving his estate, kept the ordinary country gentlemen pretty busy. But he still found time for plenty of sport.

Stag-hunting was in most counties a thing of the past: with the destruction of England's forests, the deer too had disappeared; and in any case sportsmen of modest means had hunted the hare, not the stag. But it had recently been discovered that the fox ran faster and straighter than the hare, and foxhunting was soon to be the rage, especially where enclosures provided exhilarating runs over hedge and ditch, wall, bank and timber. Hunting was the democratic sport, since one need not, under the game laws, be a 'qualified person' to follow foxhounds or harriers. The snob sport was shooting, and the recent discovery that with light, well-balanced fowling pieces partridges and pheasants could be 'shot flying' had produced a mania for this diversion among those legally qualified to pursue it, and a corresponding jealousy among those who were not.

The country squire was, of course, just as eager as the nobleman to obtain places for his sons, brothers and dependants, though it was difficult for him to do so without some aristocratic patronage. Nepotism was considered not a vice, but a family duty. G. M. Trevelyan instances the agreeable epitaph of Mrs Elizabeth Bate, 'a woman of unaffected piety and exemplary virtue. She was honourably descended, and by means of her alliance to the illustrious house of Stanhope, she had the merit to obtain for her husband and children twelve several employments in Church and State.'[3]

Election to Parliament, preferably as a county member, was the plum, attained only by a fortunate few. There was no better lottery than the House of Commons to push one's fortune.[4] An M.P. had, in his parliamentary vote, something of far more value than mere local influence. Opposition spokesmen and historians seeking to colour their narratives have no doubt exaggerated the venality of M.P.s: but certainly those who gave steady support to the Ministry expected to be rewarded for their services, not in cash but in jobs for themselves and for their protégés. Why not? Even politicians must live, and they had no parliamentary salaries, directorships, or trade union emoluments to sustain them. Outside Westminster, the country gentlemen expected to fill the commissioned ranks in the Army, less so those in the Navy, most of the preferment in the Church and (to misapply a modern expression) the 'principal grades' in the various departments of state.

In the inheritance of land, the principle of primogeniture was strictly applied, for on it the survival and increasing prosperity of innumerable families depended. If younger sons could not be provided for by Church or state, then it was thought no shame to apprentice them to a merchant in London, Liverpool, King's Lynn or Bristol. Similarly, many a country gentleman restored his depleted fortunes by a judicial alliance, marrying no doubt for love but prudently falling in love where money was, even though the money might be derived from trade. A Dorset squire might own a wool business, the mayor of a Somerset town might live on his estate a few miles outside it. So the country gentry, distinguished as they were from the rich mercantile class by the ownership of land, yet had many family, social and financial links with them.

The provincial merchants formed a class that was increasing rapidly in political and economic power. In the county towns and sea ports they were the masters, accumulating wealth, grasping at municipal control, spreading into the learned professions, infiltrating government service. Aldermen were *ex officio* justices of the peace; they had not only private wealth, but important charitable trusts at their disposal. By these, and by their control of entry into local government jobs, they exercised in the corporate towns and boroughs almost as much patronage as the Lords Lieutenant in the counties. While in the shires the number of forty-shilling freeholders, with inflation, steadily increased, in the boroughs there was a general tendency to reduce the number of freemen by charging higher 'fines' for admission, or simply by admitting no more. So power was concentrated in fewer hands and aldermen, rich merchants all, developed into an urban oligarchy exercising a decisive influence even on parliamentary elections. They generally, however, preferred their boroughs to be represented in Parliament not by one of themselves, but by the scion of some prominent county family.[5]

It has always been difficult in England to define the boundaries between classes, though a number of minute recognition signals, perceptible only to the native, fix any person, in the eyes of his neighbours, at his exact social level. In the early eighteenth century education, culture, accent, religion and political attitudes would be unreliable guides. So was wealth. Only one thing infallibly distinguished the upper from the middle classes: the ownership of land, of substantial acreages of land cultivated not by the owner and his family, but by the horny hands of tenants and hired labourers. A squire with a modest rent-roll of £300 a year might be poorer, less cultured, more of a boor than an affluent banker, lawyer or tenant farmer; but he was upper class, they were not – unless they happened also to be landowners or the sons of landowners. Marriage, however, helped to bridge the gap. Below the upper, landowning group, innumerable gradations blurred the distinction between the 'middling' and the 'lower sorts of people', though the ends of the scale were infinitely remote. In the country tenant farmers and small freeholders, minor officials of the posts and excise departments, innkeepers, wheelwrights and carpenters and artisans of all kinds, ploughmen doing a bit of shearing, woolcarders lending a hand with the harvest, all enjoyed a standard of living higher than that of the peasant on the basic agricultural wage. Similarly in the towns, small traders and shopkeepers, clerks, masons, cabinet-makers, blacksmiths, tailors, tapsters and men of many other trades lived better than the unskilled labourer, lighterman, porter or chairman.

Defoe might claim that in the country the labouring poor 'lie warm, live in plenty, work hard and know no want'. Well, perhaps they did – in comparison to the less fortunate subjects of King Louis or, for that matter, of the Elector of Hanover. But their standard of living depended largely on the last harvest. If the price of bread was low, they had money to spare for bacon, cheese and beer – the last in formidable quantities, an average of nearly a pint a day for every man, woman or child in the kingdom.[6] The greater part of the country was still not subject to Enclosure Acts, so a ploughman or rural artisan could supplement his modest wages by keeping a cow, one or two pigs or some poultry on the common land. His womenfolk could earn a few shillings at home by spinning or weaving wool. But after a bad harvest, rural labourers were hard pressed, not far above the level of starvation or at least of malnutrition. It was a great grievance that the game laws were now so strictly enforced. Before the gentry took to 'shooting flying', a poor but honest man could enrich his diet by an occasional snared hare, or a pheasant shot at roost. Now it was no longer safe to do so.

The poor in cities and towns were generally worse off. They

were crammed into appalling slums. Although the money wage might be higher in the towns than in the country* it bought less, and there were none of the fringe benefits of country life. Much of the work was subject to seasonal fluctuations. Instead of beer, the urban poor increasingly consoled themselves with rotgut gin. In every city a large criminal element preyed on rich and poor alike. Such conditions, in the absence of any police force, produced an extremely dangerous mob, destructive and homicidal, the terror of householders and politicians alike. Few had the vote, and those who did, looking back with regret to the days of Stuart paternalism, tended to use it in the Tory interest. A surprisingly high proportion of the urban poor were literate, and avidly perused political pamphlets.

As for the non-labouring poor, stigmatized as 'rogues, vagabonds and sturdy beggars', their relief and assistance was a charge on the parish, paid for out of parish funds. Consequently the first reaction of any parish officer or J.P. confronted with one of these unfortunate wretches was to hurry him over the parish boundary, with or without a whipping, so that he became someone else's charge.

More interesting to the Elector and his son were the armed forces, particularly the Army. Under Marlborough this had been raised to a strength of at least 70,000 in a high state of 'efficiency, well-trained, seasoned by war and proud with victories, supported by a strong logistic backing. But they could hardly be ignorant of the fact that the Army's efficiency and good repute would last just so long as the war lasted, not one day more. For the hostility of British public opinion to a standing army in peacetime was not conducive either to high morale or to a high standard of recruit. A private soldier in an infantry regiment received barely sixpence a week net pay, and discipline was enforced by savage floggings; so numbers were, more or less, made up by criminals and debtors released from prison on condition that they enlisted. Still, there was always money in England with which to hire Dutch, Hessians or Hanoverians.

* It has been estimated that in 1700 the average labourer's yearly wage was £25 in London, £17 10s in the West Country and £11 5s in Lancashire (E. Gilboy, *Wages in Eighteenth-century England*, Harvard University Press 1934, pp. 219–20).

The Navy in the late war had won no great battles, for the very good reason that the French battle fleet could never match it. But the nation was proud of its ships* and seamen and did not grudge the money spent on them. Moreover even peacetime service, in the Baltic or Atlantic, kept the navy alert and well-disciplined, despite brutal treatment, insanitary living conditions, poor and inadequate food and overgenerous allowances of liquor. Sea officers' training was excellent: they (in contrast to many Army officers) really knew their profession. It is doubtful, however, if the Elector or his son took much interest in the Navy.

What above all distinguished Britain from the Elector's beloved Hanover, and indeed from every other European country, was the violence, venality and treachery of its politics. His only visit to England had been at the height of the exclusion crisis, when Charles II, manœuvring desperately for his throne, his line, and even for his life, was treated by Lords and Commons with studied insolence. Politicians of all colours freely accepted bribes, both domestic and foreign – as, indeed, did the King. The trouble was that they would not stay bribed. The English had a sort of perverse pride in being the 'most divided, quarrelsome nation under the sun'; and the most intractable, turbulent class of all was the country gentry. The country gentry and closely related aristocracy were bitterly divided between the opposition or country party which was just beginning to be called Whig, and the ministerial or Court party, which was just beginning to be called Tory. But the events of 1688 gave a shake to the political kaleidoscope. A foreign king had usurped the throne on the invitation and with the assistance mainly of Whigs, and looked on them as his friends, or at least as his accomplices. So the Whigs had become the Court party, generally in power and adopting the attitudes of a party in power.

The Tories, basing their political faith on Church and King, could not regard with unmixed satisfaction a revolution in which, to preserve their Church, they had assisted in or watched passively the expulsion of their King. Confused and uneasy in conscience, split in policies and loyalties, they had now taken on the attributes of the old country party. They unquestionably represented the

* These were, however, neither as seaworthy nor as powerful as the best French ships.

great majority of countrymen and the landed interest, but their internal feuds and bad organization were such that they could seldom win a general election.[7]

It was the Whigs who were united in their determination that, on the death of Queen Anne, the throne should not pass to a Popish Pretender. The Tories were on this vital point, as on so many others, by no means singleminded, and had expressed their distaste for a German king by introducing into the Act of Settlement those insulting sections which limited his freedom of action. The Whigs were favourable to the Hanoverian succession and the composition of their party was entirely appropriate to what would now be termed an 'establishment party'. Most of the greatest and richest peers were Whigs. The same might be said of the banking and commercial world, in which Whiggery and Dissent were both very strong. The Bank of England was a Whig creation; those great corporations, the East India Company and the South Sea Company, were dominated by Whigs although the latter had, in fact, been created under a Tory administration. Since it was the Whigs whom William III delighted to honour, and the Whigs who steadily supported Marlborough and Godolphin in the early years of Queen Anne's reign, the public mind increasingly identified them with government, placemen and pensioners.[8]

Prosperous men with established positions stand above all for stability, and stability at that time was best ensured by keeping out the Pretender and maintaining the Protestant Succession. The idea of the Whigs as radical reformers is derived from the nineteenth-century Whig interpretation of history. The Whigs on whom George Augustus looked with favour were profoundly conservative in outlook and, with some reservations about a standing army, always supported the authority of the Crown. They had opposed the restrictive clauses in the Act of Settlement. They had voted for the Union with Scotland, a measure which, because of the venality and dependence of Scottish peers and M.P.s, markedly increased the Crown's power. Whenever they could, Whig Parliaments restricted the franchise in boroughs and in London itself, so as to make them accessible to 'management'. Above all, the Whigs were far more cohesive, far better organized than the Tories. It seems likely that they were generally in a minority throughout the country, and only maintained their position against the Tories by greater party discipline and political dexterity.[9]

In the eyes of the Elector, Tories were in every respect unsatisfactory. 'If you would discover a concealed Tory, Jacobite or Papist, speak but of the Dutch and you will find him out by his passionate railing.' Tory dislike of Britain's most faithful allies had been extended in full measure to poor German immigrants from the Palatine in 1709, and would hardly be moderated in favour of rich German immigrants from Hanover in 1714.[10]

It was, naturally enough, by their attitude to the great struggle against France that the Elector and his son divided English politicians into the sheep and the goats. The Allies' main object in this war was to prevent a union between France and Spain being consummated by the accession of Louis XIV's grandson to the Spanish throne. Only the Whigs gave whole-hearted support to the war effort and to Marlborough's strategy of seeking out and destroying the main French armies in the field. The Tories were on this, as in most matters, divided. Few before 1706 actually opposed the war, but most hankered after war on the cheap, at sea and in the colonies, and were, to say the least, lukewarm towards Marlborough's great victories on land. Marlborough, therefore, and his faithful friend Godolphin, the Lord Treasurer, although themselves nominally Tories, had been forced to rely increasingly on Whig support in the face of mounting resentment by the Stuart Queen who was Tory to her backbone and lent a ready ear to the whispers and intrigues of Robert Harley and Henry St John, Tory members of a coalition government which was in fact carrying out Whig policy.

The allies were fighting to preserve the balance of power. But in 1711 their counsels were confused by the accession of the Archduke Charles, their nominee for the throne of Spain, to that of the Empire, consequent on the deaths of his elder brother and father. Obviously this strengthened the Tory case for making peace.

News of these intrigues reached George Lewis, who as a subject and Elector of the new Emperor was blind to the dangers of adding to the enormous, decrepit empire of Austria the enormous decrepit empire of Spain. He, at least, was not prepared to modify his policy of 'No peace without Spain', and still hoped to win the war by an invasion of France led by Marlborough. These hopes were shattered when in July 1713 the British government made a separate peace with France. 'A storm of anger swept the allied camp, and the veterans of twenty nations cursed England, her Ministers and her General.' By this time Marlborough had been superseded in command of the army by the Duke of Ormonde, a high Tory whose sole military virtue was courage. Many British soldiers wept for shame, and when they finally marched away from their old comrades to embark for England, 'both sides looked very dejectedly on each other, neither being admitted to speak to the other, to prevent reflections that might arise'. Allied soldiers in British pay refused to accompany them, but soldiered on unpaid.[11]

The charge against the Tory ministry was not that the country did not need peace, nor that the Peace of Utrecht was a bad one for Britain. Viscount Bolingbroke, as St John should hereafter be called, drove a hard bargain, but the terms he obtained were negotiated without the knowledge of the Allies. When he had successfully obtained all that Britain wanted (including substantial commercial advantages over the Dutch) he withdrew from the war. Thus Holland and the Empire were left to negotiate from a position of weakness. When the French negotiator asked Bolingbroke what the French should do if the remaining allies took the offensive, he replied there would be nothing to do but cut them to pieces. He further informed the French of the Restraining Orders to Ormonde while British forces were still, nominally, at war and he betrayed to them the plans for Prince Eugene's last campaign.[12] Whatever the merits of that peace, this must go down in history as one of the basest deeds ever done by an English statesman. The Commons, not without some qualms of conscience, voted for the peace; but the Lords turned it down, and it was only forced through by the creation of twelve new Tory peers. (Of these, when they took their seats, the Whig Lord Wharton asked blandly whether 'they voted by their foreman'.)

The Tories in office as in opposition, had no cohesion. They were divided into roughly three sections: The 'Hanover Tories', or 'Whimsicals', uneasily conscious that by the Tory doctrine of Divine Right no one but King James could succeed Queen Anne, thought nevertheless that a Papist king would be a greater menace to the Church than a German Lutheran. They held to the Act of Settlement. After Good Queen Anne, they would welcome Good Queen Sophy; and even her son, George Lewis – well, if not exactly good, at least he was no Papist.

The second group were the Jacobites, secret or overt, who wanted the true Stuart line to be restored in the person of James III the Pretender, after the death of Queen Anne. Their leader was Bolingbroke, who was entirely devoted to the Pretender and actively planned with the French for his return while negotiating the peace. It is still sometimes claimed that his negotiations with the French to bring back the Pretender are 'not proven'. That was the case in 1715, but the publication of documents in the French archives have since removed all doubts.

Thirdly, there was the Tory centre, larger than either the Hanoverian or the Jacobite wing, uncommitted as yet either for or against the Pretender, Jacobite when drunk, Hanoverian when sober: much would depend on whether the Pretender would renounce the religion in which he had been bred and enter the Church of England. Their leader was the Earl of Oxford, better known as Harley, Bolingbroke's colleague and now hated rival.

As for Queen Anne, no one really knows what she thought about the one question which was agitating everybody from 1713 onwards. The succession to her England after her demise was something which she preferred not to contemplate, and never discussed. She had a strong aversion to George Lewis, dating back to their unfortunate meeting thirty years earlier. For the Pretender, her half-brother, she seems to have had some family feeling, and she probably corresponded with him: but on the whole she seems to have agreed with the Hanoverian Tories that it was unthinkable to have a Papist on the throne.

One did not have to be a Jacobite to want peace: nevertheless, there was a connection between the peace party and the Jacobite party. People who longed for the restoration of the true royal line were naturally lukewarm about fighting the French to prevent this. George Lewis, by taking the lead among the minor powers determined on 'No peace without Spain' had made himself particularly odious in Jacobite circles.

Many Tory doubts were settled by 'the young gentleman' himself who in 1713 and 1714, with an admirable but impolitic constancy to his faith, refused to turn Protestant.

No one followed the ups and downs of the Jacobite cause with more interest than Sophia, who longed to sit on the throne of England. She was now aged eighty-four, but was confident that she would outlive Queen Anne and that 'Queen of England' would be inscribed on her tombstone even if she was too ill to cross the sea. '*Krakende wagens gaan lang*', she used to quote the Dutch proverb, 'Creaking carts last long'. It was her idea that, to watch his family's interests, the Electoral Prince, George Augustus, should go to London to take his seat in the House of Lords under his English title of Duke of Cambridge. His exploits at Oudenarde had not been forgotten, and he had learned some English from Mrs Howard. She wrote to Schütz, the Hanoverian envoy in London, in characteristically vigorous prose, requiring him to inform the Lord Chancellor of her astonishment that no one had seen fit to send her grandson a writ to attend in his place at the House of Lords. Obviously this was a somewhat delicate matter, on which Schütz should have sounded politicians of various opinions and which he should certainly have referred to the Queen: but he consulted only the safe Hanoverians, and never mentioned it to Her Majesty. When he applied for the Duke of Cambridge's writ to the Lord Chancellor, the latter prudently referred the application to the Queen who, primed by Bolingbroke, returned an indignant refusal.

To Hanover she wrote in her own handwriting (but in words probably suggested by Bolingbroke):

I cannot imagine that a Prince who possesses the knowledge and penetration of your Electoral Highness can ever contribute to such an attempt; and I believe you are too just to allow that any infringement shall be made on my sovereignty which you would not choose should be made on your own . . . I am determined to oppose such a project so contrary to my royal authority.[13]

Sophia was at the card table when she was handed this unreasonable and objectionable letter. She went out, very agitated, and walked up and down for three hours. Two days later, walking with her granddaughter-in-law, the Electoral Princess, she again worked herself into a state about it, and fainted. Her son tried in vain to revive her. She died only two months before Queen Anne, and thus just failed to acheive her ambition.[14]

The Queen's refusal to allow George Augustus to take his seat in the House of Lords made everyone at the Court of Hanover very angry. The philosopher Leibnitz, who enjoyed a sort of general licence to interfere in public affairs, strongly advised Caroline 'to attribute the cause of the delay to the English Ministers' public and ill-founded resentment . . . If the English Court can make the nation believe there is a dislike of or indifference to England at the Court of Hanover, it will have a bad effect.' Caroline replied warmly,

It is not the Electoral Prince's fault, or desired by all honest folk, that he has not gone to London before now. He has moved heaven and earth in the matter . . . [He has received] letters from the Queen of a violence worthy of my lord Bolinbroke. The Electoral Prince is now in despair about going to take his seat in the English Parliament . . . Never has any annoyance seemed to me so keen and insupportable as this. I fear for the health of the Electoral Prince, and perhaps even for his life.[15]

The phlegmatic Elector, who disliked George Augustus as much as ever, bore his son's disappointment with fortitude. It had not been his idea in any case. He withdrew the bungling Schütz from London, and sent the able, intelligent Baron Bothmar to give Queen Anne formal news of his mother's death. She was persuaded with some difficulty to insert his name in the Prayer Book as heir to the throne, but thought it wholly unnecessary

that one of the Electoral family should reside in Great Britain to take care of the security of her royal person . . . To admit any person into a share of the cares with Her Majesty would be dangerous to the public tranquility as it is inconsistent with the constitution of the monarchy. When Her Majesty considers the use that has been endeavoured to be made of the titles she has already conferred, she has little encouragement to grant more.[16]

The Queen was sinking fast. The legend of 'Brandy Nan' is exaggerated; she was not particularly addicted to the bottle. But she was a desperately worried and unhappy woman: her husband was dead; their numerous children all died in childhood; she had quarrelled and finally broken with Sarah Marlborough, her oldest and best friend, and with the illustrious commander whose victories had illuminated the early years of her reign; her Lord Treasurer was a wine-drenched wreck of a man who could not even hold his liquor in the royal presence, and her principal Secretary of State a corrupt libertine who did not even pretend to a Christian belief. Their unseemly quarrels were more than she could bear. She was grievously afflicted with gout and with a variety of undiagnosed maladies which added up to premature senile decay. She could not last much longer, and when she died, what next?

All men imagined the worse. Whigs in particular feared a Jacobite conspiracy embracing the Queen's principal ministers and perhaps even the Queen herself. Galvanized by the hateful prospect of a Jacobite coup, many of Marlborough's old officers began organizing their disbanded veterans for a countercoup. He himself, still in self-imposed exile in Holland, arranged with the Elector that on the Queen's death he would immediately proclaim King George I to the British troops in Holland and lead them across the North Sea to safeguard the Protestant Succession. He even offered his future sovereign a loan of £20,000.

On the morning of 30 July the Queen was plainly dying, and a meeting of the Privy Council was called. But it was a packed meeting, with a disproportionate number of Jacobites and only three resolute Hanoverians. While they were waiting on the inevitable event, two more councillors arrived who had not been sent notice of the meeting, yet had a perfect right to attend, the Dukes of Argyll and Somerset. It is thought that Shrewsbury had tipped them off. These three dukes, Shrewsbury, Somerset and Argyll, were steady champions of the Protestant Succession. They represented not just the landed interest, nor the moneyed interest, nor Whigs nor Tories, but the nation at large, concerned not for party advantage, but the realm, the constitution and the Protestant religion. In their strong presence Bolingbroke lost his nerve and the half-formed resolutions of the Jacobites wilted. On Bolingbroke's own motion, the Council unanimously agreed to 'move the Queen that she should constitute the Duke of Shrewsbury Lord Treasurer'. It was found that 'Her Majesty was in a condition to be spoke to'.

Probably the Council's recommendation coincided with what, in the circumstances, she would herself have wished to do. 'The Queen about one o'clock gave the Treasurer's staff to the Duke of Shrewsbury, my Lord Chancellor holding her hand to direct it to the Duke.'[17]

As though they had never contemplated anything else, the Tory Ministry proceeded systematically to implement the Act of Settlement and safeguard the Protestant succession. Troops were ordered home from Flanders and those in home stations were alerted; lords lieutenant, fortress governors and officers commanding armies and fleets were warned; the militia was embodied, and regular units concentrated round London; the Dutch were reminded of their treaty obligations; an embargo was placed on shipping; prominent suspects were relieved of their horses and arms. It was a sustained effort of efficient administration, and by one of the ironies of history it was Bolingbroke, the Jacobite Tory, rather than Oxford, committed to Hanover, who presided over it.

The remaining Jacobites were confused and ineffective. In a secret meeting held on 1 August 1714, the morning of the Queen's death, Atterbury, Bishop of Rochester, was the only one ready to risk his neck, undertaking that he would at the Royal Exchange read, in his lawn sleeves, the Proclamation of King James III.

Upon this Lord Bolingbroke said that all our throats would be cut. To which the Bishop replied that, if a speedy resolution be not taken, by God all will be lost. Lord Bolingbroke harangued upon this subject, and the Bishop fell into a great passion and said that this pusillanimous fellow would ruin our country; so he quitted them.

'Never,' he declared, 'was a better cause lost for want of spirit.' But Bolingbroke was a politician, with a keen sense of what was possible. In the present state of the country, he said, 'England would as soon have a Turk as a Roman Catholic for King.'[18]

Instead they had George Lewis, Elector of Hanover, proclaimed as King George the First. Primed by Bothmar, he sent to London a list of notables, four Hanoverian Tories and fourteen Whigs, to act as regents until his arrival. Bolingbroke was dismissed from office by a curt note which shocked him, he said, 'for at least two minutes'.[19]

It was not without misgivings that the Elector and his Court contemplated the greatness now thrust upon them. We are inclined to divide English history into compartments labelled 'Seventeenth century: Age of Revolution' or 'Eighteenth century: Age of Stability'. But in 1714 people did not feel it was conspicuously stable. There were plenty of men still alive who as adults had seen Charles II's Restoration. Any middle-aged man would have a clear recollection of Monmouth's Rising and the Glorious Revolution. Old Scrope, Secretary to the Treasury, had fought for Monmouth at Sedgemoor. The elderly ex-mistresses of Charles II, James II and William III, now bearing the titles of Portsmouth, Dorchester, Orkney, used to meet at Court. 'Who would have thought,' said the last, 'that we three old whores would meet here.' To us the Glorious Revolution was England's last violent upheaval, but to the men of 1714 it was only the most recent.[20]

Even more apprehensive were the new King's ladies. Baroness von Schulenberg was sure they would all have their heads chopped off in the first fortnight, though George, again well briefed by Bothmar, assured her, 'All the king-killers are on my side.' The Kielmansegge, eager to better her finances in England, was at first detained in Hanover by debts which her protector ungallantly refused to meet. Eventually she left the town in disguise and both ladies made their way to the Promised Land.[21]

The King entered upon his inheritance without noticeable pleasure.
After a rough crossing, he was further delayed by fog, and the ship
wallowed off shore for several hours while the passengers longed
only for release. At six o'clock in the evening of 18 September
1714, he disembarked, tired and cross. In no mood for courtesies,
ceremonies and speeches, he went off to bed.

Next day he met the regents who had been acting for him.
Marlborough was there, home from exile. Although England's
greatest soldier had never shown much appreciation of Hanover's,
he was granted a full hour of the King's time and reappointed
Captain-General. Ormonde was notified of his dismissal, received
no supper invitation, and departed in a huff. 'Here,' announced
the Lord Chamberlain, 'is the Earl of Oxford, of whom Your
Majesty will have heard.' Oxford was given a royal hand to kiss, a
glance of contempt and a silent snub as the King turned to talk
to someone else.[1]

The move to London was made with pomp and ceremony, the
King and his son travelling in a coach escorted by the Life Guards
and preceded by some two hundred coaches of the gentry and
nobility, each with six horses, in reverse order of precedence. At
Southwark they were met by the Lord Mayor and civic dignitaries,
and drove on through the crammed, beflagged and decorated
streets. 'The royal pomp continued until his arrival at the palace
of St James's, and was favoured by as fair a day as was ever known
at that season of the year.' A million and a half of George's new

subjects, from London and Kent, travelled out to watch the show, huzzaing not so much for the Elector of Hanover, as to express their relief that there was to be no disputed succession, no civil war. The law had prevailed, albeit in a somewhat unlikeable guise.[2]

The countenance the Londoners saw, framed in a dark periwig, was commonplace. A big nose, an ugly mouth, a surly expression showed no liveliness or interest. George I's eyes, slightly bulging, were dull and vacant; he bowed to the cheers, but did not permit himself a smile. His son, all smiles, was not permitted to bow. Their mutual dislike was well known, for Hanover had for weeks been swarming with English visitors eager for early access to the loaves and fishes.

The day after his arrival in London, in words which must almost have choked him, the King formally invested with the title of Prince of Wales 'our most dear son, a Prince whose eminent filial piety hath always endeared him to us'. On 15 October the Prince's wife, Caroline, arrived with their two daughters, Amelia and Caroline. Their only son, Frederick, was left behind like an unwanted puppy in Hanover, to be looked after by tutors and lackeys. The seeds of resentment thus sown were to bear bitter fruit.

It is reasonable to suppose that in the nine years since George Augustus's marriage his character had both developed and hardened. Aged thirty-one, he probably had no very clear memory of the mother he had loved as a child and not seen since he was twelve. But it is known that he secretly treasured her portrait which, with his distant childhood memories, stoked up his resentment against his father, who had deprived him of her love. Rigorously excluded from the smallest share in the government of Hanover, denied even a modest military command, he could indulge only in his own passion for order, regularity and routine, and had become in consequence somewhat of a domestic tyrant, 'looking upon all men and women he saw as creatures he might kick or kiss for his diversion'. 'Whenever he met with any opposition to his designs, he thought the opposers insolent rebels to the will of God.' In public business his designs had been constantly opposed, or, rather, he had been allowed no designs of his own. It would be natural to work off his frustration by hectoring those who had to obey him.[3]

No sense of discretion moderated his fiery temper and sharp tongue, and the most convenient scapegoat was generally his wife, whom he bullied mercilessly while never ceasing to adore her and look upon her as 'the most meritorious of her sex'. He liked to preen himself as a man of pleasure, a great lover, even a sexual athlete; he usually had a mistress or two and regarded any attractive lady at his court as a candidate for that honour. He even fancied Lady Mary Wortley Montagu, surely an unpromising subject, and once in rapture he called his wife from her card-table to see how becomingly the lady was dressed.

'Lady Mary always dresses well,' replied Caroline drily, and returned to her cards.[4]

But these casual infidelities had no effect on his passion, physical and emotional, for his Junoesque Princess. Undoubtedly she had, in every sense of the expression, 'a lot to put up with'. But she found her compensation in the knowledge that, despite all his blustering, she generally got her own way. Lady Mary, who seldom failed to put things at their worst, wrote that

she had that genius which qualified her for the government of a fool, and made her despicable in the eyes of all men of sense; I mean a low cunning, which gave her an inclination to cheat all the people she conversed with and often cheated herself . . . She counterfeited an extravagant fondness for his person.[5]

On this one can only comment that Caroline's fondness for her husband's dapper little person, although unclouded by illusions, was probably quite sincere; and she was certainly not despicable in the eyes of all men of sense. Indeed a Dutch diplomat reported on her arrival in London that she 'discusses the most important questions in a judicious manner such as is rarely found in a woman'.[6] During forty years of married life, their relationship changed and developed. We must beware of applying to the year 1714 comments made by Hervey and Chesterfield twenty years later.

At least the Prince and Princess had taken the trouble to learn English. He spoke it loudly and fluently, with much gesticulation and an atrocious accent. London society appreciated this, and within a few days of the Princess's arrival Peter Wentworth, a page at Court, was writing to his cousin, Lord Strafford,

I find all backward in speaking to the King, but ready enough to speak to the Prince . . . The Princess came into the drawing-room at seven o'clock and stayed until ten. There was a basset table and ombre table, but the Princess sitting down to picquet, all the company flocked about to that table and the others were not used.[7]

The Coronation, on 20 October, produced the usual crop of comic incidents to enliven its solemn splendour. Since George was crowned King of France, as well as of England and Ireland, two hired play-actors represented the dukedoms of Picardy and Normandy. The Archbishop, addressing in turn the north, east, south and west, called out in the time-honoured form, 'Sirs, I here present to you George, your undoubted King. Wherefore all you who are come this day to do homage, are you willing to do the same?' It could have been an awkward moment if any Jacobites had chosen to make trouble; but, as Lady Dorchester, James II's old mistress, remarked, 'Does the old fool think anyone will say "No" to his question, when there are so many drawn swords?' In the event, no one did. Instead, they cried 'God save the King!' and all the trumpets blared.

The Earl of Nottingham's position was shaky under the new regime, since, though a supporter of the House of Hanover, he was a Tory and a High Churchman. His wife, a woman of exemplary piety and an enormous family (can she really have borne thirty children?) thought the Coronation an occasion to display her loyalty. At the start of the Litany 'she broke from behind the rest of the company where she was placed, and kneeled down before them all (though none of the rest did) facing the King and repeating the Litany. Everyone,' wrote the Whig, Lady Cowper, 'stared at her and thought she overdid the High Church part.'

Of this splendid ceremony the central figure understood not one word. But he understood well enough when Bolingbroke did homage. Seeing a face he did not know, the King asked who it was; and Bolingbroke, 'hearing it as he went down the steps of the throne, turned round and bowed three times to the very ground'.[8]

The Coronation was closely followed by the Lord Mayor's Show. The Lord Mayor, Sir William Humphreys, was an amiable vulgarian, whose wife, 'My poor Lady Humphreys made a sad figure in her black velvet and did make a most violent bawling to her page to hold up her train before the Princess, being loth to lose the privilege of her mayoralty'. It seems that the Hanovers were becoming socially accepted, enough at any rate for them to be the object of a mild practical joke; for 'the greatest jest was that the King and Princess had both been told that My Lord Mayor had borrowed her for that day only'.[9]

In forming his new Government his Majesty did not lack advice. Lord Cowper, a reliable Whig with Tory and even Jacobite family connections, favoured him with one *Treatise on the State of the Parties*, and Bothmer, while he was still in Hanover, with another. Naturally he relied mainly on the latter for sound and impartial advice.[10]

Here a disquisition is necessary into the development of the cabinet system. There were three overlapping councils with names which are confusingly similar. There was the Privy Council: but this was no longer what its name implied, since by Queen Anne's reign it included some eighty members of all parties and shades of opinions. Its functions were purely formal: pardons, for instance, and certain proclamations could be issued only by the King in Council, that is to say in Privy Council. William III had distilled from this amorphous body one of about fifteen Ministers and Household dignitaries, over which he presided, to discuss and decide policy: this was known as the Cabinet Council or, simply, Cabinet. But it was still too large, in the absence of a strong chairman such as William III, for policy-making. Queen Anne was not a strong chairman. Her health and her intellectual limitations alike precluded her from lengthy discussions of policy and the minutiae of administration. The custom therefore developed in her reign of the eight principal members of the Cabinet – the Lord Treasurer, Lord Chancellor, Lord Privy Seal, Lord President of the Council, two Secretaries of State, Chancellor of the Exchequer, and First Lord of the Admiralty* – meeting on their own, without the Queen, as a committee of the Cabinet, to discuss and formulate

* But the membership was fluid, informal and variable.

42

policy, which would then be submitted as their unanimous recommendation to the full Cabinet over which the Queen presided. In the interests of clarity these three bodies will be known henceforth as the Privy Council; the Cabinet; and the Cabinet Committee or Inner Cabinet.*

Everything depended, wrote Bothmar, on the selection of the great officers of state and Household, about eight in number, who formed the Cabinet Committee. William III, having made a bad selection at the beginning of his reign, no doubt from lack of sound impartial advice, was plagued by party squabbles throughout his reign. George I must not make the same mistake. He must choose his Ministers 'without regard to whether a man be Whig or Tory', solely according to merit, loyalty and fitness for office. But these criteria naturally excluded from consideration all who, serving in the previous Government, had disgusted the nation, 'turned everything upside down and maliciously endangered the peace of Europe', solely in order to exclude his Majesty from the throne. It must, therefore, be a Whig Government, though one or two well-affected Tories might perhaps be included, such as ran no risk of impeachment by the Whigs for their part in the disgraceful peace treaty.[11]

The key positions were the Lord Treasurer who controlled the country's finances, and the two Secretaries of State. The last were 'maids of all work', the linch pins of any administration. Foreign affairs, strategy, law and order, liaison between different departments were all their responsibility. They were the channels through which the royal will was directed; they drafted and signed executive orders to ambassadors, military and naval commanders, colonial governors, the lords lieutenant of Ireland and of the shires, justices of the peace and mayors. In state prosecutions for seditious libel or treason it was they who customarily issued warrants of arrest and examined witnesses. Their duties were inconveniently and irrationally divided between the Northern Department responsible for, among other tasks, all the countries with coastlines on the Baltic and the North Sea; and the Southern Department, the responsibilities of which included Ireland, France, the colonies and

* It was also known as the Lords of Committee, and sometimes even as the Cabinet Council, a term properly applied to the full Cabinet.

all countries around the Mediterranean. Internal affairs – law and order, instructions to lords lieutenant, J.P.s and sheriffs – they shared. Their external duties, too, often overlapped, particularly when one Secretary accompanied the King to Hanover or was more forceful and diligent than the other.

In what might almost be termed Bothmar's administration the Lord Treasurer was the Duke of Shrewsbury, and the Secretaries were Viscount Townshend for the Northern Department and James Stanhope for the Southern. Offices of less importance though still conferring on their holders the right of attendance in the Inner Cabinet, were bestowed on Lord Cowper (Lord Chancellor), the Marquess of Wharton (Lord Privy Seal); the Earl of Nottingham (Lord President of the Council); Sir Richard Onslow (Chancellor of the Exchequer) and the Earl of Orford, a naval officer (First Lord of the Admiralty). Soon after his arrival in England the King was persuaded by Bothmar to place the office of Lord Treasurer in commission, lest its holder become a sort of *de facto* prime minister, 'troublesome for the King himself'.[12] Shrewsbury was then made Lord Chamberlain and the office of First Commissioner for the Treasury was bestowed on the Earl of Halifax.

These men – Townshend, Stanhope, Cowper, Wharton, Nottingham, Onslow, Orford and Halifax – comprised the Cabinet Committee or Inner Cabinet. Shrewsbury and Nottingham were recommended by Bothmar as safe Hanover Tories. The remainder were Whigs, even safer.

There was, of course, a scramble for lesser places in the Ministry and in the Household. 'The Ministry,' commented Lady Mary Wartley Montagu soon after the King's arrival,

is like a play at Court. There's a little door to get in and a great crowd without, shoving and thrusting who shall be the foremost; people who knock others with their elbows, disregard a little kick of the shins, and still thrust heartily forward, are sure of a good place. Your modest man stands behind in the crowd, is shoved about by everybody, his clothes tore, almost squeezed to death, and sees a thousand get in before him that do not make so good a figure as himself. I do not say it is impossible for an impudent man not to rise in the world; but a modest merit, with a large share of impudence, is more probable to be advanced than the greatest qualification without it.[13]

'A modest merit, with a large share of impudence': that, in the eyes of his numerous detractors, might well have described Robert Walpole who barged through the scrum to secure the obscure but lucrative office of Paymaster to the Forces, with the undisputed right to invest for his own profit the undisbursed balance of the forces' pay. A bawdy, bucolic Norfolk squire, he had shown himself a competent administrator as Secretary at War in the days of Marlborough's supremacy. After the Tory triumph in 1710, he had suffered for his Whiggery by imprisonment in the Tower on a charge of peculation. His present appointment, like all others at the lower levels, was made mainly with an eye to the general election which must take place at the start of a new reign.

George I has been criticized for not including more Tories in his first administration. Tories were, after all, in a majority in both Houses of Parliament, and probably in the country as a whole. While no one denied that the King had an unrestricted right to choose whom he liked as his Ministers, it was obviously prudent to choose those who could harmonize the Crown's policies with the prejudices of Parliament, particularly of the Commons because of their control over taxation. Such a sensible observer as the Duke of Berwick* thought that by bringing more Tories into the Inner Cabinet, George I might have united his people.[14] But the very fact that Tories had a majority in both Houses made the King and Bothmar reluctant to take a chance on their loyalty. It seemed wiser to keep power in Whig hands until the general election, which should effectively ensure a Whig majority. After all, Lord Cowper told the King, it was solely up to him to decide 'who shall have the chief share in his confidence', and it was wholly in his power 'by showing favours in due time', to procure a parliamentary majority.[15]

Parliament was dissolved on 5 January 1715, and the King's proclamation for the ensuing election read more like a party manifesto. Voters were urged to choose 'such as had shown firmness to the Protestant Succession when it was in danger'. This clear

* James II's illegitimate son by Arabella Churchill, and so Marlborough's nephew. He accompanied his father into exile and became a distinguished Marshal in the French Army.

indication of the royal wishes, together with the exertions of the Secretaries of State and other Whig Ministers and magistrates, turned a Tory majority of 152 into a Whig majority of, by a curious coincidence, 152, later strengthened by Whig victories over several election petitions. The change was most marked in those areas where Treasury influence could most easily be brought to bear: of the 141 Whig gains, 112 were in the easily manipulated English boroughs. In the English counties and other constituencies with large numbers of voters, the Tories generally held their own, and it is not improbable that there was over the whole country an overall Tory majority, though we only have details of about a third of the votes cast.[16]

The Whigs now proceeded with zest to the rout of their enemies, especially Bolingbroke, Oxford and Ormonde, whom it was decided to impeach for treason. Bolingbroke lost his nerve: believing, as a result of a politic hint from Marlborough, that his neck was in danger, in March he slipped out of his box in the middle of a play and departed to France disguised as a valet. He had, in fact, overestimated the emergency which so stirred him, since his enemies were in possession of no evidence which could possibly bring him to the block. All he risked by staying was a few months of comfortable incarceration in the Tower, whereas by fleeing he ruined his political career for ever. Oxford displayed more courage and dignity by staying to face his accusers. He was held for two years in the Tower, and then released for lack of evidence.

From all these political measures the Prince of Wales was rigorously excluded. He sat, with his father, at full Cabinet meetings, but so did the Master of Horse, the Groom of the Stole, the Master of the Wardrobe, the equerries and all manner of Household understrappers. No important discussions took place at these meetings: they were called merely to give formal endorsement to decisions made by the Cabinet Committee, sitting, as in the days of Queen Anne, without the sovereign and, of course, without the Prince of Wales. There was no recent precedent for an heir to the throne who was the King's eldest son and himself father of a family. Except as a social figure he had no part to play in public life, not even in 1715 when the Jacobite rebellion directly threatened his line.

The Pretender's Court at Plombières in Lorraine* had, since the death of Queen Anne, been busy as bees, but far less effective. On 29 August 1714 he complained in a royal proclamation to his 'loving subjects' that:

Contrary to our expectation upon the death of the Princess, our Royal sister, of whose good intentions toward us we could not for some time well doubt, and which was the reason we then sat still, expecting the good effects thereof, which were unfortunately prevented by her deplorable death, we found our people, instead of taking this favourable opportunity of retrieving the honour and true interest of their country by doing us and themselves justice, had immediately proclaimed for their King a foreign Prince, to our prejudice contrary to the fundamental and incontestable laws of hereditary right, which their pretended Acts of Settlement can never abrogate. After this height of injustice, we thought ourselves bound in honour and duty so indispensably obliged by what we owe to our self, to our posterity, and to our people, to endeavour to assert our right in the best manner we could; accordingly upon the first notice sent to us we parted from our ordinary residence, in order to repair to some part of our dominions, and there to put our self, at the head of such of our loyal subjects as were disposed to stand by us and defend us and themselves from all foreign invasions; but in our passing through France to the sea-coast, we were there not only refused all succour and assistance, upon account of the engagement that Monarch is under by the late Treaty of Peace, but we were even debarred passage and obliged to return back to Lorraine.[17]

However, since this proclamation was issued James Edward's prospects had sensibly brightened. Many of his 'loving subjects' had become disenchanted with the Hanoverian usurper: there had been Jacobite riots in London, Oxford and the Midlands. The French government was being more cooperative, even allowing the bags of the French ambassador in London to be used for the transmission of correspondence between the Pretender and his adherents in Britain. But the Jacobite cause suffered from two fatal weaknesses. The first was the refusal of James Edward to abandon his own faith, or even to give what Anglicans considered adequate guarantees for his toleration of theirs. The second was the

* By the terms of the peace treaty of 1713 he was not allowed to reside in France.

uninspiring character of the Pretender himself and the mediocrity of his principal advisers.

This was to some extent remedied in July 1715 by the arrival in Paris of Bolingbroke,[18] who accepted office as the Pretender's Secretary of State. Being well informed of the situation in Britain he urged James Edward to rely on 'the purse and strength of England' rather than on the windy promises of Scottish and Irish Jacobites. He was not, however, the most discreet of men, and the Jacobite plans became common knowledge almost as soon as they were made, probably through Bolingbroke's mistress, a high-class Parisian prostitute. The main effort, commanded by Ormonde, was to be in the south-west of England, the scene, ironically enough, of Monmouth's rebellion, the last stirring of 'the Good Old Cause' of republicanism and dissent against James II. The Scottish rebellion, under the Earl of Mar, was to be a mere diversion.[19]

The British Government, informed of all these preparations by its able envoy in Paris, took the obvious precautions. Twenty-one new regiments were raised, garrisons were established in Bath, Oxford, Bristol and Plymouth; the Channel Fleet was put on the alert. *Habeas corpus* was suspended and a number of known Jacobites, including five M.P.s and two peers, were put temporarily out of circulation. The lords lieutenant were ordered to requisition horses and to put the militia into 'such a posture as to be in readiness to meet upon the first orders'. Papists, non-jurors and such disaffected persons were put under house arrest, disarmed and deprived of their horses. But the heaviest blow to the rebellion was the death of Louis XIV, which occurred on 1 September. His successor was a child, and the Regent, the Duke of Orleans, was by no means disposed to exert himself and risk a renewal of the war in the Pretender's cause.[20]

The country as a whole took the emergency lightly:

> God bless the King! God bless the Faith's Defender!
> God bless – no harm in blessing – the Pretender.
> But who Pretender is, and who is King,
> God bless us all! That's quite another thing![21]

And the country as a whole was right. The main Jacobite effort fizzled out. In Scotland and the English border counties there were premature, uncoordinated risings of some Highland clans, some Lowland peers and some impoverished country gentry, but they were badly led. These forces were quickly rounded up and the southward advance was checked.

Characteristically arriving on the scene three months too late, the Pretender established his Court at Perth. 'My whole life,' he informed his subjects, 'even from the cradle has shown a constant series of misfortunes, and I am prepared, if so it please God, to suffer the threats of my enemies and yours.' It was hardly a speech to rouse Macdonalds and Camerons to fighting fury, and a Jacobite officer afterwards recorded:

I must not conceal from you that when we saw the man whom they called our King, we found ourselves not at all animated by his presence, and if he was disappointed in us, we were tenfold more in him. We saw nothing in him that looked like spirit. He never appeared with cheerfulness and vigour to animate us. Our men began to despise him; some asked if he could speak. His countenance looked extremely heavy. He cared not to go abroad amongst us soldiers to see us handle our arms and do our exercise.

On 2 January 1716 he started his march towards England. He was acclaimed at Dundee and half-hearted preparations were made for his coronation. But on rumours that Argyll was advancing against him, his Council debated all night but could not decide whether to advance or retreat.

'What would you have us do?' a councillor asked the crowd in the street.

'Do?' replied an angry Highlander. 'What did you call us to arms for? Was it to run away? What did the King come hither for? Was it to see his people butchered by hangmen? and not to strike one stroke for our lives? Let us die like men and not like dogs.'[22]

But James Edward was not the man to lead a forlorn hope. With his army seeping away like a river in a desert of sand, on 9 February he packed his bags and slipped off to France. He had already quarrelled with his very able half-brother, the Duke of Berwick. Now he sent for Bolingbroke and received him graciously: 'No Italian ever embraced the man he was going to stab', wrote Bolingbroke,

49

'with a greater show of affection and confidence.' Next day he sent Ormonde with a message dismissing the man whom Berwick described as 'the sole Englishman capable of managing his affairs'. Lord Stair, the British envoy in Paris, was not without sympathy for the fallen Lucifer. 'They use poor Harry most unmercifully, and call him knave and traitor and God knows what. I believe all poor Harry's fault was, that he could not play his part with a grave enough face; he could not help laughing now and then at such kings and queens.' Bolingbroke himself said he hoped his arm would drop off and his brain fail if he ever again devoted either to the Stuart cause.[23]

Lady Cowper saw some of the rebel prisoners led through the streets of London to the Tower. Their arms were tied and their horses, without bridles, were led. The mob insulted them, carrying-warming-pans and saying a thousand barbarous things 'which some of the prisoners returned with spirit'.[24] Seven peers were brought to London to stand their trial, thereby causing the Government considerable embarrassment.

While the Pretender cut such an unheroic figure, it might have been thought that his rival, 'Young Hanover Brave', might have been given the chance to do rather better. But nothing of the sort occurred. Instead, the King took the rebellion as a chance to humiliate his son. The Prince may not have been a military genius, but he had shown himself at Oudenarde perfectly capable of performing an officer's basic duty, that of riding in front of his men and getting shot at first. It would, of course, never do for the heir to a precarious throne to be cut down by a bare-bummed Highlander; but some field command could surely have been found in which he could lose neither his own life nor too many of his men's, and the dividends in popularity would have been enormous. Instead he spent the months of crisis in inglorious ease at St James's.

The fact was that the Prince's popularity was already causing his father a good deal of concern. To those whose opinion of George Augustus is formed by unflattering accounts of his middle age this may seem a surprising statement. Perhaps his popularity was only relative, for the King was undeniably dull, and the elderly men and women whom he liked to see at Court did not exactly sparkle. Moreover the King could do no right. When, to celebrate his birthday, he issued the Guards with brand new uniforms, they complained that the excellent shirts were too coarse, and wore them outside their breeches, inviting Londoners to 'see our Hanover shirts'. He complained of well-established customs which did no harm and were designed to sweeten and ease his relations with his subjects. 'I must give five guineas to Lord Chetwynd's man for bringing me my own carp, out of my own canal, in my own park.'

Parsimony is unbecoming in a king, particularly a newly-arrived one. What was worse he was an unmitigated bore. Lady Mary declared somewhat unfairly that in private life he would have been called an honest blockhead.[25] In fact he was pretty shrewd about matters which interested him, such as army reforms, or the tangled politics of northern Europe. But his expertise on these matters was hardly a quality which commended itself to his English subjects. It would be more fair to say that he did not behave as a king should. He dined not in state, served by the great officers of the household, but privately in his bedchamber; he never went on tour through his kingdom; he never even showed himself to Londoners in the parks. He had no communication with his subjects. It was hardly an exaggeration to say that he lived in two rooms in his palace. He spent his evenings at cards, playing for paltry stakes; or he would go to the theatre in a chair, like any merchant, and lurk there in the back corner of a private box. It was by such shortcomings that the English judged their monarch, not by the alliance and treaties which his Ministers negotiated with a pack of foreigners. 'Our customs and laws were all mysteries to him, which he neither tried to understand or was capable of understanding if he had endeavoured it.' So little did he understand England that in his early days he actually wanted to close St James's Park to the public, plough it up and grow turnips there. How much, he asked his Secretary of State, would this cost? 'Only three crowns, Sir,' Charles Townshend replied. He even insisted on keeping Colchester oysters until they were stale before eating them.[26]

With our language he was equally unfamiliar, and too old to

learn. He spoke tolerable French, which any person of birth and breeding was expected to know, but many a courtier's mastery of the language was incomplete. The Duchess of Bolton, Monmouth's illegitimate daughter, praised Colley Cibber's play, *Love's Last Shift*:

'*Comment?*' asked His Majesty.

'*La dernière chemise de l'amour,*' she desperately improvised.

When to linguistic difference is added the lack of any common interest, it is no wonder that his subjects found George I dull.

He was, not without reason, harsh to his wife and bullied his son, but outside his family he had a surly, passive good nature, 'and wished all mankind enjoyed quiet if they would let him do so'. This and his complete honesty were about all the English could find to praise in him: the honesty and its drawbacks, for it led him to regard his 'acceptance of the Crown as an act of usurpation which was always uneasy to him'. We have this on the dubious authority of Lady Mary Wortley Montagu, but it is partially confirmed by his refusal ever to touch for the King's Evil. All English sovereigns before William III had conscientiously performed this tiresome insanitary duty; even Monmouth was reputed to have done so. William III had not, advising sufferers to apply to his predecessor, a clear indication of his views on his right to the throne. Queen Anne revived the ancient custom, but George I dropped it, without even covering the omission by any Dutch irony. Count Broglie, the French Ambassador, reported that he 'rather considers England as a temporary possession to be made the most of while it lasts than a perpetual inheritance to himself and his family'.[27]

His private life was disreputable. Most people sympathized with poor, erring Sophia Dorothea, still a prisoner at Ahlden, her name excluded from the Liturgy. A King must, of course, keep mistresses, but need they be such figures of fun? Could he not find ladies who were handsome, witty or both? The scrawny, bald, dull Schulenberg was, on her arrival, promptly dubbed 'the Hop Pole'. Kielmansegge 'was as corpulent and ample as the Duchess* was long and emaciated. Two fierce black eyes, large and rolling be-

* Of Munster, and later of Kendal, titles given to Madame von Schulenberg.

neath two lofty arched eyebrows, two acres of cheeks spread with crimson, an ocean of neck that overflowed and was not distinguished from the lower part of her body, and no part restrained by stays.'[28] She must have resembled a pantomime dame rather than a *femme fatale*, and irreverent cockneys dubbed her 'the Elephant and Castle'. But she was gay and amusing, and rather an asset at Court. The most personable of the King's ladies, a second Countess von Platen, stayed behind in Hanover. All three soaked up money like sponges, together with titles, places, pensions and jewellery for themselves, their friends and anyone who made the right approach to them. They were universal channels of corruption.

'Goot pipple,' called The Hop Pole from her coach surrounded by a hostile crowd, 'what for you abuse us? We came for all your goots.'

'Yes, damn ye, and for all our chattels too.'

The Gentlemen of the Bedchamber had the right and duty, jealously treasured, of assisting the King to dress and undress, and serving him at table on bended knee – all semipublic functions. Now they still held the titles, still drew the pay; but the King was dressed and undressed by German valets and served at meals by two Turks, Mohamed and Mustapha, captured by George Lewis in the Balkan wars of his youth. Faithful, astute and influential, they were the most reliable channel between the King and the outer world and, as such, bitterly resented.[29]

His close advisers were all foreigners. Jean de Robethon, a Huguenot who had served William III in a confidential capacity, had a detailed knowledge of English and continental politics. A man of secrets, a man of intrigue and behind-the-scenes negotiation, he was far from popular among English grandees, but seems on the whole to have used his influence for good. Baron Bothmar, who supervised the King's personal expenditure, was even more influential and singularly disinterested. He was in close touch with the Whigs and with reliable Tories, and it was mainly on him that the King relied when it came to choosing his Ministers. He and other foreigners formed a sort of second Household, which made George I's household expenses more than double those of Queen Anne. Two other Germans, Bernstorff and Goertz, landed at Greenwich with the King. They were ministers of the Elector of

Hanover, not of the King of England. It was an important distinction and they were supposed to mind their own business; but no Englishman ever thought they did.

The King found it very difficult to unbend before a subject, even a handsome woman. When the attractive Lady Cowper was presented to him he could only mumble, five or six times, '*Oh, je l'ai vue: elle est de ma connaissance.*'[30]

Life was a good deal gayer at the Prince's Court where there was dancing, for 'the Princess danced in slippers very well, and the Prince better than any', and masquerades at regular intervals. The stakes at ombre and other card games were high enough to make them interesting, but not so high as to ruin anybody. Lady Cowper was delighted to win, 'for a miracle, eight guineas'.[31]

The young Hanovers' art collection catered for all tastes. Caroline's was educated and orthodox, inclining to Van Dyck and the classic masters. George Augustus did not know much about pictures, but knew what he liked, and what he liked were nymphs with big behinds and round, rosy-nippled breasts.[32]

George I could not understand one word of the Book of Common Prayer, and did not pretend to, enduring the services with a stoic sense of duty. His son and daughter-in-law followed the prayers, sermons and hymns apparently with attention, and the eighteenth century was not so far advanced that this could fail to make a good impression. Like most of the fashionable world, George Augustus was no bigot, and he made history by attending a Jewish wedding. Unfortunately the man in the street was not so tolerant.[33]

Although George Augustus was almost an anti-reader, Caroline read a great deal, mastering even such solid matter as the collected works of Bacon. This, with an excellent memory, gave her a sound knowledge of history, ancient and modern, and a sense of poetry and prose style, even in the English language which she never learned to speak like a native. All this enriched her conversation, as did the bawdy humour which she exercised on occasion. Her knowledge of theology and metaphysics may have been, as Hervey alleged, rather superficial, but she could draw clever men into intelligent and interesting conversation.[34] For several years the Prince and Princess had been patrons of Handel, who followed them from Hanover. They were constant patrons of the opera and of river fêtes where his music was performed, and he no doubt gave private performances at their Court. When the little Princesses were old enough, he was their music master.[35] The Prince and Princess were also regular theatre-goers. Understanding English well, they could appreciate the salacities of some contemporary drama. Advised by a prude that no one with a good reputation would see *The Wanton Wife*, they preferred to take the advice of Lady Cowper and venture on it. They greatly enjoyed it, and 'it certainly is not more obscene than all comedies are'.[36]

All this variety, this mixture of gaiety, gossip, fine arts and intellectualism, for which Caroline was mainly responsible, made their Court a lively place, much frequented by the young, the wits and the world of fashion. The morning drawing-rooms and the twice-weekly receptions were crammed, while the King's dull Court was half-empty. The Princess's vivacity pleased everyone, as did the freedom and frankness with which the Prince spoke and their sociability in holding Court every day.

They professed a liking for England and the English. It was greatly appreciated that all the Princess's bedchamber women were English. 'I have not,' declared George Augustus, 'one drop of blood in my veins dat is not English.' In fact he was five-eighths German, a quarter French and one-eighth Scot; his loud voice and gesticulations sometimes grated on the phlegmatic islanders, who noticed that he was really more fluent in French. But remarks like this showed at least that his heart was in the right place.[37]

The native courtiers were

in rapture at all the kind things the Prince had been saying of the English – that he thought them the best, the handsomest, the best-shaped, the best-natured, the lovingest people in the world, and that if anybody would make their court to him, it must be by telling him he was like an Englishman. This did not at all please the foreigners at our table; they could not contain themselves, but fell into the violentest, silliest, ill-mannered invective against the English that ever was heard, and nothing could make Monsieur Schütz believe there was one handsome woman in England.[38]

Nor was his conduct at Oudenarde forgotten. Lady Cowper was one of his most fervent admirers, as befitted a Lady-in-Waiting to the Princess from whom she 'received a thousand marks of my mistress's favour, as embracing me, kissing me, saying the kindest things . . . I am so charmed with her good nature and good qualities.' In return for these marks of favour, she disclosed that never a meal passed without her drinking the Prince's health, under the honourable title of 'Young Hanover Brave', given him by Congreve. George Augustus replied graciously, 'I do not wonder I have enjoyed such good health since I came to England, since you took so much part in it.'[39]

It was indeed a pleasing instance of royal condescension, though the effect was rather spoilt when he betrayed his total ignorance of England's premier playwright. Clearly, for all his enthusiasm, his knowledge of his adopted country was incomplete.

George Augustus and Caroline affected a great distrust for the King's foreign imports, which was faithfully reflected by their own set. The Princess thought 'Monsieur Robethon a rogue, and Baron Bothmar another'. She was 'terribly vexed with Baron Bernstorff', and her ladies were delighted to repeat what she said about him. Everyone in the Prince's Court, from George Augustus downwards, disliked Mlle Schütz, Bernstorff's pretty but bumptious niece. One day this young lady sought to borrow Lady Cowper's diamonds to put in her hair, kindly explaining, ' "I make no scruple in borrowing them from you because you are best in your state of nature, and always worse when you are dressed out, your jewels not becoming you." "Commend me," commented Lady Cowper, "to the assurance of their foreigners." '[40]

Anglo-German relations were always tricky, and the Prince's Court always took the English side.

The Countess of Buckenburgh said the English women did not look like women of quality, but made themselves look as pitifully and sneakingly as they could; that they always held their heads down and look in a fright, whereas those that are foreigners hold up their heads and hold up their breasts, and make themselves look as great and stately as they can, and more nobly and more like quality than the others.

To this Lady Deloraine, a pretty, drunken, promiscuous little slut, replied, 'We show our quality by our birth and titles, Madame, and not by sticking out our bosoms.'[41]

Sophia, Electress Dowager of Brunswick:
engraving by I. Smith

2. George I

Johann Gaspar, Count von Bothmer

4. Queen Caroline *by Enoch Seeman*

5. George II, 1744: *portrait from the studio of Thomas Hudson*

But it was by their aversion to the King's ladies that George Augustus and Caroline most gained the favour of the natives, and this aversion was fully shared by their Court. Lady Cowper considered Schulenberg and Kielmansegge 'no better than they should be'. Mrs Howard particularly disliked Madame Kielmansegge 'who never stuck a pin into her gown without a design'. The Prince said, or was reputed to have said, that she lay with every man in Hanover. Word of this reached 'the Elephant and Castle' who, massive and seething with injured innocence – or, at least, with a sense of injury – complained to the Princess, though there was a 'mortal hatred between them'. Caroline merely replied that this was not the sort of thing the Prince would say, though in fact it was.

The slandered lady would not be appeased, and drew forth out of her pocket a document under her husband's hand, in which he certified, in all due forms, that she had always been a faithful wife to him and that he never had cause to suspect her honesty. '"It is a very bad reputation, Madame," replied the Princess drily, "which needs such support."' Lady Cowper believed, as well she might, that it was the first certificate of the kind that was ever given.[42]

Where the Prince's Court undoubtedly excelled was in its feminine attractions. His wife could hardly fail to compare favourably with the King's senior mistress. Henrietta Howard, whose precise status at the Prince's Court was still enigmatic, was a woman of charm and tact. It appears that she was able successfully to combine the roles of mistress or friend of the Prince, dresser and friend of the Princess, and confidante and friend of the very lively Maids of Honour.

Senior lady of the Prince's Court was the Chancellor's wife, Lady Cowper. Her position was somewhat equivocal, for on the one hand she professed utter devotion to the Prince and Princess; on the other, she secretly passed to Bernstorff information, derived from her husband, of proceedings in the Inner Cabinet. It was, she writes, 'an employment I was not fond of, but as it was at the request of B. Bernstorff and that I thought he was right in getting all the information I could I consented to it, as did my Lord Cowper'.[43] Apart from her addiction to political intrigue, Lady Cowper was handsome enough to attract the amatory attentions of the King, but bold enough to repulse them. With the Prince she was on platonic kissing terms.

The jewels of the Court were the Princess's Maids of Honour, a chattering, mischievous bevy of beauties barely kept in order by the senior Maid, Miss Meadows, whose fiercely guarded virginity was the jest of St James's.

The most beautiful was Molly Lepel, whose praise was sung in one of Chesterfield's more indelicate works. The naughtiest was Sophia Howe, who was one day reproved by the Duchess of St Albans for giggling in the Chapel Royal. 'You could not do a worse thing!'

'I beg Your Grace's pardon,' she cheekily retorted, 'I can do many worse things.' And so she did.[44]

The brightest and liveliest of the Maids was Mary Bellenden, later described by Lord Hervey (husband, by that time, of Molly Lepel) as 'incomparably the most insinuating and the most likeable woman of her time, made up of every ingredient likely to engage or attach a lover'.[45] Horace Walpole wrote of her: 'Above all, for universal admiration, was Miss Bellenden. Her face and person were charming – lively she was almost to *étourderie*, and so agreeable that she was never mentioned by her contemporaries but as the most perfect creature they had ever known.' That she was not a slim, classic beauty may be surmised from her rueful description of a hefty bill she had to pay, 'as long as my arm and as broad as my —'.[46] That her conversation was not free of *étourderies* may be judged from the abundant anatomical references in her correspondence with Mrs Howard. The possibilities in this lively young lady did not, of course, escape the notice of George Augustus, but 'nobody belonging to the Court ever believed he had been happy with her'. Holding, as he did, that his wife's Maids of Honour were fair game, his approach to her was less than subtle, and her retorts were sharp and to the point. When he reproached her for crossing her arms in his presence instead of putting them to a more agreeable use, she replied, 'Sir, I am not cold. I prefer to stand so.' When, using somewhat cruder tactics, he took out his purse and began slowly counting its contents, over and over again, she said, 'Sir, I can bear it no longer. If you count your money once more, I shall leave the room.' He did, so with a sudden kick she sent the guineas spinning and ran out. To his credit, George Augustus took the rebuff well, and promised her she could make her own choice of husband, provided she confided in him.[47]

The place to see the Maids of Honour displayed to the best advantage was the Chapel Royal, and there was much ogling and giggling between them and the Court bloods who were drawn like bees to honey. Bishop Burnet complained, and Lord Peterborough recorded the consequences in verse.

> Bishop Burnet perceived that the beautiful dames
> Who flocked to the Chapel of hilly St James
> On their lovers alone their kind looks did bestow,
> And smiled not on him while he bellowed below.
> To the Princess he went, with pious intent,
> This dangerous ill to the Church to prevent.
> 'Oh, madam,' he said, 'our religion is lost
> If the ladies thus ogle the knights of the toast.
> These practices, madam, my preaching disgrace:
> Shall laymen enjoy the first rights of my place?
> Then all may lament my condition so hard,
> Who thrash in the pulpit without a reward
> Then pray condescend such disorders to end,
> And to the ripe vineyard the labourers send
> To build up the seats that the beauties may see
> The face of no bawling pretender but me.'
> The Princess by rude importunity press'd,
> Though she laughed at his reasons, allow'd his request;
> And now Britain's nymphs in a Protestant reign
> Are boxed up at prayers like the virgins of Spain.[48]

They were also to be viewed in Kensington Gardens, whither the Princess sometimes took them for a walk and a breath of fresh air; for she was as great a walker as the Electress Sophia, and complained that St James's 'stank of people'.

> Here England's daughter, darling of the land,
> Sometimes, surrounded with her virgin band,
> Gleams through the shade. She, towering o'er the rest,
> Stands fairest of the fair kind confessed;
> Formed to gain hearts that Brunswick's cause denied
> And charm a people to her father's side.[49]

'Formed to gain hearts that Brunswick's cause denied.' Well, she and her husband could hardly expect to gain the Jacobites, or even dedicated Tories, who persisted in huzzaing for 'Oxford, Ormonde and High Church' and told the most atrocious lies about him, some of which came, in April 1715, to the ears of Great-Aunt Liselotte in Paris.

I have heard such a strange story from England; I wonder if it is true? I heard that the Prince of Wales saw a play where some actress, supposed to be impersonating the late Queen Anne, pretended to get drunk and flung herself into a chair. Then a milord climbed onto the stage and laid about the actors with a sword, and the Prince is supposed to have ordered his Guards to shoot him down. The entire pit shouted that if a single shot was fired, they would do away with the King's whole party, and the captain of the guards is supposed to have said to the Prince that shooting might be the thing in Hanover, but in England it just wasn't done.

There was not the smallest truth in this ludicrous story, of which there is no hint in English letters, newspapers and pamphlets.

People here say [continued Liselotte with the zest of a born gossip] that the Prince is on very bad terms with his father, and that they won't speak to one another. The Princess of Wales is supposed to have received a sort of petition asking her to consider, just and God-fearing as she is known to be, that the only rightful heir to the kingdom is the one known as the Pretender, as he was King James II's son as surely as her husband was Count Königsmarks's. How unspeakably insolent, if this really was said to the Princess! England is a mad country . . . People like the English are not to be found anywhere else in the world, specially if what I have written is true. I can hardly believe it.[50]

Nothing in Tory eyes could make the young Hanovers English. They were *not* Stuarts, and even Whig ladies felt more honoured by a single word from Queen Anne, who was truly royal, than by all their long, cosy chats with the Princess. But Queen Anne was dead, and the young Hanovers were infinitely better than the old King.[51]

It was natural, therefore, that moderate Tories, finding themselves unwelcome at the father's Court, frequented that of the son. The Countess of Nottingham, always 'holier than thou', positively ran from church to carry the Princess's train, 'preferring to make her court to an earthly rather than a heavenly power'. Her husband, noted the Whig Lady Cowper in February, 1716, 'takes great pains to insinuate the Tories into the Princess's favour. The same game is played by Lord Finch.' It was played, evidently, with some success, for Lady Cowper asked her mistress 'if she continued in the resolution of being a Tory. She told me that [she would] till I could give her convincing arguments that a Whig was more than a Tory for the King's prerogative. I said I hoped to do so.'[52]

But this affair with the Tories was a mere flirtation, as Bonet, the astute Prussian envoy, makes clear. In a report to his master written in July 1716 he described as a gross exaggeration the story that the Prince of Wales had sided entirely with the Tories. He had neither the liberty to do so because the King would not allow him so much as to engage a valet without paternal permission; nor the will, for he well knew that Tory zealots disliked him even more than they disliked the King.[53]

Caroline had, however, developed a personal aversion to the rough, earthy, forthright Lord Townshend and his brother-in-law, Robert Walpole. She actually told the King that he was an old fool to be led by the nose by them. She chided the King and told him he was grown lazy. He laughed, and said he was busy from morning to night. 'Sir, I tell you, the Ministry does everything, and you nothing.' The King, not surprisingly, spoke of her as *'cette diablesse la Princesse'*.[54]

In the reconstructed Ministry after the 1715 rising Walpole had been promoted to the posts of First Commissioner of the Treasury and Chancellor of the Exchequer. He, his brother-in-law Townshend, and General Stanhope, the Secretaries of State, thus became the most powerful members of the government. Their Ministry now proceeded to insure itself against a defeat in the general election due in 1718 by passing the Septennial Act, which laid down that seven years instead of three should be the normal life of a Parliament. While in opposition the Whigs had invariably pressed for shorter parliaments, biennial or even annual: now they were in power and likely to remain so, they stabilised their position by introducing long parliaments. This would, the preamble to the

Bill explained, reduce not only the heats and animosities of party, but the electoral expenses of Members. It was equally advantageous to the Ministry, now secure for the next six years, and for the owners of close boroughs who saw the value of their property doubled, simply by one Act of Parliament. The Tories, of course, complained that they had been cheated, and now demanded annual parliaments.[55]

These two phenomena of 1716, a one-party government and seven-year parliaments, set the political scene for most of the eighteenth century, though their results were not immediately apparent.

In the early summer of 1716 relations between the King and the Prince of Wales were worse than ever. They neither conversed nor ate together nor visited one another's apartments. If they went to the theatre, they sat in different boxes. They met neither in the palace, nor in private houses, nor walking in the park, nor hunting – only in full Cabinet meetings, in chapel and in the Princess's evening salon, and then without exchanging a word.[1]

Their mutual aversion made it very difficult for the King to pursue a project very close to his heart – a return to Hanover. It was nearly two years since he had left home, and he longed for it every hour of every day. But if he was to be in Hanover for six months, a Regent must be appointed to rule England, and the only possible choice was the Prince of Wales.

This was a prospect abhorrent to the King. The Prince had hitherto attended only the meetings of the full Cabinet, called merely to give formal agreement to decisions taken by the Cabinet Committee. From meetings of the latter body the King absented himself. In doing so, he simply followed the precedent set by Queen Anne. It may be an exaggeration to say that he was also influenced by linguistic difficulties. Although he never learned more than a few words of English, he could communicate with his Ministers in French, and frequently did so at private audiences. With those who, like Walpole and Cowper, were not at their ease in colloquial French, he could no doubt resort to dog-Latin, though Horace Walpole's tale that he habitually did so is now rather discounted. Obviously however they could discuss matters far more freely in English in his absence.

The King's non-attendance at Cabinet Committee sittings weakened his position because he heard only the final results of their discussions, not the pros and cons of the arguments which had led up to it – except in so far as he was secretly informed of these through Cowper, Lady Cowper and Bernstorff.[2] Such absence was certainly not hallowed by tradition, and there was no particular reason why it should continue to be honoured by a Regent who was avid for responsibility and fluent, if inaccurate, in English. Alternatively, if he did not wish to breach recent custom by attending Committee meetings, the Prince of Wales could very easily, and without the slightest impropriety, insist on full discussions and important decisions being made not in Committee, but in full Cabinet, under his chairmanship. In either case he would have more power than the King himself enjoyed, and he might even confide Cabinet secrets to his friends in opposition.

The arguments are unsupported by contemporary evidence, but there is nothing improbable in them and they serve to explain the King's attitude, which is inexplicable if one accepts the premise that policy-making was and must be the function of the Inner Cabinet sitting without the King or Regent.

Neither Ministers nor Parliament wished the King to leave the country before the ripples of the rebellion had subsided. But, as he made a point of it, they repealed the clause in the Act of Settlement which forbade him doing so without their consent. They would not, however, agree to the King's first suggestion that the Prince should be curbed by setting up a Council of Regency: according to precedent, they advised him, an adult regent should reign alone; the regency could not be put into commission. The King decided, therefore, to leave his son as a sort of caretaker, with very limited powers and the title 'Guardian of the Realm and Lieutenant' – an office unknown in England since it was enjoyed by the Black Prince. Not unnaturally, George Augustus angrily objected to being so restricted. 'They are all mad,' wrote Lady Cowper, who was herself in the thick of it, and the Princess was 'all in flame'.[3]

The personal quarrel between father and son was further aggravated by the vexed question of appointing a new Commander-in-Chief of the Army, the Duke of Marlborough having suffered a stroke. Rival candidates for the post were General Cadogan and the Duke of Argyll. Both were able and gallant soldiers, but Argyll was something of a politician too, and held the office of Chamberlain to the Prince. Partly out of sheer irascibility and a desire to humiliate his son, partly because he felt that the Prince and Argyll would, in his absence, make too strong a combination, the King not only promoted Cadogan to the vacant post of Captain-General, but insisted on the Prince dismissing Argyll from his Household.

The Prince protested furiously and even asked for Townshend's support. He had, however, no choice but to obey, especially when the King threatened to send for his brother, Ernest Augustus, from Hanover and make him Guardian of the Realm instead. On 4 July he surrendered, informing Bernstorff that 'he is resolved to sacrifice everything to please and live well with the King, so will part with the Duke of Argyll'. He decided, too, that it would be prudent to give a pension of £300 a year to Robethon, who might be bought 'if it is done artfully'. It was not in fact done very artfully, because though promised it was not paid until Robethon complained of the delay.[4]

The King could now go, leaving Bothmar to 'keep all things in order and to give him an account of everything that was doing'. He was in a 'mighty good humour'. When Lady Cowper wished him a good journey and a quick return, he looked as if the last part of the speech was needless as he did not think of it.[5]

So, like a schoolboy setting off on his holidays, the King embarked for his beloved Hanover. There the people were placid and respectful, the deer plump and slow. There, without distraction, he could concentrate on the important affairs of north Europe and the Empire. There, too, was the youngest and most personable of his mistresses, the Countess von Platen. He was leaving behind him Jacobite rebels, Tories who baited him, Ministers bothering him with incomprehensible business, tiresome parliaments, London fogs, importunate placehunters and the tedium of sitting through long church services of which he understood not a word. Above all, he was leaving behind his son. For six months he would be away from it all. He took with him General Stanhope, who spoke German and had an understanding of Europe rare among British politicians. The King arranged for Bothmar to keep an eye and report secretly on the Prince, while the Prince thought he had arranged for Stanhope and Robethon to keep an eye and report secretly on the King.[6]

Robethon, before being sweetened with £300 a year, had told Lady Cowper that the Prince 'only wanted power to displace everybody the King liked, and dissolve Parliament'. However that might be, the Prince's powers were severely restricted. He could take no decision in foreign policy: he was, so far as possible, to postpone assent to parliamentary Bills until the King's return. Even more galling, he was forbidden to make any appointments to the Cabinet, the Privy Council, the Royal Household, the Treasury, the Board of Admiralty or colonial governorships. In the line regiments he could not make any promotions above colonel, and in the Guards, above lieutenant. It was no great exaggeration of Bonet to say the Prince could not engage even a footman.[7]

Having always been totally excluded from public life, the Prince now made the best of his meagre opportunities. He assiduously attended Cabinet meetings, mastered the subjects under discussion and kept the Ministers, Robert Walpole wrote, 'chained to the oar, like slaves'. Lady Cowper too noticed that 'the King was no sooner gone than the Prince took a turn of being kind and civil to everyone, and applied himself to be well with the King's Ministers and to understand the state of the nation'.[8] He reviewed the Guards in Hyde Park and moved out to the rural salubrity of Hampton Court, where he held Court every day. He dined in public and saw company every evening. What with a redecorated Hampton Court, balls, river fêtes, bowls, picnics beside the bowling green and every kind of entertainment, London society had not known such a summer for years. In September the Prince and Princess – although she was heavily pregnant – made a tour of the south-eastern counties, where they tasted the water at Tunbridge Wells, presented five guineas to the dipper at the well and three more to the women strewing flowers along their path and six to the chapel for the poor. They even braced themselves – supreme sacrifice – to be civil to Lord Townshend, whom Caroline privately thought 'the sneeringest, fawningest knave that ever was'.[9] (Most people, on the other hand, found him too rough, rustic, rude and overbearing.) Townshend in return, while finding 'means to insinuate himself mightily into the favour of the Prince, left the Princess quite out, even to showing her all the contempt in the world', and paid his court instead to Mrs Howard and Mary Bellenden. It was a mistake others were to make, wrongly supposing that the Prince's philanderings indicated a waning of his wife's influence. Lord Cowper and others warned him that he was seriously underestimating her, so he 'quite altered his conduct to the Princess, to the great pleasure of those who had been concerned in the thing. This brought the Princess into perfect tranquility.'[10]

Townshend did not consider that the Prince was abusing his position or undermining the authority of the King. Bothmar did, reporting to Hanover that the Prince was deliberately receiving at his Court recalcitrant Whigs like Argyll, Tories and even Jacobites.[11]

What in fact they were seeing, though they did not realize it, was the first, tentative appearance of a phenomenon which was to be characteristic of British politics for most of the eighteenth century, an adult heir to the throne heading the opposition to his father's government, much to the annoyance and embarrassment of the Ministry. Perhaps the Prince was not consciously aiming at this, but all his actions tended that way. Robert Walpole was astute enough to see the danger, writing on the 30 July to Stanhope:

Instead of pretty extraordinary treatment, we meet civil receptions. He seems very intent upon holding the Parliament, very inquisitive about the revenue, calls daily for papers, which may tend to very particular informations; and I am not sure, they are not more for other people's perusal than his own. By some things that daily drop from him, he seems to be preparing to keep an interest of his own in Parliament independent of the King's . . . As for our behaviour to His Highness we take care not to be wanting in duty and respect, nor to give any offence or handle to such as are ready to take any opportunity to render business impracticable, and we hope we demean ourselves so that neither they who would misrepresent us to the King for making our court too much to the Prince, nor they who would hurt us with the Prince for doing it too little, can have any fair advantage over us, but this is a game not to be managed without difficulty.[12]

Robert Walpole's outward appearance and manner completely concealed his true character.[13] He was short and very corpulent, with a pink-and-white face and twinkling brown eyes. He loved good food, he loved good drink and he loved a bawdy story: indeed at his own table he generally talked bawdy, 'so that everyone can join in'. Above all, he loved money for he was a compulsive spender. He transformed Houghton, his plain old Norfolk manor house, into a provincial palace crammed with expensive objets d'art. Nor were expenses grudged on his pack of harriers, his pheasant coverts and his partridges. When in London, he always opened his gamekeeper's letters before any official dispatches. Endlessly in debt, no matter what his income, endlessly beset by creditors, he was a crafty, persistent borrower and fertile in subterfuge to delay and evade repayment. Vulgar and ostentatious in his clothes, entertainment and way of life, he bitterly resented criticism. But he had an instinctive understanding of other people's thoughts and feelings, a rare knack of divining their intentions which, experience taught him, were generally governed by pursuit of the main chance.

All this was, by 1716, well known to his colleagues. What they did not perhaps appreciate was that under his soft, genial exterior was a core of steel. He had, wrote Hervey, 'a strength of parts equal to any advancement, a spirit to struggle with any difficulties, a steadiness of temper immovable by any disappointment'.[14] Although suffering in middle age from gravel and the stone, he had terrific physical energy, riding hard to hounds, tramping all day after partridges. Mentally too he was indefatigable, capable of mastering the intricacies not only of financial questions which he thoroughly understood, but also of matters outside his normal interests.

His political career had hitherto given evidence of a sound adherence to the Hanoverian succession and a determined pursuit of wealth, rather than of any marked genius. In 1701 he had entered Parliament, inheriting from his father the family seat of Castle Rising. This he had transferred in 1703 to his uncle Horace (incidentally a Tory) and sat instead for King's Lynn, which he had represented ever since. He had been an efficient Secretary at War but had been impeached in 1712, and imprisoned briefly in the Tower, for giving his friend, Robert Mann, a cut of the army forage contract. From this he got no personal gain, but he owed Mann a lot of money, which no doubt influenced him in a transaction which was undoubtedly improper, but not particularly heinous by the standards of the day. He was regarded less as a miscreant than as a victim of Tory spite; and in 1715 was recompensed for his sufferings by an appointment coveted by all but the most affluent and disinterested politicians. There he made proper (or improper) use of his opportunities: huge sums were paid into his account in bank notes while he was Paymaster. Before 1714 he was poor: after 1717 he was rich.[15]

At first this plain but far from simple Norfolk squire was somewhat overshadowed in the Ministry by his brother-in-law, Charles, Viscount Townshend, who cut a far more important figure in a country where titles and broad acres have always been venerated. Townshend's nickname, 'Turnip', testifies to his interest in agricultural improvements, particularly in the use of root crops as winter feed for stock. He was a pioneer in the new four-crop rotation. Not only his interests, but his manners were rustic, and his temper was unreliable. 'No man,' wrote Lord Hervey, 'was ever a greater slave to his passions.'

... He was rash in his undertakings, violent in his proceedings, haughty in his carriage, brutal in his expressions, and cruel in his disposition; impatient of the least contradiction, and as slow to pardon as he was quick to resent. He was so captious that he would often take offence where nobody meant to give it; and, when he had done so, was too obstinate in such jealousies, though never so lightly founded, to see his error, and too implacable ever to forgive those against whom they were conceived. He was much more tenacious of his opinion than of his word; for the one he never gave up, and the other he seldom kept; anybody could get promises from him, but few could prevail with him to perform them ... He endeavoured to temper the natural insolence of his behaviour with an affected affability, which sat so ill upon him that the insinuating grin he wore upon those occasions was more formidable than his severest frown.[16]

No man, it may be added, was ever less likely to hit it off with Lord Hervey, a delicate, scented and powdered courtier whose health and inclination alike precluded him from any contact with the soil. 'Beef?' exclaimed 'Lord Fanny' in disgust when offered a helping of Townshend's favourite sustenance, 'Oh, no! Faugh! Don't you know I never eat beef, nor *horse*, nor any of those things?'[17] It is probable, therefore, that his description of Townshend is coloured by personal incompatibility, though other contemporaries confirm that it is at least a clever caricature. It should be added that, though a bad enemy, Townshend was a good friend, a kind and faithful husband, an affectionate father and an able administrator.[18] Such a man, a sort of aristocratic John Bull, was bound to grate on a German king, and to be a difficult colleague for his fellow Secretary of State, General James Stanhope. This gallant officer was far from being a simple soldier; he was gifted with high intelligence, fluent French, Spanish and German and an excellent understanding of Europe. His was indeed, as Horatio Walpole (Robert's brother) remarked, 'a fruitful and luxurious genius in foreign affairs'. His success in diplomacy was achieved by the novelty of the methods he adopted. 'Nothing is so useful,' he wrote, 'as explaining oneself clearly. I have not at all hidden the basis of affairs.' Foreign ministers were disconcerted in negotiation by Stanhope's practice of telling them the exact truth.[19]

When in September 1714 Stanhope accepted the seals of office for the Southern Department from the new King, he found that as a result of the treaty secretly negotiated by Bolingbroke, Britain was without a friend in western Europe. To end her isolation, it was obviously necessary to restore the alliance between Britain, the Empire and the United Provinces. But this was easier said than done; for while the Emperor would gladly receive British naval help in his vendetta against King Philip of Spain, he did not at all wish to guarantee the Hanoverian succession or risk a war with France. His Majesty's Government, however, for the sake of its American trade, had no wish to become embroiled with Spain. It was largely as a result of Stanhope's patient and skilful diplomacy that on 25 May 1716 good relations between Britain and the Empire were restored by the Treaty of Westminster, an agreement for maintaining the *status quo* in Britain, the Austrian Netherlands, Italy and Spain.

The situation in the north was complicated by the new link with Hanover. The area was important for Britain, as a principal source of iron, timber, hemp, tar and other naval stores. To safeguard these, it was in the British interest that no single power should dominate the Baltic and control its narrow exit through the Sound between Denmark and Sweden. But here the interests of Hanover clashed with those of Britain, for in 1715 Hanover came into conflict with Sweden over the question of access to the sea. Unfortunately British public opinion had long been pro-Swedish, and indeed since 1700 Britain had been allied to Sweden, committed to helping her against her enemies. So here was the King of England bound by treaty to help his ally against the Elector of Hanover. The situation could hardly have been more unsatisfactory.

George I picked his way with some skill through this morass, but it put his Secretaries of State in a position of peculiar difficulty. Their main task in foreign affairs was always to reconcile the wishes of the King with the prejudices of the Commons, and here these were diametrically opposed. However, both Secretaries loyally carried out the King's policy, without stirring up too much trouble in Parliament. It was a game more suited to Stanhope's political genius than to Townshend's, so there was no doubt which of them the King would take to Hanover: he took Stanhope, whose prodigious consumption of wine and brandy 'as if it had been syrup' earned him a general respect and a present of nine thousand bottles of champagne, burgundy and Volnay.[20]

Meanwhile the death of Louis XIV and the ineptitude of the Jacobites had prepared the ground for a switch in French policy, and the reconciliation of Britain, the Empire, Holland and Spain seemed to leave France dangerously isolated. Moreover the child King, Louis XV, was sickly, and the Regent Orléans wished, in case he should die, to secure support for his own succession to the throne against a possible claim by King Philip of Spain, Louis XIV's grandson, who was not markedly inhibited by the renunciation of his claim to the French throne, which he had made as part of the Peace of Utrecht.

He therefore sent his wily old tutor, the Abbé Dubois, in the guise of a bibliophile, to make contact with Stanhope on his way through Holland to Hanover in July 1716. Dubois suggested an Anglo–French treaty, to which the Dutch might accede, and which would among other things guarantee the Hanoverian succession in Britain and the Regent's succession in case Louis XV died. By the end of August he had settled an outline treaty which was to be referred to the authorities in London and Paris.

Unfortunately 'the authorities in London' meant Townshend and Walpole. They were not favourably impressed by the draft treaty, for francophobia was a basic article of Whig faith and it appeared that Hanoverian rather than British interests were being served. If they were to persuade the Commons they would need the full support of the Regent. Thus they seemed from Hanover to be bent more on ingratiating themselves with the Prince than on serving the King. If Stanhope, who was more concerned with pleasing the King, had met Townshend, whose aim was to keep the Commons quiet, their differences might have been resolved. But they could not meet.

The Earl of Sunderland now took a hand in the game. As Marlborough's nephew and a leading member of the Junto he had been a key figure in the politics of the previous reign, and Secretary of State from 1706 to 1710. But George I had not seemed to appreciate his merits. In the summer of 1716, therefore, he decided to better his fortune in Hanover, going abroad on the pretext of taking the waters at Aix. He took leave of Lord Townshend declaring that his main intention was to persuade the King to come back soon.[21] In fact, having arrived in Hanover, he industriously represented Townshend as caballing with the Prince of Wales against the King, which confirmed reports already received from Bothmar. The King and Stanhope, thinking that this was the explanation for the vexatious delays, decided to ease Townshend out, to the Lord Lieutenancy of Ireland, a polite form of rustication. Walpole, a friend to both Stanhope and Townshend, sent the former a dignified but spirited protest, writing on 12 December 1716:

What could prevail on you to enter into such a scheme as this, and appear to be the chief actor in it, and undertake to carry it through in all events, without which it could not have been undertaken, is unaccountable. I do swear to you, that Lord Townshend has no way deserved it of you . . . What is given out here and published, from letters from among you, in regard to the Prince, I cannot but take notice of, and will stake my all upon this single issue, if one instance can be given of our behaviour to the Prince, but what was necessary to carry on the King's service; and we never had a thought, but with a just and due regard to the King as our King and master.[22]

Later, in April of the following year, Walpole, in protest at his brother-in-law's dismissal, resigned. He was much criticized for doing so. 'The throwing up (of office) *de gaieté de coeur* is a manner of acting towards a sovereign pretty singular . . . Not thought very solid.'[23] Townshend and Walpole from now on headed a spirited and effective opposition.

Stanhope may be considered to have treated them unfairly and not, perhaps, quite honourably, but his foreign policy served his country well. The signature of the Anglo–French treaty at the end of November 1716, and the accession of Holland two months later, was a considerable diplomatic achievement and the Triple Alliance, as it came to be called, was to be the cornerstone of Europe's peace and Britain's security for fifteen years.

In the autumn of 1716 a personal tragedy overtook the Prince and Princess of Wales. The details are related by Lady Cowper:

The 28th October the Court left Hampton Court. The Ladies came with the Prince and Princess by water in a barge. The day was wonderfully fine, and nothing in the world could be pleasanter than the passage, nor give one a better idea of the riches and happiness of this kingdom. The Sunday se'nnight following, being the 4th of November, the Princess fell into labour, upon which the Council was called. There was a German midwife (whose countenance prognosticated ill, she being the very picture of the French Resident), and Sir David Hamilton waited as physician. The English Ladies all pressed to have the Princess laid by Sir David Hamilton, but she would not hear of it. The Council, as well as the family, sat up all night, but there were no signs of delivery. On Tuesday the Princess had a shivering fit, which held her a good while, and violently. Everybody but the Princess and the Germans were now in a great fright, which caused the Council to send down for the Countess of Buckenburgh, to desire her to let the Prince know that they were to beseech him to have the Princess laid by Sir D. Hamilton; which he was angry at, and when I came on Wednesday morning I was in amaze to see the hurly-burly there was about this affair. The midwife had refused to touch the Princess unless she and the Prince would stand by her against the English 'frows', who, she said, were high dames, and had threatened to hang her if the Princess miscarried. This put the Prince into such a passion, that he swore he would fling out of window whoever had said so, or pretended to meddle. The Duchesses of St Albans and Bolton happened to come into the room, and were saluted with these expressions. Everybody's tone was now changed, and nothing was talked of but the Princess's good labour and safety. Nay, Lord Townshend, to show his readiness to comply, met the midwife in the outward room, and ran and shook and squeezed her by the hand, and made kind faces at her: for she understood no language but German. This I think the tip-top of all policy and making one's court. The poor Princess continued in a languishing condition till Friday night, when she was delivered of a dead Prince.[1]

The year 1717 brought one of the great crises in the life of George Augustus, his most reverberating row with his father. It was important, for it did much to shape the pattern of politics in the eighteenth century; and, like most crises in his life, it was flavoured with farce.

The King on his return from Hanover had taken alarm at the popularity of the Prince and Princess of Wales. Clearly if he was to compete with them, he must show himself to his people. So in the summer of 1717 he too moved out to Hampton Court and dined every day in company. In August – surely a month too soon – he went partridge-shooting in Bushey Park and actually bagged a brace. He went stag-hunting for the first time in Windsor Great Park. He 'obliged the nobility very much at Hampton Court by inviting them to sit down with him at table, and by his affable behaviour on those occasions'. Hearing that his son was going to Newmarket Races in October, the King made haste to forestall him there. He 'gained many hearts by his affable and condescending way of life'. He was 'much pleased with Kensington and the easy way of living there', he 'liked Kensington mightily, 'tis so much like his gardens at Hanover than those at any other place'. All in all, he was 'more at ease and tranquillity than ever before in England'. But he was certainly not at ease with his son; indeed he was extremely vexed with him, and in September there was a total failure in communication between the two.[2]

Such was the family atmosphere when, on 2 November, Caroline was delivered of a boy. The Prince sent a Court understrapper to acquaint the King of this happy event; when the King called to offer his congratulations, the baby's father 'wasted little ceremony', and declined even to put in an appearance. But he very properly asked his father and his uncle, Ernest Augustus, to stand as godfathers. The King graciously consented, but at the last moment insisted that the Duke of Newcastle, as Lord Chamberlain, replace Ernest Augustus. Newcastle, of whom more will be heard, was at the beginning of a very long career in which he was to personify all that was most mercenary and least idealistic in politics. In the Prince's circle he was in disrepute, 'it being his peculiarity ever to turn his back on those he has any obligations to'. All through the christening ceremony, which took place in the Princess's bedchamber, George Augustus was steaming with indignation. As soon as the King had departed, he dashed up to Newcastle (treading, according to Jacobite sources, on his toes), exclaiming in his thickly accented English, 'Rascal, I find you out!'[3]

If the Prince's reaction was characteristic, so was Newcastle's. Never one to underestimate an emergency, he thought the Prince had said, 'I fight you', and dashed off to make an agitated, incoherent complaint to the King that he had been challenged, in the execution of his duty, to a duel.

The Elector of Hanover had a short way with mutineers, but in this strange country a certain circumspection would be prudent. He summoned a Cabinet Council and, observing ominously that if this sort of thing happened in Hanover he would know what to do, asked their advice. Everyone present must have been well aware that the Tsar Peter the Great had put his son to death; and the King's nephew, Frederick William of Prussia, had imprisoned his son after forcing him to witness the execution of his best friend. The King's own wife had been in jail for nearly thirty years. Stanhope, who was no ogre but occasionally 'let himself be carried away by the hastiness of his temper', on this or a similar occasion is supposed to have advised the King, in writing, 'It is true that he is your son, but the Son of God himself was sacrificed for the good of mankind.' Sunderland had even suggested, 'He must be carried off and my lord (Admiral) Berkeley will take him on board and carry him to any part of the world Your Majesty will order him, whence he would never be heard of more.'[4]

A deputation of embarrassed Ministers waited on the royal miscreant to inquire if Newcastle's allegations were true. They found the choleric little man in a state of high dudgeon and excitement.

'I said I would *find* him, and I will find him, for he has often failed in his respect for me, particularly on the late occasion by insisting on standing godfather to my son when he knew it was against my will.'

'But, Sir, the Duke did not thrust himself forward. He merely acted as godfather because the King commanded it.'

His Royal Highness retorted that he did not believe a word of this.

They returned to report to the King, whom they found in a mood closed to reason. He promptly put the heir to the throne under close arrest in his wife's quarters. Well might Mrs Howard be astonished when she was prevented from entering the Princess's apartments by two Yeomen of the Guard pointing their halberds at her breast. 'I urged that it was my duty to attend the Princess, but they said no matter, I must not pass that way.'

Stifling his furious indignation, the Prince wrote a mild and conciliatory reply to the peremptory order confining him to barracks. Writing, as usual, in French, he assured his father,

I have received with due submission Your Majesty's orders to remain in my apartment until Your Majesty inform me of his further wishes. The strong mark of Your Majesty's indignation has infinitely astonished me, never having had any sentiments towards Your Majesty other than those of a dutiful son . . . The action of the Duke of Newcastle shocked me, and I was so indignant that I could not prevent myself showing it . . . If I have had the misfortune to give unintentional offence to Your Majesty, I ask pardon.

He followed this up with another letter promising to bear no grudge against the Duke of Newcastle. But this too failed to soften the royal heart.

The general opinion in political and court circles was that His Majesty had overreacted, and the fact that the culprit's wife was confined with him added to the situation's absurdity. Though His Majesty was hardly in a receptive mood, some of the Ministers took it upon themselves to explain to him the provisions of the Habeas Corpus Act, and to recommend that His Royal Highness be released from durance vile by an act of paternal clemency rather than by a judge's order. Persuaded at last that it would be impolitic to send them both to the Tower, he ordered the Prince out of St James's Palace, but graciously conceded that the Princess, who had scarcely recovered from her confinement, might stay with her children provided she neither saw nor communicated with her husband.

She sent a defiant reply, that 'her children were not a grain of sand compared with him', and went into exile with her sorrowing ladies. The Prince curtly informed his father, 'I have just obeyed Your Majesty's orders in quitting St James's. The Princess accompanies me, and our servants are leaving the palace as soon as possible.' But their children had to remain, and their mother 'went into one faint after another as her weeping little Princesses said goodbye'. Only one Maid of Honour was undaunted, Mary Bellenden, who cheered their flight into the wilderness by a spirited rendering of 'Over the hills and far away'.

So long as the Prince did not directly disobey his orders, the King was singularly helpless. He could not cut him from succession to the throne: it was Parliament, not he, who settled the Prince's allowance; he could not, it appeared, even place him under arrest. And the Prince's communications with his father were always dutifully, indeed humbly, worded. (The publication of these letters, by the Prince, infuriated the King.) But professions, said the King, were one thing, performance another, and the Prince's professions were enough to 'make him vomit'. He drew up a paper to the effect that the Prince and Princess should hand their children over to his guardianship and cease to hold communication with, or to employ, 'any person or persons distasteful to the King'. They refused to sign this document, so he put the Chapel Royal out of bounds to them. Instead, they attended the parish church of St James's, frequented by Tories, and were treated to a sermon on the text, 'Now I say, that the heir, as long as he is a child, differeth nothing from a servant, though he be lord of all; but is under tutors and governors, until the time appointed by his father.' 'You may imagine', wrote a contemporary, 'how uppish the Jacobites are upon this disaster, and it must be owned they never had so much reason.' Gleefully Jacobites reported to Paris on 'the father being so stupidly stubborn, the son so arrogant in prosperity and mean in adversity, the wife a very —'. They even reported on 'a design by Hopeful to turn out his pretended father' and suggested that Walpole might be involved.[5]

George Augustus and Caroline set up house in Leicester Fields, on the north side of what is now Leicester Square. The house was long and two-storeyed, with a large courtyard in front and a large garden behind. It was an ill-lighted, ill-found district with a bad repute for duels, brothels, footpads, 'Mohawks', nose-slitting and other contemporary blemishes, but it was just becoming fashionable. At first their levée was 'very slender, not above three or four noblemen and they such as have not appeared at St James's for a long time. All such as are admitted to the King's court are under strict orders not to go at any time to the Prince's and Princess's.' Peers and their wives, foreign ambassadors, Privy Councillors were formally warned that if they waited on the Prince, they would not be received by the King: even casual visitors to the Prince's court were *personae non gratae* at St James's. Those who held places from the King and the Prince must dispose of one or the other. But soon, despite the royal displeasure, Leicester House became a magnet for those out of office, a veritable Cave of Adullam where Townshend and Walpole foregathered even with Tories. ('You know we are very fond in this country of forbidden fruit.') Caroline knew how to keep them. 'Balls, assemblies and masquerades have taken the place of dull, formal visiting days . . . Puns are extremely in vogue, and the licence very great.' To counter the social attractions of Leicester House, the King forced himself to become much more social in public and to take large parties to the opera.[6]

Unable to send them to Coventry, the King contemplated gaining control of the Prince's household and income. But the Ministers with difficulty convinced him that the Prince's right to appoint his own household, conferred by letters patent, was inalienable, and no one but Parliament could cut his income. The Prince was jubilant. When the King indicated that he should give up £40,000 of his income of £100,000 for the education of Prince Frederick, still in Hanover, George Augustus called George Lewis's bluff: nothing would please him better, he said, than that his son should finish his education in England, and if His Majesty would arrange this, he, the father, would provide whatever money was necessary. He knew well that the King would not want two heirs in the kingdom. However, at least the King could, and did, withdraw the Prince's guard – a shrewd blow, no doubt.[7]

The most effective form of harassment was separating the Prince and Princess from their three little girls and a baby boy who remained at St James's. A clandestine visit was sharply rebuked, the King instructing his Vice-Chamberlain to inform the Prince of his displeasure 'that he has come to St James's without my permission, and that he and the Princess must ask me in advance when they want to see the children, which will be permitted once a week'. When the Princess on one of these visits wished to see her daughters alone, their governess replied with 'many expressions of regret that she could not permit it, having His Majesty's strict orders to the contrary. Upon this the Prince flew into such a rage that he would literally have kicked her out of the room if the Princess had not thrown herself between them.'[8]

'We've such a good Papa and such a good Mama,' said one of the little girls, 'and yet we are orphans.' Asked if her grandfather never visited them, she replied, 'Oh no, he doesn't love us enough.' Hearing this, the King, 'by way of compensation, diverted himself above an hour in the nursery', which must have greatly consoled his grandchildren, and afterwards paid them regular visits. But when he was announced while their mother was with them, they all fled to the next room.[9]

Even in February when the baby Prince was seriously ill (supposedly for lack of nourishment at nature's founts) the King was obdurate. At length he had the poor little fellow sent to Kensington Palace, where his mother could visit him without friction. There, in the presence of his parents, the baby was seized by 'an oppression upon his breast, accompanied by a cough, which increasing, a fever succeeded with convulsions, which put an end to his precious life'. 'My God!' wrote Great-Aunt Liselotte from Paris, 'how I pity the poor dear Princess of Wales! She saw him at Kensington Palace before the end, but I wish she had not, for it will be still more painful for her now . . . God forgive me, but I think the King of England does not believe that the Prince of Wales is his son, because if he did, he couldn't possibly treat him as he does.'[10]

The conflicting strains of self-interest, family ties and loyalty placed considerable strains on many people.

Our courtiers looked so amazed and thunderstruck, and knew so little how to behave themselves, that they betrayed the mercenary principles upon which they acted by the confusion they were in. Those who were for the Prince do not speak their minds because the father was King. Those who were for the King were equally backward because the son would be King; these because the King might resent; these because the Prince might remember.[11]

Banned from St James's, Windsor, Hampton Court and Kensington Palace, the Prince and Princess moved in the summer of 1718 to Richmond Lodge in the Old Park. Their life here was gay, with many visitors, hunting and horse-races.

There was a horse-race for a saddle the Prince gave; 'twas run under the terrace wall for Their Royal Highnesses to see. There was an infinite number of people to see them all along the bank, and the river full of boats with people of fashion. They all stayed until it was late upon the water to hear the Prince's music, which sounded much sweeter than from the shore.[12]

Hitherto George Augustus had not shown any great enthusiasm for sport, but now he hunted two or three days a week. The usual quarry was the stag, but a letter of Pope's suggests that they might on occasion have tried the new and far more testing sport of fox-hunting.

I met the Prince, with all his ladies on horseback, coming from hunting. Mrs Bellenden and Mrs Lepel took me under their protection. We all agreed that the life of a Maid of Honour was of all things the most miserable, and wished that every woman who envied it had a specimen of it. To eat Westphalian ham in a morning, ride over hedges and ditches on borrowed hacks, come home in the heat of the day with a fever and (what is a hundred times worse) with a red mark on the forehead from an uneasy hat; all this may qualify them to make excellent wives for fox-hunters, and bear abundance of ruddy-complexioned children. As soon as they can wipe off the heat of the day, they must simper for an hour and catch cold in the Princess's apartments, from thence to dinner with what appetite they may, and after that walk, work or think, which they please.[13]

It seems that His Royal Highness's hounds had a poor day.

However, if the Princess's ladies sometimes groused, the King's court had far more to complain of. As Pope wrote to Lady Mary

Wortley Montagu: 'No lone house in Wales is more contemplative than Hampton Court. I walked there the other day by the moon and saw no creature of any quality but the King, who was giving audience all alone to the birds under the garden wall.'[14]

But the Prince's court, at Richmond Lodge in summer and Leicester House in winter, was far more than a social and sporting centre. The political influence of the Prince of Wales, as a rival centre of power, had been briefly glimpsed during the King's absence in Hanover when the heir to the throne was feeling his way towards a certain degree of political independence. Now, with the open breach between King and Prince of Wales, it took a more definite shape. Walpole and Townshend, and many other aspiring young politicians, knew well enough that the King was an elderly man and the Prince a young one, and though the road to office might at present be through the King's favour, the King would die and the future lay with the Prince. So they frequented not St James's and Hampton Court, but Leicester House and Richmond Lodge. So did Argyll and lesser opposition luminaries such as the young Earl of Chesterfield, already gaining a repute for cynicism and wit; the erratic genius, Lord Peterborough; and, curiously enough, Sir Spencer Compton, Speaker of the Commons, a man who displayed an unusual degree of stupidity, sycophancy and ineptitude. Caroline also took pains to enlist the Tories.

We have all the country gentlemen of the Tories with us, even against the head of their party, all of Suffolk, Cornwall, Devonshire, Yorkshire, Nottinghamshire, and all those with Sir Thomas Hammer, Northampton-shire, and all those of the City, in short the greatest number, and it begins to grow better every minute. Pray see what can be done with Carteret, I am afraid of him. Lord Malpas ought also to have three of Cheshire who depend entirely upon him. Ask Bishop Neville what he expects of the Amber Club . . . Say to your good friend this is the time when he may show the love he has for his country. If others don't see the matter already in that light, he must show it them. Preach this, I conjure you, this is the time, come to me tomorrow, my dear Clayton. My Lord Halifax has 4 that depend upon him.[15]

One recognizes the authentic haste and urgency of opposition politics: little did they know that it was to be over eighty years before the heady hopes of the Tory country gentry were to be realized.

For light relief at Leicester House there was always young Lord Chesterfield's feline witticisms. This 'wit among lords and lord among wits' delighted the Prince and Princess by ridiculing the King's mistresses, 'two considerable specimens of the King's bad taste and strong stomach'. Caroline remarked of the Kielmansegge's painted face: 'She looks young, if one may judge from her complexion, not more than eighteen or twenty.'

'Aye, madam,' replied the greatest wit of his day, on this occasion somewhat below his usual form, 'eighteen or twenty stone.' He enlarged on the subject: 'The standard of His Majesty's taste, as exemplified in his mistress, makes all ladies who aspire to his favour, and who are near the suitable age, strain and swell themselves, like the frogs in the fable, to rival the bulk and dignity of the ox. Some succeed, and others – burst.'

But when she heard that Chesterfield was mimicking herself, Her Royal Highness was not amused. 'You have more wit, my lord, than I, but I have a bitter tongue, and always repay my debts with exorbitant interest.'[16]

Peterborough, a somewhat rusty hero and roué, haunted Leicester House in hot but unsuccessful pursuit of Mrs Howard. The lady, now in her fortieth year, was unkindly described:

She is made up of negatives, and has not character enough to say a downright No. A tall and fine figure in a green taffety dress, set off with rose-coloured ribands; fair hair and skin; a white muslin apron, trimmed with delicate lace, ruffles of same; a white and rounded arm. A chip hat with flowers, placed quite at the back of the light hair, which leaves the white broad forehead exposed.[17]

Although nearly seventy and a grandfather of several years' standing, Peterborough addressed Mrs Howard in verse which might have done credit to a sixteen year old boy.

I said to my heart, between sleeping and waking,
'Thou wild thing, that always art leaping or aching,
What black, brown, or fair, in what clime, in what nation,
By turns has not brought thee a pit-a-patation?'

But Chloe so lively, so easy, so fair,
Her wit so genteel, without art, without care,
When she comes in my way – the motion, the pain,
The leapings and achings, return all again.[18]

She evaded his advances with practised ease, but it was some time before he gave up the struggle.

In the spring of 1719 the Court devised for the erring Prince a new instrument of chastisement. This was the Peerage Bill. Its ostensible object was to prevent the constitution being subverted by the creation of a batch of peers as had been done in 1711. This precedent, it was pointed out, was dangerous, and could be used by an unscrupulous King and Court for any purpose. Besides there had recently been too many peers created, not for political purposes but to gratify the German ladies who were believed to charge up to £12,000 from aspirants to a coronet. The real object of the Bill was, however, to ensure that George Augustus, either as Regent or after his father's death, would always be limited in his powers of patronage and shackled by a hostile majority in the House of Lords. The House at that time consisted of twenty-six bishops, 178 English peers and sixteen representative Scottish peers out of 156, elected by their fellows for each parliament. The Bill would have allowed the creation of six new English peers – no more, except princes of the blood and to replace extinct peerages. Scotland would be represented in the Upper House not by sixteen representative peers, liable to be changed if the wind blew the wrong way, but by twenty-five hereditary peers, unchangeable except by death. Thus the present Ministry could entrench themselves impregnably by making thirty-one new peers from among their own supporters, and they closing the doors to further creations. They would be secure forever – and this prerogative of the Crown would be almost extinguished.

The Prince well understood the issue, and was indignant at the attempt to deprive him, when he should come to the throne, of one of the principal ingredients of political power. Nor was he greatly reassured by Lord Cowper who, wrote Caroline in an agitated missive to Mrs Clayton, did 'not conceive that with all the advantages they have the ugly bill can pass, without the consent of the Scotch lords, by which they would so entirely affect their best property. He believes it would raise a rebellion in Scotland.' (Cowper, indeed, attacked the Bill in the House of Lords on these grounds.)

For myself who am obliged to the lower house for all the Prince enjoys of his possessions, that interests me, that they should not part with their property in this because it will be the means to lay them aside [i.e. the Commons should not vote away their chances of a peerage]. I have seen a man whom I won't name who tells me, if this Bill passes, the lower house will be obliged to return to their ancient vassalage with respect to the Lords ... I laughed heartily that you could not read one of my letters, the Prince said to me you write like a cat.[19]

The Princess's information was not quite correct: on the whole the Lords liked the Bill, which would ensure that their privileges would not be devalued by the creation of too many peers, and Scottish votes were generally for sale. Thoroughly steamed up, she wrote in March to Mrs Clayton: 'The Prince has certain intelligence that if the Bill passes the lower house they will attack him and perhaps go so far as to exclude him the crown. This is not to be mentioned but to you three, the life of the person depends on it.'[20]

In the event it was Walpole who was chiefly responsible for the Bill being rejected in the Commons. Quoting, or perhaps inventing, a plain country gentleman of about £800 a year, of a rank only equal to that and with no expectations or views to himself beyond what his condition at that time gave him, Walpole had that paragon of disinterested Roman rectitude exclaim, 'with heart and some oaths (which was what Mr Walpole overheard and catched at), "What, shall I consent to the shutting the door upon my family ever coming into the House of Lords!"' Faced with the prospect of being excluded forever from the most glittering rewards of political fidelity, the Commons at length rejected the Bill.

To agitate against the Peerage Bill a new journal, *The Plebeian*, had been started by Sir Richard Steele, an ex-officer turned essayist and political journalist who won the election at Wendover 'by a merry trick. He scooped an apple and put ten guineas in it, and said it would be deposited for the wife of any of the voters that should first be brought to bed that day nine months. Upon this several that would have been against him and who lived some miles from the town posted home to capacitate their wives to claim the apple.' *The Plebeian* was an ephemeral publication, but contributed to the political education of George Augustus. The Princess was delighted with his progress. 'Has not the Prince made a good beginning?... *The Plebeian* has contributed much to it. We drank his [Steele's] health last night. His paper we then received was delightful, the Prince has it by heart.'[21]

The Prince's suspicion that there was a move afoot to exclude him from the succession was not entirely without foundation, though he had the details wrong. What the King and his Ministry had in mind was to separate the crowns of England and Hanover. This was neither a new nor a bad idea, and was to recur several times during the reigns of George I and II. In 1716, George I had drawn up his testament by which his two kingdoms should pass undivided first to George Augustus, then to Frederick, but that on the latter's death his elder son should inherit England, his younger son Hanover. This he wanted to do lest the electoral dominions become a 'perpetual annex' of the Crown, which would 'be very disadvantageous to the interests of Hanover'.

The English Ministers saw difficulties in implementing this testament by Act of Parliament. How could the Parliament of Great Britain legislate for the succession to Hanover? They discussed the possibility of making the succession to the throne of England conditional on the renunciation of that of Hanover, but this seemed full of difficulties. If the renunciation took place on the death of the King before the succession of the new King, there would be an interregnum which, however short, would be fraught with dangers; if after, the new King could easily secure the repeal of the Act of Parliament. The proposed Act might give rise to domestic disputes, even to Jacobite and foreign intervention. The King took their advice to pursue the matter no further, but did not, apparently, revoke the will.[22]

So the Prince had got hold of the wrong end of the stick. His father's machinations had been aimed at restricting not his rights, but those of his unborn grandson; and they had, moreover, been abandoned on ministerial advice. But the suspicions remained, and indeed they strengthened him in his position as leader and paymaster of the opposition group, which was all the time increasing in popularity. He was, after all, in the happy position of being able to promise without having immediately to perform.

But if the Prince was the leader – or figurehead – of the opposition, its real inspiration was the Princess, and Walpole was its brains and mouthpiece in the Commons. There was a close friendship between Walpole and Caroline, based on an affinity of mind and temperament, which lasted all their lives. Both were earthy, worldly and cynical in outlook : both loved the realities of power, and to secure these were quite happy to allow the Prince to enjoy its appearances. They formed a united trio, in which two (without his knowledge) ruled the third. There was no physical element in the friendship of Walpole and Caroline: indeed she found him, with his gross person, his 'dirty mouth and great belly', physically repulsive.[23] Lady Cowper alleged that, to gain an ascendancy over George Augustus, 'Walpole let the Prince lie with his wife which both he and the Princess knew'.[24] This is not impossible : Walpole had long ceased to love his promiscuous, extravagant, unstable wife: the Prince posed as an ardent and successful man of pleasure, on which his rank conferred a *droit de seigneur* over any attractive woman he chanced to meet ; while Caroline, confident that wherever he strayed he would always return to her, was contemptuously tolerant of his amours and by no means squeamish in the use she made of other people's weaknesses.

The personal popularity of the young Hanovers was dramatically displayed when a chairman, perhaps rather drunk, insulted Caroline in Leicester Fields. The mob almost lynched him before he could be brought before a justice for sentencing to appropriate chastisement :

On Thursday morning last, Moore the chairman, who insulted the Princess, was whipped, pursuant to his sentence, from Somerset House to the end of the Haymarket ... The respect Her Royal Highness has among all parties was remarkable in the general cry there was all way he pass'd of 'Whip him', 'Whip him'; and by the great numbers of people that caressed and applauded the executioner after his work was over, who made him cry, 'God bless King George' before he had done with him.[25]

The Ministers' 'complaint against the Prince was that he spoilt and opposed the King's affairs; and they used to say to the King that the Prince's friends were like a battalion that broke through all their measures'.[26] They resolved to try to bring about a reconciliation between the King and the Prince of Wales, and at the same time buy off his most able supporters. The King did not see it in this way. He was willing to have Walpole and Townshend back in Whitehall, but drew the line at having the Prince back in St James's. 'Can't the Whigs come back without him?' he asked. If the Prince was to come back, he must be 'bound hand and foot'. The Ministers finally persuaded the King by convincing him that Walpole alone could talk the Commons into voting £600,000 to clear the royal debts.[27]

The Prince was far from eager to be clasped to the paternal bosom. He adored his younger children and longed to be reunited with them. He missed his guards, his mounted escorts, his salutes, all the honours due to the heir to the throne, and would give a lot to have them back. He would even write his father a letter of apology. But to ask him to live under his father's roof was too much. Rather than that, he would allow the rift to continue. He was at last persuaded to agree by the assurance that, provided he put in an occasional appearance at St James's, he need not resume residence – a concession the King was only too willing to grant. If he refused to cooperate with this plan approved by his friends, Walpole and Townshend, then the Ministry would not scruple to bring in the enemies of his House, the Tories.[28]

Caroline took even more persuasion. Above all things she wanted the custody of her daughters, but this was no part of the bargain. Walpole persuaded her to trust to the reconstituted Ministry's good will after the reconciliation, but later she regretted her concession. 'She weeps and tells me she was betrayed; that they have bribed the Prince with consenting he should stay where he was,' to agree to drop the question of the children. But Walpole promised upon his faith and honour it should be done within a few days. The Princess said to him, 'Mr Walpole, this will be no jesting matter for me; you will hear of me and my complaints every day and hour, in every place, if I have not my children again.'[29]

However, she respected Walpole's sagacity, and agreed at last

6. 'A Music Party': Frederick Prince of Wales and his sisters: (*left to right*) Anne, Caroline and Amelia; in the background the Dutch House at Kew: by *Philip Mercier*

7. Henrietta Howard, Countess of Suffolk *by Charles Jervas*

8. Molly Lepel, later Lady Hervey: *engraving by Heath*

9. A satire on the marriage of Frederick, Prince of Wales, to Augusta
of Saxe-Coburg-Gotha, 25 April 1736: 'View here . . . the *Pimp*, the
Miss forsaken and the *Wife*', the former either Walpole or Charles
Boden and the second Frederick's reputed mistress Miss Vane with
her son Cornwall Fitz-Frederick Vane

to take his advice, seeing clearly what harm the quarrel could do
to the dynasty.

Once the agreement was made, Townshend was to become Lord
President of the Council and Walpole would resume the lucrative
office of Paymaster.

The drafting of the Prince's letter to the King required ample
discussion with his friends, especially with Lord Cowper, for it
must contain the bare minimum of apology which the King would
find acceptable, and no legal commitments as to future conduct :
'he would write to the King nothing that shall tie his hands'.
Eventually it was worded to the Prince's and Cowper's satisfaction.[30]

William Pulteney, an opposition Whig, asked Walpole what
terms he had obtained for the Prince.

'Why, he is to go to Court again, and he will have his drums
and guards and such fine things.'

'But is the Prince to be left Regent as he was when the King
first left England?'

'Certainly not,' Walpole replied. 'He does not deserve it, we
have done more than enough for him; and if it were to be done
again, we should not do so much.'[31]

Pulteney, in a huff at being omitted from the reconstructed
Ministry, repeated this to Prince George, who did not forgive or
forget. Indeed he was already beginning to think that Walpole
had been indecently eager to make his own terms, but far less
solicitous for his patron's interests. Gossip in his circle was to the
same effect. Lady Cowper grumbled rather incoherently,

The Prince and Princess get nothing in reality by this agreement, but
leave to come sometimes to Court ; and for that they give up their children,
suffer their friends to betray and quit them, and take service where, in
a little time, they will hear it is a fault to be civil to those they have
betrayed: ... I fear, as now it is too plain, they only made the Prince
their cat's foot to compass their own ends, since he is thus betrayed into
this most infamous way of making peace, without any real benefit for
himself and the kingdom . . .

The Princess says we are to trust to them – 'tis in their own interest,
Walpole says, to keep their words with the Prince and Princess – but
methinks 'tis a good old English saying, that the less you believe, the

less you'll be cheated . . . I verily believe Townshend and Walpole have agreed for themselves only.[32]

Nor was the King at all pleased with the terms finally agreed. 'Did you not always promise to bring me the Prince bound hand and foot, and don't you bring him back without my having power to put any one servant in or out about his person?' Mohamed, the Turk, told people that the King was thoroughly displeased with his Ministers for pushing him into this reconciliation.[33]

The Prince took his chair and went to St James's, where he saw the King in his closet. The Prince made him a short compliment, saying it had been a great grief to him to have been in his displeasure so long; that he was infinitely obliged to H.M. for this permission of waiting upon him, and that he hoped the rest of his life would be such as the King would never have cause to complain of. The King was much dismayed, pale, and could not speak to be heard but by broken sentences, and said several times, '*Votre conduite, votre conduite*'; but the Prince said he could not hear distinctly anything but those words. The Prince went after he had stayed about five minutes in the closet . . . The Prince came back, with the Beefeaters round his chair, and hallooing and all marks of joy which could be shown by the multitude. He looked grave, and his eyes were red and swelled, as one has seen him upon other occasions when he is mightily ruffled. He immediately dismissed all the company, and I was ordered to be there at five in the afternoon.

At five I went, and found the Guards before the door, and the square full of coaches; the rooms full of company; everything gay and laughing; nothing but kissing and wishing of joy; and, in short, so different a face of things, nobody could conceive that so much joy should be after so many resolutions never to come to this, as I have heard . . .

I wished the Prince joy and comfort of what had been doing. He embraced and kissed me five or six times, and with his usual heartiness when he means sincerely. He said he knew the part I took in all his good or ill fortune, and he knew my good heart so well, he was sure I was pleased with this. The Princess burst out into a loud laugh, and said, 'So! I think you two always kiss upon great occasions.'

All the town, feignedly or unfeignedly, transported . . . The King could not be brought to see the Princess that night, and said, when he was pressed to it several times, '*L'occasion se trouvera!*'[34]

A gratifying feature of the whole business was that the Germans were kept out of it. So ignorant were they of the negotiations that

Bernstorff, when he heard Stanhope speak of '*la paix*' thought that the peace mentioned was in the Baltic.

None of the Germans knew of this except the Duchess of Kendal, whom English money and an English title had made true to the English Ministers.

Stanhope came up to the two German Ministers in the outward room, and said in French to them in his shrill scream,

'*Eh bien! Messieurs, la Paix est faite . . . la Paix est faite.*'

B. '*Les lettres sont-elles arrivées?*'

S. '*Non, non, c'est la Paix ici. Nous allons revoir notre Prince.*'

B. '*Notre Prince?*'

S. '*Oui, notre Prince, notre Prince; nous l'attendons pour être reconcilié avec le Roi.*'

B. '*Monsieur, vous avez été bien secret dans vos affaires.*'

S. '*Oui, oui, nous l'avons été . . . le secret est toujours necessaire pour faire les bonnes choses.*'

Bernstorff could not bear the insult, nor the being given up by his old master, and burst into tears, which was very faithfully reported to the Prince and Princess.[35]

It was the old man's final defeat. When next the King went to Hanover, Bernstorff accompanied him and did not return.

Next day at church the King and the Prince met, but exchanged not a word. 'When the King came out, the Prince stood by him. The King spoke to most people except the Prince: they to only looked grave and out of humour.'[36]

Most non-Jacobites were pleased with what had happened, particularly those who, not being present, had not seen the sulkiness and reluctance with which father and son formally made up their differences. The general reaction was exemplified by an honest country gentleman and militia captain, Mr Molesworth, who, wrote his wife,

was not satisfied to make his men drunk, but got drunk himself, and it was no fault of his that I was not so too; in short, he celebrated the news in a manner that alarmed the country people, for after he had made them ring the bells all day, in the evening he made his troop draw up before his lodging and he at the head of them, and began the King and Prince's healths together, and the Princess, and after, the rest of the royal family; at every health he made his troop fire round a volley of shot: he invited several gentlemen to pledge these healths, and when they had done they threw the glasses over their heads. When this was done he carried them all with him to drink a bowl of punch. As to his men, after they had despatched a barrel of ale they thought themselves not glad enough, and he, to make them so, went amongst them and gave them money to finish in wine. He is at present a little disordered with that night's work, and desires his best service to you.[37]

But some of those closest to the Prince were less well pleased. Lord Cowper, for instance, who felt that he had been bypassed and his sage advice neglected in the negotiations, went into retirement. Not so his wife to whom the King had taken a fancy.

The Princess said to me that . . . the King could not help liking me as well as ever; and that she saw plainly by the King's manner last night that I could do as I pleased, and that it was my fault if I did not rule them all. I answered, for the thing itself, I did not believe it at all; and, supposing it were true, power was too dear bought when one was to do such dishonourable work for it.[38]

The King was in a dejected mood not only because he must now be civil to his son, but because his sister, the Queen of Prussia, perhaps the only person of whom he was really fond, died at this time. She was suspected of having been poisoned with a diamond powder, the symptoms of which were graphically described by Mohamed,

for when she was opened her stomach was so worn that you could thrust your fingers through at any place, as did Mohamed. The King, he said, was in such sorrow that he was without eating or drinking, or sleeping, but kept walking and wailing all the time, and by hitting his toes against the wainscot (which he ever does when he walks) he had worn out his shoes till the toes came out two inches at the foot.

In this black mood, according to Walpole, 'he was very rough with the Princess – chid her very severely in a cruel way. He told her she might say what she pleased to excuse herself; that she could have made the Prince better if she would, and that he expected from henceforward she would use all her power to make him behave well.' But the Princess herself put a good face on it, and came out of the closet 'transported at the King's mighty kind reception and told everybody how mighty kind he had been to her'.[39]

92

There was 'great hugging and kissing between the two old and two new Ministers. They walk all four, with their arms round one another, to show they are all one.' But this rapture was confined to Sunderland, Stanhope, Townshend and Walpole. The rank and file of the two Courts were far from reconciled, which

made the whole thing look like two armies drawn up in battle array; for the King's Court was all at the top of the room behind the King, and the Prince's Court behind him. The Prince looked down and behaved prodigious well. The King cast an angry look that way every now and then; and one could not help thinking 'twas like a little dog and a cat – whenever the dog stirs a foot, the cat sets up her back and is ready to fly at him . . . Walpole has undertaken to make the Prince do everything the King pleases. The Prince knows nothing of this, but thinks he governs everything.[40]

The Princess's chief *bête noire* was young Craggs* who had played a large and, she thought, crafty part in the peace negotiations. 'He makes many professions and tells many lies. He says he was not for taking the children from the Princess. He said the quarrel had been made by under-servants, who had repeated abundance of things about the Prince's opposition to His Majesty's Government.'

The Princess said, '"I was told you had condescended so low as to call me a bitch."

'At which he began a volley of oaths and curses at the falseness of the assertion, for so long a time, and with so much vehemence, that she said to him, "Fie! Mr. Craggs; you renounce God like a woman that's caught in the fact."'[41]

The strange phenomenon of the Prince of Wales heading the opposition to His Majesty's Government was generally attributed to the unnatural and lamentable feud between father and son. But, while personal antipathies no doubt sharpened political differenced, these differences themselves were inevitable in the circumstances of the time. These may be summarized as follows.

From 1715 until the last decade of the eighteenth century Britain was virtually a single party state.† Not only all the

* James Craggs, Junior, Secretary of State.
† This is best instanced by the Parliamentary Papers of John Robinson

93

members of the Government, but all members of the Opposition who had the slightest chance of becoming members of the Government, were Whigs. The once great Tory Party, although from time to time it probably voiced the opinions of most people in the country, was represented in Parliament by a small, noisy group of country gentlemen, embittered by the barren politics of resentment, railing against the extravagance and corruption of the Ministry and concerned mainly with the burden of the land tax and the iniquity of a standing army. Because of their leaders' follies and quarrels and because Walpole and his colleagues succeeded in implanting in the Kings' minds the conviction that all Tories were potential Jacobites, they had only a certain nuisance value with no possibility whatsoever of joining, let alone forming, an alternative government.

As for the Whigs, those in the Government and those in the Opposition were divided by no differences of principle or policy, which meant that an opposition Whig could without a qualm at any time accept office. All that divided them was that some were in and some were out, and the principal ambition of the latter was to join the former.

The next factor setting the pattern of politics for most of the period 1715–60 was that the Kings were elderly or infirm, while the heirs to the throne were young and healthy.

Finally the franchise was such that the Crown could, by means of patronage, exercise an overwhelming influence on elections except on the rare occasions when political passions ran so high that patronage, family pressure and naked corruption were at a discount. This will be discussed in more detail in a later chapter.

These factors governed politics throughout the reigns of the first two Georges, and from about 1782 to about 1793, that is to say, for over half the eighteenth century. They were in abeyance during the reign of Queen Anne when the heir to the throne was older than the Queen and resident in Hanover and when fierce differences divided Whig and Tory; while George III's eldest son was a child or a minor; and during the wars of American Inde-

who, describing in 1782 the political loyalties and affiliations of every single Member of Parliament, never once mentions the words Whig and Tory.

pendence and the French Revolution when, again, Government and opposition were deeply divided on questions of principle and an honourable man could not easily be induced to cross the floor.

In such circumstances an ambitious politician who saw no immediate prospect of office in His Majesty's Government had no alternative but to make his court to the Prince of Wales in the hope of a reversion. He might, if he was very fortunate, obtain some lucrative employment in the Prince's household, but what he really sought was a reversion. 'Everyone,' remarked Walpole – and who should know better? – 'comes to Court to get; and if there is nothing to be got in the present, it is natural to look for reversions.'[42] As the King grew older or more infirm, so the value of actual jobs fell and that of reversions rose, and desertions from the King's to the Prince's party increased. Eventually the Prince's opposition grew so formidable that the Ministry was forced to buy off some of its more dangerous members by taking them into the Government. This, of course, infuriated the Prince. It was inherent in the politics of reversion that his followers, by taking thought of the morrow and not worrying too much about the next day, could add considerably to their stature; but he could never do so; so long as his father lived, he could never join the Ministry. However great his talent and capacity for mischief, he had no constructive role to play.

When Sunderland and Stanhope cursed the Prince's battalions, and lured Walpole and Townshend to their side, when the Prince then inveighed against the ingratitude and treachery of the deserters, they were unconsciously enacting the first performance of a drama (or comedy) which was to be re-enacted many times in the course of the century.

Soon after the reconciliation, the Prince and Princess did at last secure custody of and free access to their own children. In April, while negotiations were still in progress, Anne had contracted smallpox, and to the Princess's request to see her the King had replied, through Mohamed, that 'she might go, but she must carry neither doctor nor physic', for he had himself made appropriate arrangements. Her parents were for some days, at the height of the political crisis, in a state of desperate anxiety; but the attack was a light one, and the little girl soon recovered and was very little marked. Caroline, too, caught the disease, but recovered quickly, with no permanent disfigurement. Throughout her illness George Augustus remained at her side, risking an infection which so often proved fatal.[43]

6

The royal reconciliation was not the only matter to engage public attention in the spring of 1720. All classes, high and low, were absorbed in the fascinating pursuit of capital gain. It was quite easy: one simply bought shares, any shares, as many as possible, and then saw their value rise two-, three- or four-fold in a few months. It was rather like loo, faro or basset, with the gratifying difference that one could not lose. Small squires and tenant farmers, wrote Defoe, flocked to town, 'each expecting no less than to ride down again in his coach and six'.

'How long have you been a gentleman?' someone asked a young fellow in a fine laced coat.

He replied with commendable frankness, 'Only a week, madam.'

Mrs Molesworth, whose husband celebrated with such conspicuous loyalty the happy return of His Royal Highness to His Majesty's Court, was typical of thousands who, totally ignorant of such matters, invested every halfpenny they had, and lamented only their inability to raise more.

I am [she confessed to her friend, Mrs Howard] almost South Sea mad . . . and I cannot, without great regret, reflect that, for want of a little money, I am forced to let slip an opportunity which is never likely to happen again. Good Lady Sunderland was so mindful of her absent friends as to secure us a five hundred pound subscription . . . and it is now doubled; but this has given me a taste of fortune which makes me more eager to pursue it . . . I should have been satisfied if I could by any means have raised the sum of five hundred or a thousand pounds more, but the vast price that money bears, and our not being able to make any security according to law, has made me reject the scheme I had laid of borrowing such a sum of a moneyed friend.[1]

It had all started nine years ago when the Tory Ministry of Harley and St John, anxious to win over some of the moneyed interests to their side, had granted a charter to the South Sea Company, which they hoped would be a counterpoise to the Whig-dominated East India Company and Bank of England. It was promised a monopoly of trade with Spanish America, which would be extracted from Spain as part of the price of peace; and holders of £9 million of gilt-edged stock were compelled to exchange this for stock at par in the new company.[2]

The South Seas trade, which meant essentially trade with the Spanish Main, had always had in English eyes the peculiar fascination of forbidden fruit. The exploits of the buccaneers stimulated this interest, as did the directors of the company, with rumours, quite without foundation but industriously circulated, that four ports in Chile and Peru were to be ceded by Spain. The prospect of exchanging English woollens for gold, silver, gems and precious drugs was indeed an alluring one.[3]

In the event, the company's fortunes proved rather disappointing. All the Spaniards actually conceded, in the Assiento of 1713, was a thirty years' monopoly of the slave trade and the right to send to South America one trading ship a year, of a limited tonnage, of which 28·75 per cent of the profits would accrue to the King of Spain. But it was one thing to negotiate an agreement with the Spaniards, another thing to hold them to it. Because of their procrastination, the first trading ship did not actually set sail until 1717; and next year, in the course of a quarrel between the two countries, the company's assets on Spanish soil were all seized.

No matter. What concerned people was not dividends, but capital appreciation, not the company's trade and profits but the value of its shares, and there seemed very little connection between the two. So long as people wanted to buy South Sea stock, its value would rise. So in November 1719 the directors of the South Sea Company determined on another conversion operation, bigger and better than that which had given the company so auspicious a start.

It was not pure public spirit that moved the directors to offer to take over the huge National Debt. Holders of this Government stock would be invited to exchange it for new South Sea stock (which the company was authorized to create, £1 for £1, for the debt it took over) at current prices. Since current prices were adroitly boosted to well above par by optimistic 'leaks' about future trading prospects, the directors would then have extra stock to sell on the open market. Everyone would thus be satisfied. Most pleased of all were the politicians, courtiers and royal mistresses who received, to impress them with the virtues of this scheme, some £1·5 million worth of South Sea stock free, gratis and for nothing.

The directors' proposals were put to the Commons on the 20 January. Walpole, still in opposition, was concerned mainly with ensuring that the Bank of England's rival offer did not go by default, since its directors were his personal friends. He played for time by warning the House that the company's scheme had its dangers, since it 'countenanced the pernicious practice of stock-jobbing by diverting the genius of the nation from trade and industry' – and so on. He suggested that at least the South Sea directors should be obliged to put a ceiling on the price of their stock, as the Bank had undertaken to do. But when the Bank dropped out of the bidding, Walpole went along with the rest of the House in approving unanimously the South Sea directors' improved offer.[4] Walpole was neither more nor less prescient than the rest, but being out of office, bore no personal responsibility for what might ensue. He accepted office only on 4 June, when the issue had long been determined, South Sea stock was soaring and no one envisaged anything but continued, glittering prosperity.

> What need have we of Indian wealth,
> Of commerce with our neighbours?
> Our constitution is in health
> And riches crown our labours.
> Our South Sea ships have golden shrouds,
> They bring us wealth, 'tis granted ;
> But lodge their treasure in the clouds,
> To hide till it is wanted.[5]

It was, of course, the essence of the whole scheme, that stock should continue to rise, so that people should continue to buy it.

To stimulate the public's cupidity, 'groundless and mysterious reports were circulated concerning valuable acquisitions in the South Sea and hidden treasures'; dividends of ten, thirty, even fifty per cent were voted, which the directors knew could never be paid. To prime the pump the directors contrived a series of new issues, four in all, and even lent to people who had bought £100 worth of stock money at five per cent to buy £250 worth more. Stock of £100 face value, worth £126 at Christmas 1719, rose at the first new issue in April 1720 to £300 and £400 ; by the end of June it was worth £1000, and John Blunt, the most prominent of the directors, was made a baronet for enriching himself and so many others.[6]

Defoe in the *Original Weekly Journal* wrote that:

Since the late hurly-burly of stock-jobbing there had appeared in London 200 new coaches and chariots besides as many more now on the stocks in coach-makers' yards ; about 4000 embroidered coats; about 3000 gold watches at the sides of whores and wives ; some few private acts of charity; and about 2000 broken tradesmen.[7]

The Prince's friends were as eager as any to invest. Mrs Howard was 'successful in the South Seas', nor did he and Caroline disdain a flutter.

One of Walpole's great arts to please the Princess has been making her a jobber in the South Sea. They bought in for her that very morning before the great debate, and it was used to Members of Parliament as arguments that they [the Prince and Princess] were both for the project. Since they subscribed at a hundred and fifty – he twenty thousand, she ten – many members of Parliament were struck out for this.[8]

The King himself invested from Civil List funds £20,000 at the first issue in April, £40,000 in the second and third issues. About 12 June he sold this stock for £106,400, a very tidy profit. The German ladies too were believed to have benefited to the extent of £30,000.[9] Walpole, though he had no particular apprehensions, was constitutionally disinclined to put all his eggs in one basket, and limited his South Sea investment to a modest £9000.[10] Others who, like Walpole, wished to spread their risks, or could not obtain South Sea stock, found alternative ways of making their fortunes. The Prince was so imprudent as to become Governor of a very dubious copper company, despite Walpole's apprehensions that 'the Prince of Wales's Bubble' would be hawked about in Change Alley. Not until his company was threatened with prosecution did he withdraw his patronage, taking a profit of £40,000.[11]

Those whose conscientious scruples inhibited them from investing in Puckle's Machine-gun, designed to fire round bullets against Christians and square bullets against Turks, could venture their savings in companies dedicated to trading in human hair; importing Spanish jackasses for improving English mules (quite a sensible idea, this); transmuting quicksilver into precious metals; insuring marriages from divorce; breeding silkworms in Chelsea Park; making fresh water from the sea; or constructing a wheel of perpetual motion. There was even an amiable swindler, familiar to every schoolboy, who set up shop in Cornhill for receiving subscriptions for a project of great profit, 'but no one to know what it is'. The profit amounted to over £1000, collected in cash from confiding investors, with which he absconded, and was heard of no more.[12]

The directors and politicians deplored these muddy channels, which diverted investment from the limpid waters of the South Sea. On 11 June a proclamation was issued prohibiting unchartered corporations from offering their stock. This flung a cold douche over investors, and the more prudent began unobtrusively to sell and take their profits. The Duchess of Marlborough persuaded her Duke, now grievously decayed in understanding, to sell out at a profit of £100,000. When the King in mid-June, the price having risen to nearly £1000, rashly determined to reinvest the money he had realized so handsomely a few days earlier, Aislabie, the Chancellor of the Exchequer,

used my endeavour to divert His Majesty from this resolution, for that the stock was carried up to an exorbitant height by the madness of people, and that it was impossible it could stand, but must fall . . . His Majesty was pleased to tell me that I had the character of a timorous man, and that he was assured the stock would rise to 1500 per cent, and positively commanded me to lay it out in the purchase of stock and subscriptions.

By August the wise and far seeing were getting cold feet.[13] The balloon – a far more appropriate metaphor than a bubble – which had been quietly and unobtrusively leaking for six weeks, now collapsed with a startling rapidity. By early September hundreds of investors were selling out for anything they could get, bringing down South Sea prices with a run. Thousands of ordinary people who had bought, or contracted to buy, saw their lifetimes' savings disappear in a few weeks: gone was the glittering dream of affluence; in its place, the stark prospect of ruin. It was, wrote a contributor to *The Freethinker*, 'a pain to convene in public places . . . a torment to visit private houses'.

Thus in the course of eight months we have seen the rise and progress of that mighty fabric, which being wound up by mysterious springs and artificial machines to a stupendous height, had fixed the eyes and expectations of all Europe; but whose main foundations being fraud, illusion, credulity and intoxication, tumbled to the ground as soon as this ambidexterous and selfish management of its principal projectors was discovered. With its fall multitudes of unwary but covetous persons were unfortunately crushed, and not a few ancient and honourable families almost entirely ruined.

Yet the country's wealth was still there: it had not been immolated in a furnace or sunk literally in the South or any other sea. What, then, had become of it? *The Freethinker*, and a score of other journals, had the answer. 'The wealth and inheritance of the island are transferred to the meanest of the people . . . the nobility, the gentry, the merchants have become a prey to the idle, the licentious, the spendthrifts; men whose habitations are not known.'[14]

In November the King returned from Hanover to a panic-stricken capital, but his appearance did nothing to allay his subjects' alarm. There was a clamour for the blood of the guilty men. 'You may at present load every gallows in England with directors and stockjobbers without the assistance of a sheriff's guard or so much as a sigh from an old woman.'[15] There were warnings that at an official inquiry 'honest gentlemen should not sit near the directors for fear of accidents . . . Several people went with pocket-pistols and a desire to use them.'[16]

At this moment of public turmoil, Walpole demurely returned from his well-timed holiday in Norfolk. In no way could he be blamed for anything that had happened. He had been in opposition in 1711 when the South Sea company was granted its charter, in opposition again in 1720 when it took over the National Debt. He had himself lost money in his South Sea investments, and was so little in the know that only the urgent representations of his banker had dissuaded him from a further disastrous plunge in August.

But although Walpole had not displayed any marked perspicacity in his South Sea investments, he saw very clearly the political dangers of the collapse. For public anger would not be directed solely against the directors and the politicians who were mainly responsible : the hunt for scapegoats might not stop short of the dynasty itself. The King and Prince of Wales were deeply involved ; the German ladies had received large blocks of South Sea shares as an inducement to use their influence in favour of the directors' proposals. The wildest rumours, although totally unfounded and often contradictory, were circulating which could benefit only the enemies of the House of Hanover; to encourage them by persecuting the directors would pave the way for a Stuart restoration. It was essential to calm people.[17] Walpole was still only Paymaster, but his reputation for financial sagacity and his non-involvement in the South Sea scandal gave his views great weight. His objects were, in order of priority, to preserve the dynasty by whitewashing the King ; to allow public confidence to recover by minimizing the directors' errors ; and to restore whatever could be restored to those who had suffered. To this end he first proposed to the King a plan, devised by his banker, for strengthening South Sea stock by engrafting it with that of the East India Company and the Bank of England (both sound Whig institutions). These proposals were in the end so altered and modified as to bear little resemblance to the originals, but the knowledge that Walpole had hastened from Houghton to the rescue was enough to lift South Sea stock from its rock bottom price of 125 to 200.[18]

When Parliament met on 8 December there were loud cries for vengeance. One honourable member recommended that, as no present laws could touch the directors,

the example of the Romans ought to be followed who, because their laws were defective in not having provided a penalty for parricide, made one to punish the crime after it had been committed, and adjudged the guilty wretch to be sewn up in a sack and thrown alive into the Tiber . . . He would be satisfied to see the directors suffer the same fate.

Walpole deprecated such draconian measures and steered the House towards a harmless resolution, passed unanimously, which condemned 'the infamous practice of stock-jobbing'. Having thus taken the heat out of the issue, he persuaded the House that all contracts with the company must be honoured: those who had made fools of themselves could not escape the consequences simply by dishonouring their debts and hanging the directors.[19]

He could not, of course, prevent a parliamentary inquiry into the company's affairs, though he did nothing to expedite it: nor could he prevent an Act forbidding the directors to leave the country or alienate their estates, which might be required to compensate the victims. Evidence placed before the inquiry included aspersions on the personal honour of Stanhope, who in fact was less to blame than any Minister. So enraged was he that in answering the allegations in the House of Lords he died of a stroke. The older Craggs committed suicide and the younger died of smallpox.

Generations of historians have credited Walpole with the financial genius which restored the situation after the bursting of the Bubble. Modern research shows that he produced no panacea. 'Time, not Walpole, was the healer. The prime necessity, as he saw it, was to avoid panic and restore confidence . . . The trade of the nation was in a flourishing condition. The danger, if any, was psychological.'[20] So, indeed, was the cure. Walpole's so-called genius in this instance may be compared to that of the officer who, armed with no more than a walking stick, strolls up and down in front of his men under heavy fire. By baulking innocent victims of their senseless revenge, he gave an impressive demonstration of nerve, imperturbability and resistance to popular clamour. His reward from the King was to be made, in April 1721, First Lord of the Treasury in place of Sunderland and Chancellor of the Exchequer in place of Aislabie. From the people Walpole's reward was execration for shielding the guilty men and the derisive nickname of the Skreen Master General.

Holding two of the principal offices in the Cabinet Committee, with his brother-in-law, Townshend, Secretary of State in the vacancy made by the death of Stanhope, Walpole was now for the first time within reach of real power. But he was not yet supreme : Stanhope's able protégé, John Carteret, was Townshend's colleague as Secretary of State; and when Sunderland died suddenly in April 1722, his mantle fell on Carteret. But Walpole's chance had come. Steadily he strengthened his grip on power and for twenty years nothing could prise it loose. His system was not built in a day : it was the product of circumstances and of his own patient, determined application. But the Parliament of 1722 saw the rapid growth of what his enemies were to call 'Robinocracy' or 'the Robinarchy', so this is a convenient point at which to examine it.

The principal duty of a Minister, the performance of which marked him as a success or a failure, was to reconcile the wishes of the King with the prejudices of Parliament. George I had not dropped out of politics: far from it: he took an intense and active interest in government, in foreign affairs, and in particular those which related to Hanover. He alone had the unfettered right to employ or dismiss Ministers of the Crown; he could give personal orders to generals and admirals. Above all he had powers, unrivalled by any Minister or combination of Ministers, of patronage. It was the King who promoted naval and military officers, who chose bishops, who made all appointments on the Civil List, and many in the colonies, who created peers, who distributed pensions on the English or Irish establishment. Hundreds of minor jobs in the Excise and Revenue Departments, the Post Office, Admiralty, and Board of Trade were ultimately in the gift of the Crown. These were the realities of power, and it was accepted that the King chose his Ministers and then delegated to them the patronage they needed to run the country – though he still retained much in his own hands. However restricted his power, his Court was the heart of political life.

At the very beginning of his reign Cowper told the King, ''Tis wholly in Your Majesty's power, by showing your favour in due time [i.e. before a general election] to one or other of them to give whichever of them you please a clear majority in all succeeding Parliaments.'[21]

Two generations later Burke, in his *Thoughts on the Causes of the Present Discontent*, elaborated on the same theme, and showed how the prevailing political morality operated mainly to the benefit of the Crown.

On the side of the Court will be all honours, offices, emoluments; every sort of personal gratification to avarice or vanity; and what is of more moment to most gentlemen, the means of growing, by innumerable petty services to individuals, into a spreading interest in their country. On the other hand, let us suppose a person unconnected with the Court, and in opposition to its system. For his own person, no office, or emolument, or title ; no promotion ecclesiastical, or civil, or military, or naval, for children, or brothers, or kindred. In vain an expiring interest in a borough calls for offices, or small livings, for the children of mayors and aldermen and capital burgesses. His court rival has them all. He can do an infinite number of acts of generosity and kindness, and even of public spirit. He can procure indemnity from quarters. He can procure advantages in trade. He can get pardons for offences. He can obtain a thousand favours, and avert a thousand evils. He may, while he betrays every valuable interest of the kingdom, be a benefactor, a patron, a father, a guardian angel to his borough. The unfortunate independent member has nothing to offer but harsh refusal, or pitiful excuse, or despondent representation of a hopeless interest. Except from his private fortune, in which he may be equalled, perhaps exceeded, by his court competitor, he has no way of showing any one good quality or making a single friend.[22]

'Give any man the Crown on his side,' said Lord Granville,* 'and he can defy everything.' Well, not perhaps quite everything, for it was no use a King choosing Ministers who could not get on with Parliament, especially with the Commons, who controlled Supply and without whose consent not a shilling's taxes could be raised. And Parliament, particularly the Commons, took a great deal of managing.

By 1722 the party labels, Whig and Tory, had ceased to have any significance either in Parliament or in the machinery of Government. Walpole's Robinocracy was from the first a single party state. Tories were not, in general, Jacobites, because most

* Formerly Carteret.

of them abhorred the prospect of a Popish restoration; but Walpole, Hervey and Sunderland convinced George I that the entire party was tainted with Jacobitism. 'Nothing,' the Pretender was informed in 1722, 'is so hideous and frightful to him as a Tory.'[23] This revulsion remained implanted in the Hanoverian mind for two generations, and gave rise to a ruthless purge of Tories from positions of power. Patriotism, which Tories had claimed as their hallmark, had now been stolen for a badge by the Whigs. For a Tory family there was no future but that of penurious and humiliating exclusion forever from the corridors of power, unless they turned Whig, which many did.

Tories could not be entirely eliminated from the House of Commons: a few obstinate Tory boroughmongers, a few constituencies with voters too many for easy manipulation, continued to reflect the loyalties of the lower orders and of many country gentry who remained defiantly Tory at heart.

Politicians were divided from one another not by party labels but by ties of friendship, family and territorial connections, favours given and received – all that the eighteenth century termed 'interest'. To these should be added professional and commercial connections: East Indian, West Indian and other groups of merchants formed pressure groups, small in numbers but considerable in influence, which could not safely be ignored. On many issues the lawyers, usually about seventy-five in number, formed a legal pressure group; as did occasionally fifty or sixty army officers and a dozen or so naval officers in the Commons.[24]

The extent to which an individual member was amenable to the pressure of interest depended partly on the nature of his constituency. The English county members, eighty in all with electorates averaging about 4000* prided themselves on being the most 'independent' – independent, that is, of interest, but more subject to public opinion and to the demands of their own conscience. London members also had large electorates (Westminster 9000; Southwark 4000) and consequently a reputation for independence, even for unregenerate Toryism, because the more the voters the less subject were they to manipulation.

* Rutland was the smallest with about 600, Yorkshire the largest with 15,000.

At the other end of the scale were members for small English boroughs, 146 in all each representing an average of twenty-four electors. But dependence could not in fact be gauged by the number of voters in a member's constituency: a county member might owe his election to some local magnate, the representative of Buckingham (twelve voters) or Banbury (fourteen) might be so moved by some great issue as to defy the wishes of his patron. Burke was to discover, to his surprise, that as member for Bristol, where thousands of electors all expected him to promote their individual interests, he had less real freedom of action than the representative of a pocket borough with an indulgent patron.[25]

Methods of borough management varied according to the nature and franchise of individual boroughs. Some answered best to straight or thinly disguised bribery. A fictional character in a play, complaining of a candidate's parsimony, remarks, 'I could get but thirty guineas for an old pair of jackboots, while my neighbour over the road had a fifty pound note for an old pair of leather breeches.' Voters in a close borough knew their scarcity, and were continually raising their price. They liked nothing better than an auction for their votes, and by mid-century the mere possession of a vote in a borough where two wealthy families competed was enough to put its fortunate owner almost beyond the reach of want.

In some boroughs a man might vote only if he lived in a particular quarter of the town, perhaps in the old town as it existed two or three hundred years earlier when its charter was granted. In such cases it was a simple matter for a landlord to evict unreliable tenants and replace them with those on whose votes he could rely. In others only the Corporation had the vote, or all Freemen had it. In such constituencies the party in power would limit the number of voters to secure themselves against defeat, or create scores of new freemen for a particular election – fifty-nine, for instance, at East Dulwich, or 500 in Bedford. Charity, gifts for public purposes such as a water supply, shipbuilding contracts, jobs in the Revenue, even threats of the press gang – all these methods were used to manage close boroughs. It was, therefore, a prime object of political leaders to acquire the services of the boroughmongers, men controlling one or more close boroughs. Of these there were about a hundred, most of them peers, nominating nearly two hundred M.P.s.[26] How an election campaign was conducted is shown in a candidate's instructions to his agents in Rochester which read like a military operation order.

These instructions must be thoroughly attended to, the proper persons and places pitched and a plan laid accordingly –

To fix the names of half a dozen or more stout freemen, to attend the bar, to make room for our friends to poll easily, and constantly, if possible, to keep possession of the bar.

To fix on persons who are to attend each house where freemen are, from Sunday evening till the time of polling, and they to keep constantly at those houses, and never stir out of them till the election is finished ; except it be to poll themselves.

To fix on about half a dozen active persons (whether freemen or not) to conduct about twelve or fourteen freemen at a time from the houses where they are kept, to the polling place, with directions to see them all polled before they leave them. And let the house managers always deliver out those freemen first, whom they think most doubtful, and endeavour as much as may be to keep them sober till they have polled.

By no means to make a parade with the freemen the morning of the election, but to get them as soon as may be, into your private houses, and keep them there till they are polled : to prevent the other side getting away any stragglers.

To have some sensible persons, to go about the town, and the poll house, and to the houses of entertainment of the other side, to get away any drunken, or straggling freemen, and to talk with them properly, and poll them immediately, or carry them to our private houses to be conducted from thence to the poll.

To every person employed in any office, to have his instructions in writing what part he is to take and desired strictly to adhere to it as a great deal will depend upon conduct and good management.

Towards the close of the poll to spare no expense that may seem necessary.

Between this time and the election get what doubtful persons you can into your private houses and entertain them till the election comes on.[27]

Ambitious politicians generally preferred to represent close boroughs because whenever they accepted office, they had to stand for re-election. This could be an expensive business in a county or open borough, but cheap, for instance, at Old Sarum, which was inhabited only by sheep.

It was calculated that in the Parliament of 1701 about 350 members were substantial landowners. Of the remaining 200 nearly all, whether lawyers, merchants, army officers or courtiers, were closely related to the peerage or county gentry.[28] Nearly all county gentry, Whig or Tory, Court or county, Government or Opposition, believed in their heart of hearts that the historical duty, the main purpose of the House of Commons, was to hold in check the power of the Government and the Ministry. Since the death of Queen Elizabeth these anarchic gentry had, by their obstructive tactics, made stable government almost impossible. But in Walpole they met their match. One of his great achievements was to induce a majority of them to support policies which they instinctively disliked. How did he manage it?

Partly, of course, by patronage, which he used with more skill and ruthlessness than any Ministry before or since. Every man, he believed, had his price, every appointment served a political purpose. He naturally gave the key jobs to those he could most trust, his own relatives such as his elder brother, Horatio, who held a succession of important diplomatic posts; his younger brother Galfridus, who was made Postmaster General in 1721; his son-in-law, Lord Malpas, accommodated in the Admiralty in 1727; his sons Edward and Horace who each held several sinecures; his nephew by marriage, Isaac Leheup, whom he made M.P. for Bodmin and Ambassador to Sweden. Next in priority came Norfolk friends and neighbours; then his business associates such as his banker, Robert Jacombe. Finally, for any jobs left, the ordinary peers and M.P.s who must be kept sweet. The minutiae of patronage he delegated to trusted agents, but no cornet was given a troop, no parson a deanery, unless it fitted into Walpole's political pattern.[29]

Patronage was not the whole answer, for there was never 'enough pasture for the beasts that must be fed'. The Younger Pitt was derided in his first week in office as 'a lad here with five barley-loaves and two small fishes, but what are they among so many?' It was to provide a cheap supply of loaves and fishes that Walpole in 1725 revived the Order of the Bath: thirty-eight red ribbons made a handsome addition to the Court's patronage. There was many a gratified recipient of this honour who, like Lord Bateman, 'solemnly promised and gave his great honour that he would

110

always attend the House and vote as he should be directed for the King's service'.[30]

The hard core of the ministerial strength in the Commons consisted of the 'placemen' – courtiers, naval and military officers, civil servants and the like, on whose votes the Government could rely. But there was a small group who voted with the Opposition either because they owed their place to the Prince of Wales, or because they were, though placemen, of an independent turn of mind. Also more or less susceptible to ministerial pressure were all those M.P.s whose relatives, friends and dependants had been gratified by royal or ministerial favour, and fifty or sixty members for the boroughs which were directly controlled by the Ministry – the so-called Admiralty or Treasury boroughs, or those such as Bossiney in Cornwall where of eleven voters, ten were Revenue officers. The Government could generally rely, too, on the votes of forty-five members for Scottish constituencies, 'a parcel of people of low fortunes, that could not subsist without their board-wages'.*[31]

To ensure stable government, therefore, it was absolutely necessary for a Ministry to secure the support of two or three parliamentary parties, groups of M.P.s each owing allegiance to a leader, generally a peer, for whom a place in the Cabinet must be found. These party leaders might be boroughmongers responsible for the choice of a number of M.P.s., or they might, like Carteret or Stanhope, be party leaders by virtue of their ability and personality. Politics in the Augustan Age was the art of gaining these key men by one means or another. But without a party whip it was not easy to keep their followers up to the mark, especially during the hunting and shooting season.

Finally there were the independents or 'neuters', seldom less than 100 in the Commons. They considered themselves free to vote for or against the Government, and it was the mark of a good Minister to ensure, by 'civility', 'bustle', 'management' or, in the last resort, 'expense', that most of the neuters voted with the Court for most of the time.

It was in the management of the Commons that Walpole excelled. All the decisive battles were fought in the Commons and he understood them through and through. He was part of their back-

* Ten guineas a week during the parliamentary session.

ground, he shared their tastes though he had outgrown their prejudices. Although overconfidence sometimes led him astray, he could generally anticipate their reactions. He could address them in the earthy terms they understood; he knew when to yield on detail to secure a more important point later, and when to stand like a rock – when to flatter and when to bully, when to cozen and when to bite.

He was, moreover, extremely solicitous of their economic interests. He knew where the shoe pinched and how to relieve it. He was the best businessman ever to be Prime Minister; the prosperity wrought by his enlightened fiscal policies spread far beyond the Whig commercial classes; the most crusted Tory squire, cursing a government conducted by the principles of 'Change Alley', could still approve a reduction in the National Debt and a lowering of the land tax.

However, Walpole did not neglect the House of Lords. After all, most Cabinet Ministers were or aspired to be peers or they were closely related to the peerage. It was moreover in the Upper House that ministerial pressure could most readily be exerted. The mere fact that it contained only 220 members made it easier to manage than the Commons. Besides, any Tom, Dick or Harry who owned a borough could make an M.P.; but only the King (or his Minister) could make a bishop or a baronet. Not that George I or his son did create many peers; for fear of devaluing the peerage they refrained from doing so; but the possibility of a baronetcy or a step up in the ranks of the peerage was always in the background of a politician's ambitions. Even dyed-in-the-wool Commons men like Stanhope, Walpole and Pitt ended their careers in the Lords.

It was among the twenty-six bishops that Walpole could best contrive that his seed fell on good ground. There was in the early 1720s a mortality among the predominantly Tory bishops, just when Walpole most needed it. They positively seemed to die to accommodate him. Since neither Archbishop was entirely sound, Walpole relied on Gibson of London to keep the Bench of Bishops well stocked with prelates of sound Walpolean views and, if possible, parliamentary influence. Country parsons were often – generally, perhaps – Tories, taking their politics from the patrons who had provided them with livings; but it was Walpole and Gibson who pointed the way to lucrative pluralities, deaneries and the more profitable dioceses. For some, like Bangor, were financially a dead loss; others, like Durham or Winchester, could make a man's fortune, and it was the custom to make an aspiring prelate serve his apprenticeship in one of the former and translate him to the latter only when he had proved that the labourer was worthy of his hire.

His enemies might claim that Walpole was a quack doctor who had 'cured a whole Bench of Bishops of religion', but no doubt most of his choice were good men, reasonably learned and reasonably pious – though some doubts must remain about Blackburn of York, a roistering ex-naval chaplain and, it was alleged, buccaneer who enjoyed his pipe and liquor even in the vestry and was reputed to keep a seraglio. But the worst that could be said of Gibson was that he was a 'pig of Epicurus' and of Hoadley of Winchester that he believed not a word of the Bible and during seven years as Bishop of Bangor he never set foot in his diocese.[32] Their imperfections could be overlooked so long as they never forgot their maker. Political reliability was particularly desirable in clerics who had to do with the universities. Lord Townshend 'passionately inveighed against the Dean [of Christ Church] calling him beast and wretched fellow, who being made Dean to strengthen the Whig interest there, did nothing but laze away his time and suffered the Tories to increase their power and interest in the university'.[33] But such infidelity was happily rare: at the height of his power Walpole could rely on twenty-four of the twenty-six bishops in the House of Lords.

So Walpole controlled the House of Lords and managed the Commons. But besides being 'Minister for the King in the House of Commons' he was 'Minister for the Commons in the Closet'. Here he resorted to simple bribery – George I received £600,000 which he needed to pay his debts; George II was given a very generous sum for the Civil List; the Duchess of Kendal, 'the Good Duchess', Walpole's ally against Carteret, was rewarded with a £17,500 a year pension, a lump sum of £9000 kindly provided by the Duke of Chandos,* and a patent for the manufacture of Irish

* A universal channel of corruption and one of Walpole's best managers. By this and other well-judged gratuities he obtained a dukedom for himself,

copper coinage which turned out in the end to be rather unfortunate.[34]

With one-party government the Privy Council, which contained men of all parties, dropped out of use except for formal purposes. Walpole made as little use as possible of the full Cabinet, even without the King, since it was too large and contained too many Court dignitaries who contributed little of value to its deliberations. With his personality he established such a mastery over the Cabinet Committee, that by 1726 his enemies were already accusing him of elevating himself to being a Prime Minister, though the constitution knew no such office.

In establishing his supremacy Walpole was greatly helped by the increasing cost of politics in general and elections in particular. A seat in Parliament became more and more sought after by county families for the prestige and the patronage it attracted. A single M.P. could by attaching himself to the right group, bring all sorts of minor jobs to his friends and relations. When the demand for any commodity increases while supply remains constant, the price must rise ; so the cost of treating, entertaining and generally keeping sweet the voters inexorably increased. Weobley, for example, which had cost its member £70 in treating in 1690, rose to £719 in 1717. The Septennial Act, although claiming in its preamble to reduce the cost of elections by reducing their frequency, actually had the opposite effect, for candidates would pay more and voters expected more for a seven-year seat than for three years. Many county families of modest means could no longer stand the cost of a family borough, and sold their right of nomination to the highest bidder, generally the Treasury or some great borough-monger like Newcastle. Increasing emoluments for voters whetted the appetites of the urban oligarchies which controlled innumerable boroughs and encouraged them to reduce the number of voters in order that the jam might be more thickly spread. Where, for instance, the franchise was restricted to freemen of a borough, the 'fines' (or fees) for the admission of new freemen were sharply increased; or, more simply, no new freemen were admitted.[35]

an earldom for his father, a deanery for his brother and many lesser benefits for friends and relations.

Increasing costs reduced the number of contested elections, as in counties and boroughs the great families, to save expense, divided up the seats by private treaty. The reduction is most marked in those bastions of democracy, the English counties.

Summary of contested elections, 1722–47[36]

	1722	1727	1734*	1741	1747
All seats	144	114	133	94	62
English counties	17	12	13	4	3

All this resulted in a concentration of power in fewer hands, which facilitated a dictatorship based not on force, not on terror, but on patronage and the shrewd exploitation of human weaknesses – in a word, Robinocracy.

* A year when political feeling and hostility to Walpole ran unusually high.

7

Although it was really no business of the First Lord of the Treasury and Chancellor of the Exchequer, Walpole kept a close watch on the Jacobite exiles. His spymaster penetrated the Pretender's court, and a financial arrangement with the Postmaster General in Brussels ensured that he received copies of much Jacobite correspondence.[1] Dubois and the Regent Orléans also gave him an occasional tip-off. He was therefore well aware of a plot for a rebellion in 1722. Troops were concentrated in Hyde Park, Papists and non-jurors were kept under surveillance and the King's Hanover visit was postponed. That there was a hare-brained scheme of some sort was proved from the surviving correspondence in which a clumsy cypher was easily broken. Walpole himself did not really think it serious. Townshend and Carteret were even more sceptical. But Walpole was not disposed to minimize the danger: adroitly inflated and dramatically disclosed, it would impress the King with the realization that his only salvation lay in the present Ministry. Habeas Corpus was suspended; a punitive fine was laid on Catholics and non-jurors; an unfortunate young gentleman, Christopher Layer, suffered the barbarous penalties of high treason; and Bishop Atterbury of Rochester, protesting loudly at the outrage, was incarcerated in the Tower, duly impeached, and sent into exile.[2] The Jacobites were reduced to their former state of impotence, spreading rumours that 'a new cargo of German ladies of the largest size are coming, and Mohamed is to be chief over them'.[3]

Carteret, who was by this time a rival to Townshend and Walpole in the Inner Cabinet, was not a man to jib at behind-the-scenes intrigue in an effort to counter the strong influence of Walpole. Fortunately for Walpole, the plot was discovered and a conveniently timed crisis in Ireland enabled him to send Carteret there to deal with it, since the country came into his Department. He made Carteret Lord Lieutenant of Ireland and replaced him as Secretary of State with the Duke of Newcastle.

Newcastle was near the beginning of a long political career which was noted principally for his extraordinary tenacity in retaining office. Ridiculed by his contemporaries as a timid, indecisive bungler, too nervous ever to cross the sea or even to sleep in a room alone, forever playing second fiddle to more able men, he has to some extent been reassessed by modern historians : but he lacks a modern biographer largely, one suspects, because of the Herculean task of examining more than 900 large folio volumes of his correspondence. In a celebrated passage by Horace Walpole he is described as 'exceedingly timorous. His ruling passion was the agitation, the bustle of business, but he was as dilatory in despatching it as he was eager to engage in it. He was as jealous of his power as an impotent lover of his mistress, without activity of mind enough to enjoy or to exert it.'[4] He was forever hurt by imaginary slights, forever beseeching his friends to make up his mind for him. 'I am at a loss what to do . . . Something must be done, but I know not what. Pray think of it . . . Pray pity and advise me . . . My friends must think for me . . . I leave the whole to your goodness and friendship.' Nevertheless the support of Newcastle and of his brother, Henry Pelham, was almost indispensable to any government. His political associates were ungrudgingly financed from his immense private wealth. Even in these early days he controlled seven boroughs and had the decisive say, through his huge and widely spread estates, in four county elections, besides influence in many more. In nearly forty years as Secretary of State and First Lord of the Treasury, with government patronage added to that of the Pelham family, experience and tireless attention to detail made of him a very astute operator. The fact that between 1724 and 1762 he was out of the Cabinet for only two brief years is proof enough that he mastered at least the art of political survival. His greatest political virtue was his untiring diligence and some understanding of the system of alliances on which the balance of power in Europe depended; his worst handicap was his jealousy and suspicion of his closest colleagues and even of his own brother. It was well said of him that he always seemed to have lost half an hour in the morning and to be running after it for the rest of the day. But all in all, Townshend and Walpole could hardly have picked a more accommodating partner, adept at keeping the coach in running order but far too nervous ever to take the reins.

Carteret's place might well have gone to William Pulteney, who certainly felt that his merits and his old friendship with Walpole entitled him to a post more distinguished than that of Cofferer to the Royal Household, and when cut out by the despised Duke of Newcastle, he made plain his displeasure. A useful orator with some grasp of economics, he started making a nuisance of himself in the Commons, implying that the Civil List debts were due not to royal extravagance, but to ministerial incompetence and corruption. By doing so he hoped to better his position, but Walpole was not playing by those rules, and promptly reallocated his lucrative sinecure to a relation of the Duke of Newcastle. Pulteney, therefore, transferred his talents to the Opposition.

Walpole now turned to those financial and fiscal reforms on which his fame as Prime Minister is deservedly based. At the accession of George I the National Debt, swollen by the war, had stood at the stupendous total of £54 million, raised at varying rates of interest up to nine per cent, of which the interest alone amounted to over £3·35 million a year. To reduce this burden Walpole had from 1719 set aside from revenue an annual sinking fund which within eight years reduced the capital of the debt by £6·5 million and the interest to a uniform four per cent. So great was the country's confidence in Walpole's financial acumen that in 1727 he was able to raise money at three per cent, though he did from time to time raid the sinking fund for other urgent purposes. One of the principal sources of revenue was the land tax, raised on all landed property. It was a convenient tax, easily assessed and easily collected, with every 1s of the tax bringing in some £500,000; but Walpole disliked it, for he was a landowner himself and knew how tightly the tax squeezed many a modest squire. Most of these were Tories, and it was of importance to reconcile them to Robinocracy; so in 1721 Walpole reduced land tax from 3s to 2s, and gained much popularity thereby. He also revised and simplified the excise duties on certain home products, and the customs duties levied on imported goods, notably wine, tobacco, silk and tea, which were basically those of 1660. These improvements did much to stimulate trade.

In 1726 the political scene was enlivened and Walpole's difficulties markedly increased by the return of Bolingbroke. It had taken him ten years, abject apologies, an earlier visit to London and the somewhat costly intercession of the Duchess of Kendal to achieve even a partial rehabilitation, and he was still not allowed to take his seat in the House of Lords. However, ransomed, healed, restored to his confiscated estates and more or less forgiven, he plunged with zest into the exhilarating game of legal but extra-parliamentary opposition. His wit, his charm, his reputation for gallantry, his literary flair and the gay irresponsibility of his politics made his house at Dawley, near Twickenham, a Mecca for Opposition writers whom Walpole had never bothered to conciliate or to buy. Gay, Pope, Swift, Nicholas Amhurst – they all clustered round him, finding in the ruling establishment a perfect target for satire: the King with his wife in prison for adultery and his harem of elderly adulteresses supervised by a pair of Turks; the rough, irascible Townshend and the timorous, dithering Duke of Newcastle; Walpole in his vulgar clothes strutting around his over-decorated palace, with his huge red face, his great swag-belly (he now weighed twenty stone) and his pretty, pleasant mistress, Moll Skerritt 'for whom he was said to have given (besides an annual allowance) £5000 by way of entrance-money'. The satirist could hardly miss. In December 1726 there appeared the first number of *The Craftsman*, product mainly of the poison-pen of Nicholas Amhurst (alias Caleb d'Anvers) to which Bolingbroke, under the pen-name Humphrey Oldcastle, and Pulteney were the ablest contributors. By allegory, by bogus advertisements, in verse and in prose polemics, *The Craftsman* never ceased to inveigh against the corruption, the debased standards, the political prostitution, on which the Robinocracy was alleged to be founded. 'Dr King's Golden Soporific' was advertised as 'the cure for many ills. The Patient who took it is now satisfied that England is under the best of governments.' A few months later there was described a monster on exhibit at Westminster Hall.

The body of this creature covered at least an acre of ground, was part-coloured and seemed to be swelled and bloated as though full of corruption. He had claws like a harpy, his wings resembled parchment and he had about five hundred mouths and as many tongues . . . As ostriches eat iron, his favourite diet was gold and silver. . . . He could make more than three hundred tongues at once lick his feet or any part of his body.

This was strong stuff, which made Tory squires and coffee-house politicians chortle. Walpole was depicted as a man with a purse of gold in his hand and arch malignity leering in his eye. To all problems and complaints he had but one answer: 'He threw more gold, and they were pacified.'[5] Walpole writhed under the lash, but when Amhurst and the editor were arrested and charged with seditious libel, the evidence against them would not stand up in open court and they were immediately released.

In 1726 there was published Swift's *Gulliver's Travels*. Politically conscious readers were convulsed with the description of Whig politicians ('not always of noble birth or liberal education') competing for the Emperor's favour by dancing on the tight-rope; whoever dances the highest without falling succeeds in the office . . . Flimnap, the Treasurer, is allowed to cut a caper on the straight rope at least an inch higher than any other lord in the whole Empire. I have seen him do the summerset several times together . . .'

Those who failed to secure the blue ribbon of the Garter or the red ribbon of the Bath were much amused by

another diversion which is only shown before the Emperor and Empress, and first minister, upon particular occasions. The Emperor lays on the table three fine silken threads of six inches long. One is blue, the other red and the third green. . . . The Emperor holds a stick in his hands, both ends parallel to the horizon, while the candidates, advancing one by one, sometimes leap over the stick, sometimes creep under it backwards and forwards several times, according as the stick is advanced or depressed.

10. 'Solomon in his Glory', 19 December 1738: George II, his mistress Madame
Walmoden and, on the wall, a portrait of the late Queen Caroline

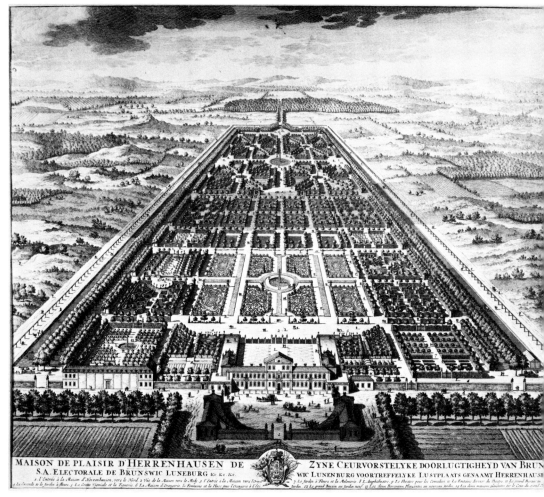

11. Schloss Herrenhausen

Whoever performs his part with most agility, and holds out the longest in leaping and creeping, is rewarded with the blue-coloured silk; the red is given to the next, and the green to the third, which they all wear girt twice round about the middle; and you see few great persons about this court who are not adorned with one of these girdles.

Opposition writers naturally gravitated to Leicester House. Pope cultivated Mrs Howard; and Gay, one of her 'led captains', wrote a book of fables for Prince William, whose mother promised to provide for him when she came to her own. Swift was graciously informed that Caroline 'loved to see odd persons, and having sent for a wild boy* from Germany, had a curiosity to see a wild dean from Ireland'. He took this well and he too became *persona grata* at Leicester House; he and Caroline exchanged presents – or rather the promise of presents, for she seems to have forgotten to send the medals she promised, a slight which this touchy man did not forgive. He claimed to have had her guarantee that he would be 'settled in England' as soon as the King was in his grave.[6]

Since his father had no wish whatsoever for him to live *en famille* at St James's Palace, George Augustus could not be deprived of a separate establishment. Besides the cooks, scullions, turnspits, cleaners, grooms and other menial servants, there were about forty-five appointments reserved for persons of a higher social status, carrying salaries varying from £100 to £1200 a year. Some of these – the Treasurer of the Household and the Master of Horse, for instance – were busy men with proper jobs to do. Other appointments were pure sinecures or partly honorific.

Gentlemen of the Bedchamber, peers and sons of peers, and the Grooms of the Bedchamber, young gentlemen of good county families, were supervised by a dignitary known as the Groom of the Stole, and received £600 and £400 a year respectively for their not very demanding duties which were generally performed in rotation. The Gentlemen in Waiting were of equivalent social status but drew smaller emoluments, as did the equerries and pages of honour who accompanied the Prince out of doors, riding and hunting. The Princess, similarly, had her ordinary domestic servants, and also the Ladies of the Bedchamber and Maids of Honour supervised by the Mistress of the Robes. Besides these

* see p. 124 below.

courtiers, there were the officials who administered the estates of the Duchy of Cornwall.[7]

It was on these household appointments, and on the reversion offices when he should come to the throne, that the Prince's political influence was founded. Moreover the unpopularity of the King's Court, in the aftermath of the South Sea Bubble, attracted support for the Prince. On the 1721 anniversary of the Restoration, *Mist's Weekly Journal* 'hesitated to return thanks for a deliverance from rogues with swords in their hands when we are ruined by Footmen, Pimps, Pathics, Parasites, Bawds, Whores, nay, what is more vexatious, old ugly Whores! Such as could not find entertainment in the most hospitable precincts of Old Bailey.'[8] Mist was quite unconscious of the fact that the most regular contributor to his ultra-Tory Journal was none other than Daniel Defoe,* the ultra-Whig, in his favourite role of literary *agent provocateur*.[9]

But although the climate was propitious for the exploitation of the reversionary factor, the Prince, during the years which followed his formal reconciliation with his father, acted with uncharacteristic circumspection. Perhaps he shrank from more family rows, with all the contempt they brought upon the House of Hanover. More probably, he was content just to wait his turn.

Nor did he take any political initiatives during the King's lengthy holidays in Hanover. He had, of course, a shadow cabinet of gentlemen to whom he had awarded the reversion of various offices; but he does not seem to have objected when its principal luminary, Sir Spencer Compton, accepted in 1722 the job of Paymaster to the Forces. He still, however, resented Walpole's earlier defection, and made his resentment very plain, not merely against Sir Robert but against his brother Horatio ('a scoundrel and a dirty buffoon'), Townshend ('a choleric blockhead') and Newcastle ('an impertinent fool'). Nevertheless Walpole remained on cosy, familiar terms with Caroline, and through his hunting and drinking crony the Duke of Devonshire, who was also a member of the Leicester House set, kept the Prince informed of Government policy and even of secret despatches.[10]

The Prince's Court was not as gay as it had once been. 'Young

* Defoe: 'As yet neither Mist nor any of those concerned with him have the least guess or suspicion.'

122

Hanover Brave' celebrated in 1723 his fortieth birthday, and 'England's daughter, darling of the land', was developing a middle-aged spread. His respect for regularity and punctuality had become an obsession: everything had to be done at a set time, for the good and sufficient reason that it had always been done at that time in the past. The 'Virgin Band', no longer virginal, had dispersed. Sophie Howe had eloped with a notorious rake in circumstances of scandalous publicity. Molly Lepel married that strange creature, Lord Hervey, whom Caroline treated like a pretty pussycat, an occasion celebrated by Lord Chesterfield in somewhat indelicate verse that must have appealed to Their Royal Highnesses' salacious tastes, especially the verse which had a dig at the King:

> Heaven keep our good King from a rising!
> But that rising who's fitter to quell
> Than some lady with beauty surprising;
> And who should that be but Lepel?[11]

The lively Mary Bellenden had also married, for love, neither confiding in nor consulting her princely admirer who had other plans for her. With her husband, Colonel John Campbell, future Duke of Argyll, she lived in the depths of the country, absorbed in rural and domestic duties, occasionally inquiring of her friend Mrs Howard, as from another world, for the latest Court and London news.

You are a base woman for, to be sure, you might have found one day to come to Coombank when His Highness goes to visit his dad, which he does sometimes as *The Evening Post* informs me . . . And pray tell me who has been baited by men and dogs in your family [i.e. at the Prince's Court] and if our Maids are like to lose what they are weary of. Pray God they will not stay with you till my son is old enough to – them all!'

But Mrs Howard, retaining the friendship of Mary Campbell, was losing that of the Prince. This was perhaps due to her becoming a little deaf, for 'Young Rattlebag' (as the Jacobites called him) liked always to have an appreciative audience. 'I was told', wrote Mrs Campbell in April 1722, 'that somebody who shall be nameless had grown sour and cross and was not so good to you as usual.'[12]

Characteristically Lady Mary Wortley Montagu heard, somewhat later, of the coolness between Mrs Howard and her protector, and found another explanation.

I, who smell a rat at a considerable distance, do believe in private that Lord Bathurst and Mrs Howard have a friendship which borders on the tender . . . the fair lady [was] given to understand by her commanding officer [the Prince] that if she showed under other colours, she must expect to have her pay retrenched. Upon which the good lord was dismissed.[13]

A streak of parsimony became increasingly apparent in George Augustus. The £100,000 a year which he received from Parliament and the £7000 or £8000 a year which the Duchy of Cornwall produced did not go very far but, rather than run large debts, he economized.

[He] had only the Lodge at Richmond and his house in Leicester Fields. He went into the country regularly for five months and came back punctually to town on a stated day. He never (during the five months) made any parties nor once lay in London, and he never condescended to invite any person to stay with him in the country, by which means all additional expenses of cold loaves, firing, diet and candles were saved. His diet [was] so plain and the quality of his roasts and dishes so little and the ingredients for dressing them so little.[14]

The Young Hanovers from 1722 to 1727 lived very quietly. They attended occasional concerts and balls, and put in an appearance at the Lord Mayor's civic procession up the Thames to Westminster, where 'some Liverymen offering wine to Their Royal Highnesses, they accepted the same and drank prosperity to the City of London, which was answered by acclamations'. They hunted a lot – at least the Prince did, and the Princess sometimes followed in a coach.

Their relations with the King were cool, but correct. His Majesty even made them a present – not, to be sure, of jewellery or other articles of value, on which the German ladies had first claim, but a 'wild boy' captured in the forests of Hanover, who

walking on all fours, running up trees like a squirrel, feeding on twigs and moss, was last night carried into the drawing room at St James's . . . They have put on him blue clothes lined with red, and red stockings, but the wearing of them seems extremely uneasy to him. He cannot be got to lie on a bed, but sits and sleeps in a corner of the room.[15]

Their children gave the Prince and Princess a good deal of anxiety. Anne and Amelia were delicate and many notes to Mrs Clayton testify to their parents' worry about their colds, catarrh, bronchitis, swollen neck-glands and occasional convulsions. The Princess was not one to accept without question the advice of the Court doctors. 'I begged them for the love of God to put on [Princess Amelia] a blister, but they must not do it . . . He was for giving her an antimony to vomit, which I absolutely refused, but Dr. Bussie agreed to give her a vomit of Hypococyana. I tremble at that.' 'Amelia is to have a blister behind her ear and to be blooded.' The little girl's father now put his foot down and 'forbad it yesterday absolutely. When I found it not done and they found me in despair, it was agreed she should be blooded at night'. So mama had her way as usual, although papa was 'possessed of an opinion that it is wind hinders her swallowing . . . My fears and the opposition I met are endless'. Finally, 'The animals have proposed a flannel shift to make her sweat, upon which I dismissed them.'[16]

In 1722 Caroline had Amelia and Caroline inoculated against smallpox with a serum brought from the East by Lady Mary Wortley Montagu. It was extraordinarily bold of her – indeed Great-Aunt Liselotte condemned it as positively rash.

If one of my children were well, I could not possibly steel myself to make them ill, even though it was for their own good . . . [with an inoculation] the pain is supposed to be less severe and to last for a shorter time, and it is believed the smallpox will never come back. That must be what made the Princess do it. God grant that she may find this is so . . . My doctor doesn't think the remedy is safe, he says he doesn't understand it.[17]

To treat the children Caroline engaged Dr Freind, a devoted Jacobite who only a year earlier had been deeply involved in the Atterbury Plot.[18] Where the health of their children was concerned, George Augustus and Caroline were remarkably open-minded about Jacobite machinations.

But although loving parents to their younger children, they were not overindulgent. One day the Duchess of Marlborough came into Leicester House just as the Princess had been administering wholesome discipline to a child who was roaring piteously. The Duchess tried to console her, but the Prince remarked, 'Ah, see there, you English are none of you well bred because you were not whipped when young.'[19]

'You English!' It was a far cry from the days when he had nothing but praise for the English and insisted in his strong German accent that he was one himself. The Duchess reflected, 'H'm, I am sure *you* could not have been whipped when young.' But she choked it in.

George Augustus saw no need to visit Hanover. He would not be allowed to see his mother, still incarcerated at Ahlden, and could hardly avoid meeting his eldest son, Prince Frederick. The arrangement suited the King very well: the Prince of Wales was safely under his eye in England, while he was represented in Hanover only by a young boy to whom he had no great objection. Frederick had spent a lonely childhood, with no relatives (except on his grandfather's visits), no friends, only grooms and pages for company. He was the centre of ceremonial, with no responsibilities. He had been educated on the cheap by a succession of indifferent tutors. No one had ever given him love, patience or understanding. Nevertheless unbiased reports suggest that there was more to him than his parents and tutors liked to admit: he was neither foolish nor vicious: his possession, at the age of seventeen, of a mistress seemed to guarantee that he had princely tastes. He was rather popular in Hanover, and Lady Mary, never one to spare criticism, reported that:

Our young Prince has all the accomplishments that it is possible to have at his age, with an air of sprightliness and understanding and something so very engaging and easy in his behaviour that he needs not the advantage of his rank to appear charming. I had the honour of a long conversation with him last night before the King came in. His governor retired in order that I might work some judgement of his genius by hearing him speak without constraint, and I was surprised at the quietness and politeness that appeared in everything he said; joined to a person perfectly agreeable and the fine hair of the Prince.

In Hanover the King was a new man, quite different from the morose bore who cast such a shadow over St James's.[20] When in

126

this receptive mood, he was persuaded by his favourite daughter, Sophia Dorothea, Queen of Prussia, to cement the Treaty of Hanover by a double marriage alliance. His grandson, Frederick, should marry her daughter, Wilhelmina ; and her son, Frederick William, an artistic, dreamy youth, should marry his granddaughter, Amelia, a hoyden who cared for nothing but horses.

The Queen of Prussia first tackled Wilhelmina, urging in her prospective bridegroom's favour, that 'he is a good-natured prince, kind-hearted but very foolish. If you will have sense enough to tolerate his mistresses, you will be able to do what you like with him.' But the good effects of this encomium were countered by King Frederick William who characteristically assured her, 'I'll not have a daughter-in-law who carries her nose in the air and fills my Court with intrigues. Your Master Fritz* will soon get a flogging at my hands, and then I'll look out for a marriage for him.' [21]

Lady Darlington, George I's Hanover mistress, gave him a bad account of Wilhelmina, telling him that she was *laide à faire peur* and deformed, as bad as she was ugly, and so violent in her rages as to have apoplectic fits. However, George was persuaded by his daughter to go and see for himself. 'She is very tall,' he commented, as though she were a marble statue. 'How old is she ?' Without another word he examined her in detail, holding a candle under her nose while she turned red and pale in turn. What he saw more or less satisfied him,[22] so it was agreed that the marriage should take place on his next visit to Hanover, in 1727. The Prince of Wales was not consulted.

In November 1726 George I's divorced wife was released by death from her thirty-three years' imprisonment. A brief, non-committal notice in the *London Gazette* mentioned the death of the Duchess of Ahlden. The King forbade any Court mourning and went to the theatre, accompanied by a couple of mistresses, on the night his wife's death was announced. He was, however, worried by a prophecy that he would not survive her by a year. A vague rumour that he now married the Duchess of Kendal is certainly without foundation. In June 1727 the King again set off for Hanover. When he reached Delden on the frontier of Holland, he overindulged at supper, consuming several water-melons. It is said

* Known to history as Frederick the Great.

127

that a letter written by his late wife was there thrown into his coach, reminding him of the prophecy that he would not long survive her. Either this or the water-melons, or both, upset the King and brought on a stroke. Rejecting advice to stop and rest, he shouted angrily to the postilions, 'To Osnabrück! To Osnabrück!' These were his last words. When the coach reached Osnabrück on 11 June 1727, George I, that unlovable but shrewd and honest monarch, was dead.

8

George Augustus and Caroline were at Richmond and had retired to bed for an afternoon nap when they were informed that the First Lord of the Treasury must see him urgently. This, like so many of the great moments of George's life, was faintly marred by farce : he was buttoning up his breeches when he heard that he was King. Neither surprise nor joy overcame for one instant his resentment against Sir Robert. When the Minister duly inquired from whom he should now take His Majesty's instructions, George II replied curtly, 'Go to Chiswick and take your directions from Sir Spencer Compton.' He then disappeared to tell Caroline the exciting news.[1]

It is said that the new King's next order was that two portraits of his unfortunate mother, which he had hitherto been obliged to hide, should now be hung in a place of honour. He hastened to examine his father's private papers. Among these he found the suggestion to George I in the handwriting of Sunderland's private secretary, Charles Stanhope, that the Prince of Wales be kidnapped and conveyed by Admiral Berkeley to a distant country 'whence he would never be heard of more'. Berkeley, required to resign his commission, retired to the continent, and Sunderland and Charles Stanhope, not without reason, forfeited all chance of royal favour.[2]

Nor did the King approve the arrangements made for his eldest son's nuptials. Princess Wilhelmina, he said, had a madman for her father, and he did not think that 'ingrafting my half-witted coxcomb upon a madwoman would improve the breed'. The wedding was again postponed until the King should himself go to Hanover in 1729 : his father's funeral seemed insufficient reason for an earlier visit.

There was also the awkward matter of his father's will, which the Archbishop of Canterbury produced at an early Council meeting. The King, without a word, pocketed the document, which was never seen again. In this testament George I had expressed the wish that after the death of his grandson, Frederick, Britain and Hanover should be divided, the former going to Frederick's elder son, the latter to the younger son, neither of whom had yet been born. Should Frederick die without issue, Hanover would go to the Duke of Wolfenbüttel. Besides that now produced by the Archbishop, one copy of the will had been deposited with the Emperor and one in the Hanover archives, whence it was later transferred to the Duke of Wolfenbüttel in his capacity of executor. But the validity of the will was more than doubtful : the Emperor had advised that the Electorate of Hanover could only pass from the eldest son by voluntary renunciation ; and the British Government, while in principle favouring the separation of the two states, had foreseen insuperable constitutional difficulties. About George Augustus's own attitude to this matter there is some doubt. It is pretty clear that he never gave his formal consent, but Lord Chancellor King recorded in his diary for 24 June 1725 that Walpole had told him that George Augustus and Caroline had both favoured Hanover going to their eldest son, Frederick, and Britain to William, but that George I had refused his consent because it would be unjust to Frederick.[3]

At all events the new King had good reason for suppressing this embarrassing document. At the best interpretation of his action, he was forestalling a thoroughly untidy situation and perhaps safeguarding the interests of the unborn children of Frederick who, although unloved, was after all his eldest son and heir. At the worst, he wished his dominions to be divided in another way – Britain to his favourite son, William, Hanover to Frederick. (He was also, it appears, safeguarding his half-sister, the Duchess of Kendal's daughter by George I, from being spoilt by a legacy which seemed to him absurdly overgenerous. Some years later the young lady married Lord Chesterfield, who threatened to sue the King for £20,000. The matter was settled out of court.[4])

It was easy enough to dispose of that copy of the will which was in England. But to persuade the Duke of Wolfenbüttel (who stood, in certain circumstances, to benefit by it) and the Emperor to give up their copies required some finesse. Fortunately the Electoral Government in Hanover gave a unanimous opinion that 'though at first sight it may appear reasonable', it was illegal and invalid. 'The Duke of Wolfenbüttel,' wrote Newcastle to Horatio Walpole in Paris, 'was in some measure apprised of the contents of the late King's will. Those about him are endeavouring to persuade him to act a right part towards His Majesty.' But he was 'uncertain what hopes and expectations he may have of the support of the Court of Vienna'.[5]

Newcastle 'feared the Emperor will support the pretensions of the family of Wolfenbüttel', and early in July instructed Horatio Walpole to lose no time in sounding Louis XV's chief Minister, Cardinal Fleury, 'not saying he is talking on orders of the King', and enlisting the support of the French Government, for 'it is [His Majesty's] firm resolution not to suffer the Court of Vienna to take any advantage from the incident'. Horatio Walpole was charged by Newcastle in a very private letter to 'mention it to the Cardinal in a way not to make him imagine the King is in any distress or uneasiness. If upon discourse with him you could procure a declaration in writing from the Cardinal upon it, it would give His Majesty the highest satisfaction.'[6]

Fortunately the aged Fleury was favourably disposed to the King, having been gratified by the most condescending and affectionate inquiries, in the royal hand, about his health. 'And had the King that goodness for me?' he asked. 'Was it possible he should know I was drinking the waters?' He expressed 'the utmost detestation and astonishment at the ill-disposition of those who could suggest to His late Majesty advice of so mischievous a nature'. The Cardinal expressed the opinion that it would be most embarrassing if the will were published. The King, he thought, should await events, see what Wolfenbüttel did and visit Hanover in the spring to reassure the Ministers there and suppress any embryonic cabals. The King was delighted with this proof of French support in case the Emperor should prove difficult. 'The Cardinal may depend upon it that no offers or threats of the Imperial Court will be able to make the least impression on His Majesty.'[7]

Eventually the Duke of Wolfenbüttel was brought to reason by a pension 'continued under cover of hiring his troops as a reward for his facility in giving up his copy'. The Emperor's copy was not handed over until Anglo–Imperial relations improved with the Treaty of Vienna in 1731; but meanwhile so long as George II was assured of French support, the Emperor could not turn it to his advantage.[8]

When Walpole left Richmond to report to Sir Spencer Compton at Chiswick he assumed that his days of power were over. 'Everything,' he told Compton, 'is in your hands: I neither could shake your power if I would, not would I if I could. One of your white sticks* or any employment of that sort is all I ask.'[9]

Compton was a worthy mediocrity of great application and dignity, but no talent save for time-serving. 'Frighted with the greatness of his undertaking, and more particularly as to what related to money matters', he begged for Walpole's advice and assistance in composing the first speech which the King would make in Council. Walpole, nothing loth, busied himself with this simple task while poor, innocent Compton went off to see the King. For the next four days Leicester House, where the King still remained, was crammed, but Walpole waddled through the throng as though he were invisible, while everyone crowded round his supposed successor.[10]

On 27 June Parliament met and proceeded immediately to vote the Civil List for the new reign. Walpole proposed that George II be treated far more generously than his father. The latter had received £700,000, with a further £100,000 going to the Prince of Wales. But the new King was guaranteed £800,000, out of which he would be expected to provide for the Prince of Wales ; and if the taxes earmarked for that purpose produced a surplus, it would not be appropriated for the Sinking Fund but would accrue to the King, a concession which was calculated to bring his income up to an average of £900,000, with a jointure of £100,000 for the Queen. With only one dissenting voice the Commons voted these sums,

* Insignia of the Comptroller of the Household, a very modest job.

and Walpole got the credit. His excuse for the increased Civil List was the King's large family and the rising cost of living. 'Good excuse', observed Hervey spitefully, 'for a farmer's backwardness in paying his rent.'[11] Later the King ordered both Walpole and Compton to draft a speech, 'and when it came to choose, shook his head at poor Sir Spencer's and approved Sir Robert's'.

There is little doubt that Caroline, who had always remained on friendly terms with Walpole, influenced the King in his favour. It was she who told Walpole that Compton had proposed only £60,000 for her jointure, thus enabling Sir Robert to outbid him, 'thereby gaining her good grace'. When the King objected to Walpole's greed for money, she replied : 'The old leeches will not be so hungry as the new ones, and will know their business better.' Others might have offered more, but no one else could have persuaded Parliament to vote so much for the Civil List. His father, she reminded George, had remarked that Walpole could convert stones into gold, and a hardly less desirable attribute was that he could keep the Tories out. As for Walpole himself, he could quietly congratulate himself that over the last few years, while his rivals had ingratiated themselves to the mistress, he, with more perspicacity, had made up to the wife. He had, he observed, the 'right sow by the ear'. Moreover brother Horatio came over from Paris and, having received a wigging from the King for quitting his post without a proper relief, made a good impression by his able summary of Anglo–French relations and by the friendly messages he brought from Fleury. Within a few days the King had decided that Walpole, not Compton, was his man. Unfortunately (for George Augustus was an honourable man) Compton had been promised the job, and must therefore be offered it. So a little pantomime was enacted. Compton was assured that he was the King's choice and Walpole promptly undertook to serve under him. At this Compton dissolved into tears, a habit of his at moments of stress, and admitted he was not up to it.[12]

As Walpole drove that day past his rival's house, crammed with courtiers, he remarked to a companion, 'Did you observe how my house is deserted, and how that door is crowded with carriages? Tomorrow the scene will be changed: that house will be deserted, and mine will be more frequented than ever.' The Queen, spotting

Lady Walpole* in the throng at Leicester House called out gaily, 'There I'm sure I see a friend!' and beckoned her to come and kiss the royal hand. In returning, Lady Walpole told her son, 'I might have walked upon their heads, so eager were they to pay their court to me.'

So on 24 July Walpole was reappointed First Lord of the Treasury and Chancellor of the Exchequer, and Townshend received the seals of the Southern Department. The Duke of Newcastle had to come in too, though his royal master judged him as 'not fit to be a chamberlain of the smallest court in Germany'. Poor Compton won only a consolation prize, a barony as Lord Wilmington, and continued in his office as Paymaster.[13]

So the King 'heaped favour on men he had so lately loaded with reproaches', while the only Walpolite to be purged was Sir William Yonge who under the soubriquet 'Stinking Yonge' was a frequent object of royal disapprobation. Indeed it was Walpole who conducted his own purge, packing off Lord Chesterfield, whom he could not stand, to be Ambassador in Holland.

Jacobite hopes had run high when George I died. Walpole, they felt, was sure to go, a mixed Whig–Tory Ministry would come in, and somehow or other events and public opinion would turn to their advantage. But on 21 June Lord Strafford had warned the Pretender,

> The same violent and corrupt measures taken by the father will be pursued by the son, who is passionate, proud and peevish, and though he talks of ruling by himself, he will just be governed as his father was. But his declarations that he will make no distinction of parties and his turning off the Germans will make him popular at present.

Two months later Lord Orrery had to tell the Pretender: 'There do not appear to be many discontented people.' But surely *The Craftsman*, describing the new King as 'mild, gentle and clement ... deeply rivetted in the affection of the people', was laying it on with a trowel. He was, in fact, extremely bad-tempered over trifles, but accepted major disasters with fortitude. The blunder of a *valet de chambre* would put him in a passion, but a Jacobite rebellion left him calm and collected.[14]

* Although estranged from her husband, they kept up appearances.

'He will just be governed as his father was.' The common report was that George Augustus, for all his hot animal courage and fiery temper, had very little will of his own. Writing many years later, in the light of afterknowledge, Hervey noted that although the King snubbed, rebuked and contradicted his wife whenever she expressed a political opinion in public, yet it was she who ruled him. While the King was Prince, some underestimated her influence. 'But as soon as ever the Prince became King the whole world began to find out that her will was the sole spring on which every movement in the Court turned; and though His Majesty lost no opportunity to declare that the Queen never meddled in business, yet nobody was simple enough to believe it'.[15] So, at least, it seemed: that was the common opinion. But it is possible that George Augustus and Walpole allowed her less of the reality of power than she realized. Certainly she had no power over Walpole, and if she ever did independently change her husband's mind, he was unaware of the fact.

One day, enumerating the people who had governed this country in other reigns, he said Charles I was governed by his wife; Charles II by his whores; King James by his priests; King William by his men, and Queen Anne by her women favourites. His father, he added, had been governed by anybody that could get at him. And at the end of his commendious history of our great and wise monarchs, with a significant, satisfied, triumphant air, he turned about, smiling, to one of his auditors and asked him: 'And who do they say governs now?'[16]

But the Opposition wits soon saw otherwise:

> You may strut, dapper George, but 'twill all be in vain;
> We know 'tis Queen Caroline, not you, that reign –
> You govern no more than Don Philip of Spain.
> Then if you would have us fall down and adore you,
> Lock up your fat spouse, as your dad did before you.[17]

Years of bullying by his father, years of insecurity and of never knowing if he would be allowed to inherit the throne had certainly made him erratic in temper and somewhat hesitant – whatever he might say – to act without ample advice, but he generally chose good advisers.

Exactitude was his passion, not merely in the detailed ordering of his life, but in his knowledge of matters which interested him. He was interested in foreign affairs, and in an age when these were often governed by dynastic considerations, his detailed knowledge of every royal family in Europe was an undeniable asset. His greatest enthusiasm, now at least allowed full scope, was for military affairs. He loved talking army 'shop' and reminiscing about campaigns. His knowledge of regiments, establishments and drill movements was precise. He had the Guards' regimental reports and returns sent to him personally every week. He characteristically set his face against the system of promotion by purchase, and earned thereby a good deal of unpopularity in fashionable circles, for this ban 'in time of peace prevents rising in the army and discontents them all from the highest to the lowest'. In the end, however, custom was too strong for him.[18]

His numerous infidelities were purely sensual. None of his mistresses had the smallest influence over him so long as Caroline was alive, and no matter how often he strayed, he always returned to her, for she really was the love of his life. But he was not the love of hers; she never yielded to him more than her body. That is clear from her discussions with Walpole and Hervey, discussions which were cool, clinical and detached: no woman could have spoken thus of a man she loved. So he shouted at her, stormed at her, bullied her in public – but was, or pretended to be, guided by her in private. Whatever the facts of the case, it was assumed among the politicians close to the throne that if one needed anything done, Walpole must first be persuaded. He would convince the Queen, who would then tackle the King, so that the Minister's recommendation came back to him in the shape of a royal command.

Both King and Minister were satisfied with their rapprochement. 'The King,' wrote Newcastle in November, 'is in a mighty good humour, very gracious to all of us and, I hope and trust, perfectly well satisfied with the management of his affairs.' 'Our Premier,' wrote Lady Lechmere in the same month, 'is in as great favour with the new King as with the old King, and in all appearance will remain so.'

For the coronation the Queen's jewellery had to be borrowed, for all that belonging to Queen Anne had passed into the hands of

Mesdames Schülenberg and Kielmansegge. Lady Mary Wortley Montagu attended the ceremony and gave a spirited account of it.

She that drew the greatest number of eyes was indisputably Lady Orkney. She exposed behind a mixture of fat and wrinkle, and before a very considerable protuberance that preceded her. Add to this the inestimable roll of her eyes, and her grey hairs which by good fortune stood directly upright, and 'tis impossible to imagine a more delightful spectacle . . . I should have thought her one of the largest things of God's making if my Lady St John had not displayed all her charms in honour of the day. The poor Duchess of Montrose crept along with a dozen black snakes playing about her face, and my lady Portland . . . represented very finely an Egyptian mummy embroidered over with hieroglyphics.[19]

The continuation of Townshend and Walpole in office meant the continuation of Townshend's foreign policy, which he based on continued friendship with France. To this he added an element of hostility to the Emperor and to Spain. He was exhilarated by the consequent complications, and concocted a plan to divide the Austrian Netherlands between France and Holland – a strange reversal of the policy under which we had fought a great war to keep them intact as a buffer state between France and Holland. But Walpole deplored such adventures and deplored even more the higher taxes they necessitated. Land tax had to be raised to four shillings, its level during the great French wars. He did not hesitate, in the Cabinet Committee, to criticize Townshend's impetuosity and what he conceived to be a rash ambition to entangle Britain in the affairs of Europe.

The Opposition, meanwhile, had scored another paper victory over Walpole without in the least loosening his grip on power. In 1728 there was produced *The Beggar's Opera* by Bolingbroke's friend, John Gay. The idea of an opera about highwaymen and whores, set in Newgate instead of in palaces, was highly original; the tunes were catchy and the political allusions most diverting. From the first night it was a roaring success. The plot centres on Peachum [Walpole], an organizer of cutpurses who augments his normal business profits by betraying his people for the reward; Locket [Townshend], a corrupt jailor; and Macheath, a highwayman, by implication a country gentleman ruined by the Whig lawyers and the materialist, money-grubbing policies of Robino-cracy. From Peachum's very first song the audience missed nothing.

> Through all the employments of life,
> Each neighbour abuses his brother;
> Whore and rogue they call husband and wife:
> All professions be-rogue one another.
> The priest calls the lawyer a cheat,
> The lawyer be-knaves the divine;
> And the statesman, because he's so great,
> Thinks his trade as honest as mine.

When Jenny, the whore, sang of ruined estates, every Tory squire, impoverished by competition with Whig magnates and self-made lawyers and merchants, loudly applauded.

> The gamesters and lawyers are jugglers alike,
> If they meddle your all is in danger:
> Like gypsies, if once they can finger a souse,
> Your pockets they pick, and they pilfer your house,
> And give your estate to a stranger.

The corruption of Court and London life – which was nothing new but which the Opposition portrayed as the hallmark of Robino-cracy – was tacitly assumed in one song after another.

> If you at an office solicit your due,
> And would not have matters neglected;
> You must quicken the clerk with the perquisite too,
> To do what his duty directed.

The art of political survival did not escape notice.

> Ourselves, like the great, to secure a retreat,
> When matters require it, must give up our gang.
> And good reason why,
> Or instead of the fry,
> Ev'n Peachum and I,
> Like poor petty rascals might hang, hang;
> Like poor petty rascals might hang.

And there was in Macheath's song a strong dash of radicalism calculated to appeal to the London mob.

> Since laws were made for ev'ry degree,
> To curb vice in others, as well as me,
> I wonder we han't better company,
> Upon Tyburn tree!
> But gold from law can take out the sting;
> And if rich men like us were to swing,
> 'Twould thin the land, such numbers to string
> Upon Tyburn tree!

This was the sort of stuff that a year earlier would have gained the author a hearty reception at Leicester House. But now George Augustus and Caroline were not amused. 'Bob the poet's foe' was the principal prop and stay of the Crown, and Gay's promised preferment dwindled to a mere £200 a year as Gentleman Usher to little Princess Louisa. It was a slight he did not forget. As for Swift, he was quickly forgotten, and in his chagrin wrote a bitter poem about his own demise.

> From Dublin soon to London spread,
> 'Tis told at Court, 'the Dean is dead.'
> And Lady Suffolk in the spleen
> Runs laughing up to tell the Queen.
> The Queen, so gracious, mild and good,
> Cries, 'Is he gone? 'Tis time he should.
> He's dead you say? Then let him rot;
> I'm glad the medals were forgot.
> I promised him, I own, but when?
> I only was the Princess then;
> And now, the Consort of the King,
> You know, 'tis quite another thing.'

But the King had a low opinion of poets. 'You ought not to write verse,' he told Hervey. 'Leave such work to little Mr Pope.'

Hunting was much more in his line, and in the summer of 1728 he discovered the delights of Windsor, where the stock of game was much increased. The Court hunted hard, once until nine o'clock in the evening; another day in pouring rain they ran the stag all the way to Weybridge. The King and the elder children always rode to hounds. Several of the nobility attended, and Sir Robert Walpole 'clothed in green as a ranger'. To Henrietta Howard's cool, detached intelligence it was a rather over-rated performance. 'We hunt with great noise and violence, and have every day a considerable chance to have a neck broke.'[20]

But the royal approbation was confined to stag-hunting: a true German, George Augustus thought the stag a worthy quarry and the fox – though he gives just as good or better run – mere vermin. When the Duke of Grafton asked to be allowed to leave the Court for a few days' fox-hunting:

The King told him it was a pretty occupation for a man of quality, and at his age, to spend all his time tormenting a poor fox, that was generally a much better beast than any of those that pursued him; for the fox hunts no other animal but for his subsistence, while those brutes who hunt him did it only for the pleasure they took in hunting. The Duke of Grafton said he did it for his health. The King asked why he could not as well walk or ride post for his health; and said, if there was any pleasure in the chase, he was sure the Duke of Grafton could know nothing of it; 'for with your great corps of twenty stone weight, no horse, I am sure,' added His Majesty, 'can carry you within hearing, much less within sight of your hounds.'[21]

Princess Amelia, now aged seventeen, masculine in appearance and spending most of her time in the stables, was the hardest rider in the family, though the King too went well. As for the Queen, who

neither saw nor cared to see much of the chase, she had undertaken to mount Lord Hervey the whole summer (who loved hunting as little as she did), so that he might ride constantly by the side of her chaise, and entertain her whilst other people were entertaining themselves with hearing dogs bark and seeing crowds gallop.[22]

But apart from the stag-hunting, the Court was not very lively. As Lady Pomfret complained to Mrs Clayton, 'All things appear to move in the same manner as before, and our actions are as mechanical as the clock which directs them'. Next to Windsor, Kensington was Their Majesties' favourite palace. Kensington Gardens was a fashionable resort, to which admission was by ticket only issued by the Lord Chamberlain. About the Gardens George Augustus and Caroline used to parade, singling out acquaintances for a bow and a few gracious words, then moving, he with his curious, strutting step, she, regal but with increasing *embonpoint*, panting along behind him.

Meanwhile in Hanover Frederick was getting impatient at the postponements of his marriage. Although he had never set eyes on the lady of his grandfather's half-hearted choice, he sent an A.D.C. to Berlin to plan an elopement. Unfortunately the secret was badly kept and news of the design reached London. George Augustus, as might be expected, was furious, and sent Colonel de Launay to fetch the Prince.[23] (Hervey tells another story. According to him, the King sent for his son only in order to forestall an Address from Parliament on the subject. 'The persuasions prevailed and the King, as children take physic, forced himself to swallow the bitter draught for fear of having it poured down his throat.')[24]

Prince Frederick of Prussia and his sister, who were quite innocent and ignorant of the plot, were soundly thrashed by their father, whom His Majesty of England now dubbed 'the Corporal'. His Majesty of Prussia referred contemptuously to his royal cousin of England, because of his formal manner, expertise in the ballroom and strutting gait, as 'the Dancing Master'. When they next met in 1729, George Augustus actually challenged Frederick William to a duel, which Townshend with some difficulty prevented.

Colonel de Launay arrived at Hanover after dark, tracked down his quarry to a Court Ball and whisked him ignominiously away that very night. They had a ghastly journey to England, late in 1728. The Prince's welcome to England was frigid. He had innocently planned to please his parents by an unexpected, unannounced arrival. His plans went awry: his father knew he was coming, but sent no one to meet him, so that he had to drive in a hackney coach to St James's Palace, where he was promptly relegated to the schoolroom.[25]

His parents at first, despite a report from his tutor in Hanover that his faults were not those of a high-spirited young gentleman but *les tours de lacquais et de coquin*, treated him at first without open hostility. The father's refusal to allow his son's birthday to be celebrated was attributed to parsimony rather than hatred. 'I think,' he is alleged to have remarked, 'this is not a son I need be much afraid of.' But the young man, who dabbled in *belles letters* himself, lost no time in making contact with the Opposition writers, already disenchanted with Caroline as Queen, and he even met Bolingbroke secretly in a mutual friend's house. Bolingbroke, bowing, slipped and fell. The Prince immediately raised him up. 'My lord, I trust this may be an omen for my succeeding in raising your fortunes.' He did not, therefore, remain long in his father's good books: he was allowed no separate establishment and an allowance of only £24,000, 'in small sums without account' (plus a further £10,000 from the Duchy of Cornwall), although the Commons in settling the Civil List at the beginning of the reign had assumed that £100,000, the sum his father had received as Prince of Wales, would be given to him by the King. His servants were to be appointed, paid and dismissed by his father.[26]

From the day of his arrival in London one finds conflicting accounts of this young man. Hervey and Horace Walpole have so blackened his character that every favourable word seems like an attempt at whitewashing. According to Hervey he was 'as false as his capacity would allow him to be, and was more capable in that walk than in any other, never having the least hesitation in telling any lie that served his present purpose'.[27] He was weak in his understanding, but obstinate in his temper; and the affability and friendliness on which people generally remarked was simply the product of a habit, unbecoming in a prince, of 'cajoling everybody'.

Others remarked on the Prince's charming manners, his easy address and generosity. He was, as his meeting with Bolingbroke shows, always prompt with *le mot juste*, which is more than can be said of his father. Wrote Lady Irwin: 'I believe you would like the Prince; there is a frankness and affability in his way very different from his rank and very engaging.' Hervey's own mother found the Prince 'the most agreeable young man it is possible to imagine, without being in the least handsome. His person little, but well made and genteel: a liveliness in his eyes that is indescribable and the most obliging address that can be conceived.' But the impression of excessive affability amounting to weakness was a false one. Frederick was a lad of spirit, for when at a masque 'a gentleman made up to him and called him abusive names, the Prince collared him and gave him a box on the ear'.[28]

He was also something of a musician, for he played the viola

142

well and enjoyed giving private concerts; nor was he a bad versifier, in English and French. In his private life he was, until marriage, modishly promiscuous, 'laying down £1,500 fee simple in the daughter of a hautboy player', taking out 'a year's subscription' to a prima donna; but he was rather an unconvincing rake, for he allowed a prostitute to rob him of his watch and his money, and one at least of his mistresses found him incredibly ignorant of sexual technique. He was undeniably a gambler, winning (or, more often, losing) as much as £1,000 in a night's session. Perhaps the worst that can truthfully be said of him was that he never really matured: too often he acted in a manner which was well-meaning but irresponsible and thoughtless. He had had, at this stage in his short life, a weak hand dealt him by fate, with 'a father that abhorred him, a mother that depised and neglected him, a sister that betrayed him and a set of servants that neither were of any use to him, nor were capable of being of use, nor desirous of being so'.[29]

All his parents' affection was lavished on his young brother, William, Duke of Cumberland, a rather bumptious boy of nine, who seems to have shown a precocious intelligence hardly apparent in his later career. One day the Queen shut him up in his room for a display of tantrums. When he was released, she asked him what he had been doing.

'Reading.'

'Reading what?'

'The Bible.'

'And what did you read there?'

'About Jesus and Mary.'

'And what about them?'

'Why, that Jesus said to Mary, "Woman, what hast thou to do with me."'

When the King asked this infant prodigy whether he would rather be King or Queen, he replied pertly, 'Sir, I have never yet tried. Let me be one of them a month and I'll tell you.'[30]

Even at the age of nine, Frederick would never have got away with such answers.

No one, when he was Prince of Wales, had charged George Augustus, 'Young Rattlebag', with being either tongue-tied or shy, but now Lord Egmont complained that 'His Majesty, knowing his dignity, is careful of what he should not say rather than of what he should . . .' 'The King speaks so very little, and to so few.' It was seldom indeed that he uttered a *bon mot*, as when he asked Walpole about parliamentary business for the week.

'I cannot tell Your Majesty all, but I will ask our Governor' (meaning the Speaker).

'Governor! I thought you was Governor!' The retort was gleefully repeated by all who complained that Walpole was making himself a 'prime minister'.[31]

Throughout his reign George Augustus was bad at chatting in a crowd, but among his own circle the complaint was that he talked too much and with too little discretion.

The Queen, however, was as quick as any person Lord Egmont ever knew, and always said exactly the right thing – inquiring after one's children, 'How is the little girl? Is she better'; another's wife, 'Have you heard from your wife, my lord? I thought you left her in Bath'; a third's pictures, 'The Queen talked in such a manner of my prints that I was obliged to send for more of my books to show her.' She had a royal knack of seeming to be interested in other people's interests.[32]

Peter Wentworth, a page, thought she was much too free with her sympathy.

As we went to Richmond last Wednesday, our grooms had a battle with a carter who would not go out of the way. The good Queen had compassion on the rascal, and ordered me to ride after him and give him a crown. I desired Her Majesty to recall that order, for the fellow was a very saucy fellow, and I saw him strike the Prince's groom first, and if we gave him anything for his beating, 'twould be an example to others to stop the way a purpose to provoke a beating . . . I got immortal fame among the liverymen, who are no small fools at this Court. I told her if she would give the crown to anybody, it should be to the Prince's groom, who had the carter's long whip over his shoulders. She laughed, but saved her crown.[33]

When the King was in Hanover,

our life is as uniform as that of a monastery. Every morning at 11 and every evening at 6 we drive in the heat to Herrenhausen through an enormous linden avenue, and twice a day cover our coats and coaches with dust. In the King's society there was never the least change. At table, at cards, he sees always the same faces, and at the game retires into his chamber. Twice a week there is a French theatre; the other days there is a play in the gallery. In this way, were the King always to stop at Hanover, one could take a ten-year calendar of his proceedings.[34]

George Augustus, Young Hanover Brave, the gallant of Richmond and Leicester House – was in middle age becoming a bore.

But while in Hanover every courtier was yawning his head off, Caroline's court in London was more lively than ever, especially as Prince Frederick was temporarily in his mother's good books. 'In the next room the Prince had the fiddles and danced ... I thought [Walpole] moved surprisingly genteelly, and his dancing really became him which I should not have believed if I had not seen.'[35]

The Queen said, 'There is honest Mr Wentworth who has not drunk enough.'

'I have drunk Your Majesty's health,' he replied.

'And my children's too, I hope?'

'Yes, Your Majesty.'

'But there is one health which you have forgot, the Duke and Duchess of Newcastle that have entertained us so well.'

'Your Majesty, I have been down among the coachmen, to see if they have obeyed my orders to keep themselves sober, and it would not have been decent for me to examine them about it without I had kept myself sober. But now that grand duty is over, I am at leisure to obey Your Majesty's commands.'

There was one remarkably riotous party reported by Peter Wentworth.

I shall be no more her jest as a lover of drink at free cost, because she has my lord Lifford* to play upon, who this day sennight got drunk at Richmond. My lord made good use of his time whilst at dinner, and before they rose the Prince came to them and drank a *bompère* to my lord Lifford, which he pledged, and began another to him, and so a third. The Duke of Grafton, to show the Prince he had done his business, gave him [Lifford] a little shove, and threw him off the chair to the ground and carried him to the Queen ... When someone told him the Queen was there and saw him, his answer was, 'What do I care for the Queen?'[36]

* An elderly and very dull Huguenot soldier, a crony of George Augustus.

In February 1729 John Gay tried to exploit the extraordinary success of *The Beggar's Opera* by writing a sequel, *Polly*, 'less pretty but more abusive, and so little disguised that Sir Robert Walpole resolved, rather than suffer himself to be produced for thirty nights together upon the stage in the person of a highwayman', to induce the Lord Chamberlain to ban the play. Gay then 'zested his work with some supplemental invections, and resolved to print it by subscription'. The Duchess of Queensberry, beautiful, fashionable and popular, set herself to soliciting subscriptions, and made even the King's servants, in the King's drawing room, 'contribute to the printing of a thing which the King had forbid being recited'.

George Augustus asked her what she was doing.

'Sir,' she replied, with a dutiful curtsey, 'it is an act of charity, and a charity so humane that I do not despair of bringing Your Majesty to contribute.'

Such insolence was not to be borne, and the King sent a verbal message requesting her not to come to Court.

Her reply, in writing, was hardly less saucy than the original offence. 'The Duchess of Queensberry is surprised and well pleased that the King has given her so agreeable a command as to stay from Court, where she never came for diversion, but to bestow a great civility on the King and Queen.' She handed this missive to the Vice Chamberlain who begged her to 'give him leave to carry an answer less rough ... Upon which she wrote another, but so much more disrespectful that he desired the first again and delivered it.'

It must be confessed that the Duchess had the best of the encounter; but the King bore no grudge against her family, and would not allow the Duke, in consequence of the incident, to resign his sinecure.[37]

The death in 1726 of Dolly, Walpole's sister and Townshend's beloved wife, and the eclipse of their common enemy, Carteret, weakened the ties which united the brothers-in-law. Jealousy played its part. Viscount Townshend was by birth and breeding a Norfolk magnate, Walpole no more than a respectable country gentleman. But now the vulgar, ostentatious splendour of Houghton put Townshend's seat of Raynham in the shade. During the last reign the channel of communication for those who sought royal favour had been through Townshend and the Duchess of Kendal: now it was Walpole's levées which were crowded, for everyone knew that he and he alone had the ear of the Queen. In short, as Walpole observed, 'So long as the firm was Townshend and Walpole, the utmost harmony prevailed; but it no sooner became Walpole and Townshend than things went all wrong.'[38]

The contrast in their private lives contributed to their differences. Townshend was scrupulously virtuous, indeed puritanical, in his relations with women: a man of choleric temper, he was not merely offended but enraged by Walpole's cynical, flagrant immorality and the bacchanalia which alternated with hunting and partridge shooting at Houghton. In 1728 there occurred, arising from these characteristics, a violent row which warned those who had eyes to see that a split between the two could not long be delayed. In a spirit of mischief Walpole frivolously accused his brother-in-law of an attempt on the virtue of Lady Trevor, wife of the Lord Privy Seal, a person of impregnable chastity, noted for the purity of her conversation and 'the most forbidding countenance that natural ugliness, age and smallpox ever compounded'.

This touched Townshend on the raw. Pale and shaking with anger, he retorted with a comparison between Walpole's morals and his own.

'What, my lord,' replied Walpole lightly, 'all this for my lady Trevor?'[39]

A sudden quarrel in 1729, concerning a mere question of parliamentary tactics, ended in Walpole, for once losing his temper, exclaiming, 'My lord, there is no man's sincerity which I doubt so much as your lordship's!' They seized one another's collars, struggled across the table and had reached for their sword-hilts when Newcastle's brother, Henry Pelham, separated them. A duel was averted, but there was no prospect thereafter of them working in harmony.[40]

Under such pressures the choleric Townshend would neither work with his brother-in-law nor go. 'He talked every day of retiring, but would not stir. The King . . . had consented to let him go, but would not force him out; the Queen wished him gone, but knew not how to make him go.' Finally the King took him up on one of his more positive threats of resignation and in May 1730 appointed William Stanhope (ennobled as Earl of Harrington) in his place. Townshend retired from politics and settled down to improve his Norfolk estates.[41]

After 1730 it was no longer Townshend and Walpole, or even Walpole and Townshend, but plain Robert Walpole Ltd. The two Secretaries of State, Newcastle and Harrington, took no initiatives themselves, and were content to endorse even his foreign policies which were more properly their business. Peace and retrench-ment – though not, of course, reform – were the objects of the Robinocracy, and the uncommitted country gentry found little to grumble about. Townshend's departure had enabled Walpole and the King to make a shift in their foreign policy towards the 'old system' of an alliance with the Empire. George Augustus had 'a natural aversion to the French' and the old alliance was the one in which he had been brought up, for which he had fought that glorious day at Oudenarde and in which he felt most comfortable.[1]

Military affairs were still his greatest interest. Hervey declares that he 'always considered soldiers as the principal supports of his grandeur and power, and were glad of any pretence to increase their number'. This, like many of Hervey's statements, is not quite true. At the beginning of his reign George II had wanted, for reasons of economy, to make great reductions in the regular army, and had been uncharacteristically dissuaded by Walpole who had told him that 'if he broke his army, he broke himself'. On this advice the army was maintained at about 30,000 men, dispersed between Ireland, Scotland, Gibraltar, Minorca and the West Indies, despite the disapproval of the country gentry and their traditional apprehension 'that there was no danger but from a standing army'.[2] In 1731, as a result of improved relations with Spain and the Empire, reductions could safely be made. 'Very cheerful countenances are worn at Court both by His Majesty and his Ministers.'[3] The fact was that thrift — some would call it parsimony — was an obsession almost as gripping as his love of military matters, and it did not redound to the King's popularity, for the English people are equally quick to blame their monarchs for spending too little as for spending too much. 'His nearness in money matters', his 'ungiving disposition', not much mentioned when he was Prince of Wales, was held against him throughout his reign. Walpole and Hervey agreed that to talk to the King of consideration for past services, charity and bounty, was 'making use of words that with him had no meaning'. He had, recorded Hervey's viperish pen, a natural 'reluctance to bestow'. He thought Englishmen in general overpaid, and he liked saving their salaries by keeping their posts vacant. 'He never had the least inclination to oblige, and I do not believe there ever lived a man to whose temper benevolence was so absolutely a stranger.'[4]

Like many another, the King was irritated by the custom of giving large tips to the servants of one's host when one went out to dinner. The Queen said she had found it a pretty large expense to visit her friends even in town.

'That is your fault,' said the King, 'for my father, when he went to people's houses in town, never was fool enough to be giving away his money.'

The Queen pleaded for her excuse that she had only done what Lord Grantham had told her she was to do; to which His Majesty replied 'that she was always asking some fool or other what she was to do, and that none but a fool would ask another fool's advice'. When Hervey, on the Queen's behalf, pleaded polite custom, the King suggested a simple solution to the problem. 'Then she may stay at home as I do. You do not see me running into every puppy's house to see his new chairs and stools. Nor is it for you,' said he, addressing himself to the Queen, 'to be running your nose everywhere, and trotting about the town to every fellow who will give you some bread and butter, like an old girl that loves to go abroad, no matter where, or whether it be proper or no.'[5]

150

Hervey's, however, is not the last word on the King's manners. Mrs Howard declared that his thrifty habits were the result of a penurious, insecure youth; he often gave, through her, small pensions from his own pocket, but told her not to let it be known. Other evidence, too, gives us a portrait more agreeable and balanced than that drawn by Hervey. Lord Percival (Egmont's son) quotes instances of the King seeing justice done in matters of charity and patronage, such as in the case of a humble chaplain who had been without reason the object of ministerial spite.

The King turned to the Queen and asked how that could be. The Queen said that she did not know, and there must be some great mistake committed. Soon after a good preferment fell, and the King bestowed it on him. My cousin Dering,* said upon this that the King was a man of much honour and justice, and had moreover a tenderness in his nature . . . The King had obtained a list of all the necessitous French [Huguenots] in order to restore them their pensions, which at the beginning of his reign he had too hastily deprived them of.[6]

Like many middle-aged soldiers the King found army 'shop' the most fascinating subject of conversation. It is a taste rarely shared by civilians, certainly not by Walpole and Hervey, whose memoirs are our main source of information on George Augustus during the 1730s. But the Huguenot, Lord Lifford, was content to reminisce for hours with him. The Queen, who liked teasing the old Frenchman, said to him one day, *à propos* the sentries from the Blue Horse Guards, 'I'll lay what you will that he of the right is a Scotsman, and he of the left an Englishman and a Yorkshireman.'

When she came to them she asked the right hand man, a handsome young gentleman volunteer, 'What countryman are you?'

'A Scotsman, Your Majesty.'

'What is your name?'

'Hamilton.'

'Of what family?'

'The Duke's of that name.'

'How long have you been in the regiment?'

'Ever since it has been the Duke of Argyll's.'

Then she asked the other sentry, 'What countryman are you?'

'An Englishman, Your Majesty.'

* Mary Dering, Dresser Extraordinary to the Princesses.

'Your name?'

'Hill.'

'What county?'

'Yorkshire.'

The Queen was pleased and said, '*N'est ce pas que j'ai dit vrai? Je connais bien la physiognomie.*'[7]

One suspects that Her Majesty had cheated, but tales such as these, improved no doubt with repetition, enhanced her reputation for intelligence, affability and a truly royal condescension.

For those who had little taste for military anecdotage, and a great deal of time to kill, gambling was the principal indoor occupation at Court, as it was in contemporary society as a whole. On a typical evening there would be a large quadrille table and another where the young people, even down to little William not yet in his teens, played with the bedchamber ladies at lottery ticket, winning and losing as much as £100 in an evening. The Maids of Honour played with the King in Mrs Howard's apartment, until he came up and, with the Queen, retired to bed.

Hervey found the Court life insufferably boring: 'No mill horse ever went on a more constant track or a more unchanging circle.' Hampton Court was particularly tedious for he hated hunting and walking. But the King was a great walker, winter and summer, and so too was the Queen, 'even in frost and snow which, before it affected Their Majesties, had made all their attendants sick.'[8] He even took to fox-hunting, or at least allowed gentlemen in his Court to indulge in this plebeian sport.

Whether through shyness, a surly temper or piles (to which he was a martyr) the King was uneasy in a gathering of people. He was criticized for 'not speaking to the country gentry when they came to Court, which tries them, and makes them declare they have no business to come there, and so they betake themselves to the discontented party'.

It were to be wished [wrote Lord Egmont] that the King had more affability, and that his sincerity in showing his resentment when he is displeased with a subject's conduct did not prejudice His Majesty's affairs in this manner. The nobility of England are proud and take fire at any slight the Crown casts on them. Besides, there are conjunctions in time when a King should take pains to please.[9]

152

12. The east front of Kensington Palace 1736: *engraving by Vivaret after John Rocque*

13. The south front of Leicester House 1720: *copy of a contemporary view by T. H. Shepherd*

14. The south front of Richmond Lodge, Kew: *watercolour by Thomas Sandby*

Importunate place-seekers he particularly resented. When Sir William Strickland badgered him about a place, the King muttered something in German which Sir William could not understand. A thoughtful friend, however, gave the translation, or perhaps mistranslation: 'Get out, you rascal!' Upon which Sir William determined to wait no more on the King, but pretended himself ill of the gout.[10]

Hervey somewhat contradicts his own tales of the King's reluctance to oblige when he writes, 'The King and Queen looked upon mankind as so many commodities in the market ... Sir Robert Walpole being sworn appraiser to Their Majesties at all these sales.' It was not so much the King as the Ministry who was blamed for the neglect shown to 'the ancient gentry and men of fortune in the disposal of employments and favours, which they choose to bestow on little and unknown persons'. Here one detects the mark of Walpole himself, who insisted on value for money. But the King was always reluctant to help Walpole by making peers for the purpose of political patronage. This was due not so much to 'the costive nature of the King's unforgiving spirit' (Hervey again) as to his dislike of diluting and cheapening the peerage.[11]

Whatever his attitude in the past to Opposition writers, now he was King, George Augustus 'neither loved learning, nor encouraged men of letters, nor were there any Maecenases about him'. The King 'often used to brag of the contempt he had for books and letters; to say how much he hated all that stuff from his infancy ... because he despised it and felt as if he was doing something mean and below him'.[12]

The Queen on the other hand fancied herself as a blue-stocking; she read copiously, if without discrimination, and remembered every word she read. But the quality of her literary judgement is instanced by the favours she lavished on Stephen Duck, a Wiltshire farm labourer and one of the more forgettable poets of the eighteenth century. She gave him a pension, a place in the Yeomen of the Guard and as custodian of her favourite grotto at Kew, Merlin's Cave. When he took Holy Orders, she made him chaplain of Kew and Rector of Byfleet: he repaid her with copious laudatory doggerel. The King often rebuked her for dabbling in all that lettered nonsense, called her a pedant and said she loved to spend her time more like a schoolmistress than a Queen.[13]

In matters of art, too, they differed. During one of his holidays in Hanover, the Queen and Hervey removed some very bad pictures from the dining-room and replaced them by some very good ones. The King, on his return, ordered his favourites to be restored. Hervey pleaded for the retention at least of two Van Dycks, and received a sharp rebuke.

My Lord, I have a great respect for your taste in what you understand, but in pictures, I beg leave to follow my own. I suppose you assisted the Queen with your fine advice when she was pulling my house to pieces and spoiling all the furniture. Thank God, at least she has left the walls standing! As for the Van Dyckes, I do not care whether they are changed or no; but for the picture with the dirty frame over the door, and the three nasty little children,* I will have them taken away, and the old ones restored; I will have it done too tomorrow morning before I go to London, or else I know it will not be done at all.

Hervey asked respectfully, 'Would Your Majesty have the gigantic fat Venus restored too?' 'Yes, my lord; I am not so nice as your lordship. I like my fat Venus much better than anything you have given me instead of her.'

His Majesty then

snubbed the Queen, who was drinking chocolate, for being always stuffing, the Princess Emily for not hearing him, the Princess Caroline for being grown fat, the Duke for standing awkwardly, Lord Hervey for not knowing what relation the Prince of Sultzbach was to the Elector Palatine, and then carried the Queen to walk, and be re-snubbed in the garden.[14]

They were both regular churchgoers, receiving the Sacrament in their bedroom when ill. The King gave great satisfaction to Churchmen by declaring soon after his succession that while he lived the Test Act should never be repealed. Less satisfaction was, perhaps, given by his general description of the bench of bishops as a 'parcel of black, canting, hypocritical rascals'.[15]

Hoadley of Winchester, a Walpolite prelate who as Bishop of Bangor had never set foot in his diocese, singularly failed to win

* Van Dyck's portrait of Charles I's children.

154

His Majesty's approbation. 'A pretty fellow for a friend,' said the King, turning to Lord Hervey,

Pray what is it that charms you in him? His pretty limping gait (and here he acted the Bishop's lameness), or his nasty, stinking breath? – paugh! – or his silly laugh, when he grins in your face for nothing and shows his nasty rotten teeth? Or is it his great honesty that charms your lordship . . . My lord, I am sorry you choose your friends so ill; but I cannot help saying that if the Bishop of Winchester is your friend, you have a great puppy and a very dull fellow and a great rascal for a friend. It is a very pretty thing for such scoundrels, when they are raised to favour so much above their desert, to be talking and writing their stuff, to give trouble to the Government that has shown them that favour; and very modest in a canting hypocritical knave to be crying, 'The Kingdom of Christ is not of this world', at the same time that he, as Christ's ambassador, received £6,000 or £7,000 a year. But he is just the same thing in the Church that he is in the Government, and as ready to receive the best pay for preaching the Bible, though he does not believe a word of it, as he is to take favours from the Crown, though, by his republican spirit and doctrine, he would be glad to abolish the power of it.[16]

The Queen, however, dabbled not merely in theology but in ecclesiastical patronage, leaning for advice in these matters on her friend and bedchamber-woman, Lady Sundon (formerly Mrs Clayton) who is variously described by Hervey as a warm, generous, friendly person, who often went out of her way to help those who could in no way return the kindness and by Lady Mary Wortley Montagu as irritating, conceited, pompous and cunning.[17]

How far Caroline was truly religious, and how far merely interested in theology, may be judged from a scene one morning with her chaplain. She ordered him to begin prayers in the room next to her bedchamber. He, observing the picture of a naked Venus over her fold-stool, remarked, 'And a very proper altarpiece is here, Madam!'

Somewhat annoyed, she ordered the door to be closed. Immediately the prayers stopped. She asked why.

'I refuse,' roared Dr Maddox,* 'to whistle the word of God through a keyhole.'

*My own family legend, no doubt incorrectly, attributes this story to our ancestor, Dr Chenevix, later Bishop of Waterford. Perhaps I may be forgiven

Hervey improved the story by an excellent skit.

1st Parson From pride, vainglory and hypocrisy, from envy, hatred and malice, and all uncharitableness . . .
2nd Parson Good Lord, deliver us.
Queen I pray, good Lady Sundon, shut a little that door: these creatures pray so loud, one cannot hear oneself speak . . . So, so, not quite so much; leave it open enough for these parsons to think we may hear, and enough shut that we may not hear quite so much.[18]

The Queen *was* amused.

The love which George Augustus bore his wife had never inhibited him from bestowing his favours more widely and with princely profusion – or so he bragged. Indeed he owed it to his position, first as Prince of Wales and now as King and Defender of the Faith, to keep a *maîtresse en titre*. But a passion of fifteen years' standing – if, indeed, it was a passion and not a mere formality[19] – had for some time been waning, and for Mrs Howard herself the tedium of two or three hours' daily *tête à tête* with George Augustus was barely mitigated by her increasing deafness. Moreover, although no political hostess, she was too friendly with Bolingbroke, Pulteney and Pope. At this point, in 1728, her ruffian of a husband determined to make what he could from a situation in which he had so long acquiesced. He ordered her to return to her conjugal duties, and even obtained from the Lord Chief Justice a warrant authorizing him to seize her person wherever he should find her. To escape a fate worse than death, she was obliged to remain day and night within the confines of the palace, 'whence she did not dare stir one moment or one inch; and the King's honour required that he continue to extend the protection which was growing irksome to both of them. Despite

for quoting from his letter to Lady Sundon asking for her niece's hand in marriage. 'My salary as chaplain to Her Royal Highness [the Princess Royal] will, I hope, be thought a reasonable earnest of future preferment . . . My birth, I may venture to add, is that of a gentleman. My father long served and was at last killed (at Blenheim) in a post in which he was very well known. One of my brothers is now in the army, a post not thought below people of the first rank: another, indeed, keeps a shop, but I hope that circumstance rather deserves compassion than contempt.'

her well-attested sense of humour, it is doubtful if she appreciated being a bone of contention between a husband who had not the least wish to secure her person, and a lover who was anxious to rid himself of it. If anything could add to the absurdity of the situation, it was the intervention of the Queen.'[20]

Caroline had never been able to see Mrs Howard's renowned charm and good sense, but realized that, were she to depart, her place would soon be taken by some other lady more ambitious and less manageable. At one point the violent Howard insolently threatened to seize his wife even from the Queen's own carriage.

'I was horribly afraid of him,' she told Lord Gervey, 'for we were *tête à tête* . . . as I knew him to be so brutal as well as a little mad, and seldom quite sober . . . But as soon as I had got near the door and thought myself safe from being thrown out of the window, *je pris mon grand ton de Reine et je disais* I would be glad to know who would dare open my coach-door and take out of it one of my servants.'

Howard threatened – surely an empty threat – to complain to the King, to which Caroline replied loftily that Mrs Howard was her employee, not His Majesty's. And so they parted.

It was suggested that the Queen buy the lady from her husband for £1200 a year. 'But I thought it was a little too much not only to keep the King's *guenipes* under my roof but to pay them too.'

Eventually the King paid Howard the £1200 a year during the lifetime of his brother, Earl of Suffolk, to whom he was heir, and Howard signed a bond

for the future to give her as little trouble in the capacity of husband as he had ever given her pleasure. And so this affair ended, the King paying £1200 a year for the possession of what he did not want to enjoy, and Mr Howard receiving them, for relinquishing what he would have been sorry to keep.

The strain had evidently been too much for Mrs Howard's composure for, said the Queen,

After all this matter was settled, the first thing the wise, prudent [lady] did was to pick a quarrel with me about holding a basin of ceremony at my dressing, and to tell me, with her fierce little eyes and cheeks as red as your coat, that positively she would not do it; to which I made her no

157

answer in anger, but calmly, as I would to a naughty child: 'Yes, my dear Howard, I am sure you will; indeed you will. Go, go! fie for shame! Go, my good Howard; we will talk of this another time.'

A week later Mrs Howard was forgiven, but reminded 'that it was in my power, if I had pleased, any hour of the day, to let her drop through my fingers – thus – '

The Opposition were encouraged by Walpole's quarrel with Townshend. Surely this would lead somehow to their advantage. Lord Hervey, who had been eighteen months abroad seeking relief from a gall-bladder complaint, returned in the autumn of 1729 and like a small, sharp-nosed rodent, feeling his way with twitching nostrils through the political jungle, sounded Pulteney on Opposition prospects. Pulteney assured him, 'The Queen is hated, the King despised, their son both the one and the other, and such a general discontent with the present Government is spread all over the Kingdom that it is absolutely impossible for things to go on in the track they are now in.'

Hervey inquired what the Opposition had in mind to replace the present arrangements. 'Not the Pretender, I hope?'

'Why, the little Duke [of Cumberland] or anyone but this puppy, this huffing military jackanapes of a king, or the timid, poor, mean, weak mortal, his son, the Prince of Wales.'

Pulteney took a sanguine view of the Opposition's prospects.

'Stout as our shitten monarch pretends to be, you will find we shall force him to truckle and make his great fat-arsed wife stink with fear before we're done with her. We shall make her give up her minion and him his myrmidon* or I am much mistaken.'[21] It is hardly surprising that in 1731 the King called for the Privy Council book and personally struck Pulteney's name from the list of members.[22]

* Walpole, in a somewhat improbable double role.

10

His Majesty's passion for economy can hardly have been satisfied by his annual payment to Mr Howard, but it was felicitously exercised at the expense of the Prince of Wales. 'He would not hear of any additions to the Prince's family'; 'there would be no more grooms of the bedchamber appointed to the Prince'; and 'as his marriage with Prussia was now at an end, his family would remain in the circumstances they were for some time'.[1] By these means he intended to clip the Prince's political wings, but in fact the Opposition had not yet begun to exploit Frederick's nuisance value, and he was (especially when his father was in Hanover) on correct terms with his mother. There was, therefore, nothing improper in his forming a friendship with Hervey, who had recently accepted the office of Vice-Chamberlain to the Household. In 1729 and 1730 their friendship was close. Caroline in later years used to suggest that her son offered Hervey a part share in his mistress, and they certainly shared, under the pen-name of Captain Bodkin, the authorship of a comedy of which Wilkes, the actor-manager, said, 'if the last two acts, which I have not seen, are exceeding better than the first three, which I have, the play might last one night'. In the event, it did not.[2]

Frederick regarded himself as part of, not opposed to, the Hanoverian Establishment, and told Egmont that he hoped

time would reconcile all to be friends of the Government: that as for the old people, it was not to be expected they should be gained, but the youth will, especially as Westminster School is gained by means of gaining

159

Dr Freind; that he looked to the gaining of one school to be worth gaining fifty families.[3]

A fruitful source of information on Poor Fred is Colonel Schutz, who had been appointed by the King to control the Prince's Privy Purse (which needed some controlling) and lost no opportunity of disparaging his master. He had, Schutz said, no reigning passion.

If there be, it is to pass the evening with six or seven others over a glass of wine and hear them talk of a variety of things, but he does not drink. He loves play and plays to win that he may supply his generosities, which last are great; but so ill-placed that he often wants the wherewithal to do one well-placed kindness by giving to unworthy objects. He has had several mistresses, and now keeps one, an apothecary's daughter at Kingston; but he is not nice in his choice and talks more of his feats in this way than he acts. He can talk gravely according to his company, but is sometimes more childish than becomes his age. He thinks he knows business, * but attends to none. He likes to be flattered, and if he meets with a good Ministry, may satisfy his people. He is extremely dutiful to his parents, who do not return it in love. They let him do as he will, but keeps him short of money.[4]

His interests were not confined to quiet conversation and play. They included music, cricket and his fine new barge, which outrowed the King's with an equal number of oars. He made unsuccessful attempts on an Italian opera-singer and the daughter of an English peer, and fathered a child on the chambermaid of Hervey's mistress.[5]

Unfortunately the pages of Hervey's memoirs which deal with his friendship with the Prince have been destroyed by his descendants; and with them, perhaps, much that would explain the virulence of the subsequent feud. For in 1731 the happy concord of the Prince, Hervey and the Queen was broken. Hervey's mistress, Miss Vane, transferred her favours to the Prince, producing a son, named FitzFrederick but reputedly the offspring of a triumvirate of the Prince, Hervey and Lord Harrington. Egmont believed that she fanned the Prince's latent resentment against his parents. Moreover the Prince had now taken as his principal adviser that grotesque parvenu and by-word for venality, George Bubb Dodington, and for one reason or another was treating

* Business meant the work of government, not buying and selling.

Hervey with some coldness. Hervey reproached Miss Vane in an angry letter, threatening to reveal all. She fell into a fit and complained to the Prince. Thereafter Frederick and Hervey were sworn foes, and it is from Hervey principally that historians have formed their opinion of 'Poor Fred'.[6]

As for Hervey, he was higher than ever in the Queen's favour, and a close friend of Walpole. 'Pretty Mr Fainlove', 'the delicate Hermaphrodite', 'the pretty little master-miss', as Pulteney called him, provoking a duel which their seconds stopped before either was badly hurt, was a power in the land.[7]

He used his power, characteristically, to further his feud against the Prince of Wales. The Queen's distaste for her elder son, dormant for the past two or three years, did not require much stoking, and the King's even less: but what was required, this spiteful creature supplied. In judging him we must not forget his health. He was desperately ill, with a ruined digestion and an agonising condition of the gall-bladder, which reduced him for years to a meagre milk and vegetarian diet. All this, together with what appears to be a totally unjustified reputation as a catamite, he bore with uncomplaining fortitude and a wry self-mockery which caricatured his own weaknesses and idiosyncrasies. But when this is said, it must be added that he was by his warped nature a malign and probably mendacious troublemaker, a bad enemy and (as his memoirs prove) a worse friend – except always to Caroline with whom he remained on terms of intimate but innocent friendship, more of a son than a lover, and more of a comrade than either.

Two years after his quarrel with the Prince, Hervey quarrelled with Pope. The poet's deadly riposte took the form of comparing Hervey with Sporus, the Emperor Nero's catamite-castrato:

> Let Sporus tremble – 'What, that thing of silk,
> Sporus, that mere white curd of asses' milk?
> Satire or sense, alas! can Sporus feel?
> Who breaks a butterfly upon a wheel?'
> Yet let me flap this bug with gilded wings,
> This painted child of dirt that stinks and stings;
> Whose buzz the witty and the fair annoys,
> Yet wit ne'er tastes, and beauty ne'er enjoys;

So well-bred spaniels civilly delight
In mumbling of the game they dare not bite.
Eternal smiles his emptiness betray,
As shallow streams run dimpling all the way.
Whether in florid impotence he speaks,
And, as the prompter breathes, the puppet squeaks;
Or at the ear of Eve,* familiar toad,
Half froth, half venom, spits himself abroad,
In puns, or politics, or tales, or lies,
Or spite, or smut, or rhymes, or blasphemies.
His wit was all see-saw between that and this,
Now high, now low, now master up, now miss,
And he himself one vile antithesis.
Amphibious thing! That acting either part,
The trifling head, or the corrupted heart!
Fop at the toilet, flatterer at the board,
Now trips a lady and now struts a lord.
Eve's tempter thus the rabbins have expressed
A cherub's face, a reptile all the rest;
Beauty that shocks you, parts that none will trust,
Wit that can creep, and pride that licks the dust.[8]

It is unfortunate and not conducive to truth that Hervey's memoirs should be eminently readable and irresistibly quotable, for it is from them that our information of Court life in the 1730s is principally drawn. His hatred of Frederick was frank and flaunted: his hatred of George Augustus only became fully apparent with the publication ninety years later of his reminiscences.

It was not altogether fair to blame the Prince for his idleness and inattention to business, since George Augustus, following his own father's example, gave his son nothing useful to do. The Prince particularly wished to make a progress through the country but this his father would never allow, 'his popularity having already given offence'.[9]

For Frederick's shortcomings Walpole blamed 'those who filled his head with odd notions'.

'Who?' asked Egmont.

'Dodington, who looks upon himself to be First Minister.'

At this even the earnest Egmont smiled.

* The prompter, Walpole, and Eve, the Queen.

162

George Bubb Dodington was the 'vilest man, vain, ambitious, loose and never satisfied'. 'He wants to be a lord, and, when he is that, he will want to be a duke.' 'I own,' he assured the Prince, 'that Your Royal Highness's favour is the pride and pleasure of my life, but, I did not owe its rise, nor will owe its continuance to flattery, I have set my whole heart on your happiness.'[10]

In 1732 the Prince and Dodington were given a golden opportunity to make trouble. Walpole decided that it was high time someone tackled the problem of smuggling. It was a national scandal: high customs duties and a tiresome tangle of controls had resulted in the smuggler being tolerated, indeed welcomed, by almost everyone in the country. No less than three million pounds of tea were run ashore each year. Naval captains brought in contraband in His Majesty's ships. The Prime Minister himself bought from smugglers at Houghton, and his personal supplies of smuggled wine and Holland linen were brought to Westminster by an Admiralty barge.

Smugglers operated in large armed gangs of a hundred or more: they had in ten years killed six customs officers, badly beaten 250: informers were tortured, strangled, whipped to death. They used hogsheads with false bottoms – brandy below and some cheap wine, duly declared, on top. Casks painted to resemble rocks and oilskin bags of tea camouflaged as mackerel pots were floated ashore with the tide: lace was carried past the noses of the searchers in coffins. Nor did they confine themselves to straight smuggling. Tobacco, for instance, imported for re-export, paid $6\frac{1}{3}$d a pound on entry, which was refunded when it left the country. So merchants imported the fine leaf bone dry, and exported it damp, heavy and adulterated with stalks and rubbish.

Walpole saw no difficulty in reconciling his private patronage of smugglers with his duty as First Lord of the Treasury. It was calculated that smuggling cost the revenue £1,050,000 a year, not much less than the total income from Customs and Excise. His plan was to extend to wine and tobacco his bonded warehouse system, introduced in 1723 for tea, coffee and chocolate; and responsibility for collecting dues, hitherto the duty of the Customs service, would be transferred to the Excise Department. Customs officers were notoriously lax, whereas the Excise men had a reputation for efficiency and highhandedness. Their accounts were frequently audited. They had the right of entry into shops, inns and taverns and could demand from any retailer proof that on the dutiable goods he was selling duty had actually been paid. It was against this proposal, that wine and tobacco be transferred to the hated Excisemen, that the kingdom erupted in spontaneous protest.[11] Bolingbroke, Pulteney, *The Craftsman* and every man with a grudge against the Prime Minister assailed the plan in a campaign of unexampled mendacity and malignity. It was put about that wine and tobacco were just the thin end of the wedge: the Minister was resolved to extend excise to all foodstuffs and clothes. It was said that soon not only shops and public houses, but private houses would be exposed to raids by insolent excisemen who would break open a gentleman's bureau and trunks, ravish his female dependants and carry him off to prison if he so much as uttered a protest.[12] If Walpole had his way, the Crown's revenue from the Excise would be so great that there would be no need for him to call Parliament. The army of excisemen* would be the Minister's private army, employed to suppress all liberty. Magna Carta would be denounced, private property destroyed. Excise was linked to a larger standing army, Popery, the abolition of juries, tyranny and even to the wearing of wooden shoes which was the hallmark of downtrodden Frenchmen while free Britons wore leather. (One enterprising merchant imported, ironically from Holland, a large consignment of sabots to be used for anti-Excise propaganda.) The Minister was depicted by the caricaturists sitting, proud and corpulent, in a coach drawn by 'the dragon, Excise' from whose orifice a stream of gold flowed into Walpole's lap.

The ballad-makers enlarged on 'this monster, God rot him, the Pope first begot him', 'with belly as big as a storehouse',

> Grant these and the glutton
> Will roar out for mutton
> Your beef, bread and bacon to boot.
> Your goose, pig and pullet
> He'll thrust down his gullet,
> Whilst the labourer munches a root.

---

* There were 126 in the whole kingdom.

And after each verse the roaring, feet-thumping chorus in every tavern throughout the land.

> Horse, foot and dragoons,
> Battalions, platoons,
> Excise, wooden shoes and no jury.
> Then taxes increasing
> While traffic is ceasing
> Would put the whole land in a fury.[13]

London, hotbed of a radicalism which at times allied itself to the Tories and Country Party, headed the opposition to Excise, and a large meeting of merchants resolved unanimously to oppose it. 'Pass what bill you like, we will not comply with it.'[14] Every town, every village followed suit.

It was strange that Walpole, always inclined to let sleeping dogs lie, had not foreseen trouble. Years of uninterrupted success seem to have blunted his political instinct. He was sure he was right: he trusted to his consummate parliamentary management to have his way. Besides, he would link it with a shilling off the land tax, a sop to the country gentry. The King backed him, believing that if smuggling could be stopped, the Civil List would surely benefit from the extra revenue. He saw opposition to Walpole as a personal insult to the Crown. When Hervey suggested that his policy would get Walpole into trouble with the Commons, 'He is a brave fellow,' said the King. 'He has more spirit than any man I ever knew.'[15]

The Prince, advised by Bubb Dodington, plunged into the fray. So damaging was his opposition to Excise that the King offered terms: if Frederick would be reconciled to Walpole, he would have the choice of his own household, the choice of three princesses to marry and £80,000 a year settled on him. To this he replied with dutiful thanks to His Majesty for conceding what were only his rights, but a pointblank refusal to make it up with the Prime Minister.[16]

'No slavery! No wooden shoes! No Excise!' bawled the London mob as they rioted around a coach full of ladies. 'We know this coach! It comes from the St James's end of town.'

'Good people,' the ladies protested, 'though we live at St James's end, we are as much against Excise as you.'

'Are you so? Then God bless you! Coachman, drive on.'

When the King, at the opening of Parliament, said he depended on the 'force of truth' to justify his Minister's measures, the wits quipped that what he meant was the 'force of troops'.[17]

Lord Stair in a long audience with the Queen inveighed against Walpole. 'In no age, in no country, was any Minister so universally odious as the man you support.' The Excise Bill, he said, although in the Commons corruption might prevail, could never be forced through the Lords. 'Madam, I think it so wicked, so dishonest, so slavish a scheme that my conscience would no more permit me to vote for it than his ought to have permitted him to project it.' At this the Queen could no longer restrain herself. 'Oh, my lord, talk to me not of your conscience. You make me feel faint.'[18] But when Lord Scarborough told her, 'I will answer for my regiment against the Pretender but not against the enemies of Excise,' she herself began to have her doubts. These were not shared by the King. He despised utterly the silly puppies who opposed his Minister. 'They did not expect to find me so firm! The fools imagined perhaps they could frighten me. But they must not think they have a Stuart upon the throne; or if they do, they will find themselves mistaken.'[19]

The Ministry's real weakness was that a general election was due next year. They might have got away with this thoroughly sound but unpopular measure near the beginning of their term of office, but not near the end. The freeholders, it seemed, would insist on voting for anyone who opposed Excise. Too many place-men – even peers and bishops – were dubious about the Excise Bill and not unwilling to see Walpole discomfited. The Ministry's majority dropped from sixty-one at the first reading of the Bill to sixteen at the third: even the placemen, fearing an outraged public opinion, were deserting to the enemy. Walpole saw the writing on the wall; he would not 'enforce taxes at the expense of blood'. On 10 April he finally admitted, privately at dinner, 'This dance, it will no longer go. I intend to sound a retreat.'[20]

He extricated himself adroitly and took vengeance on those who had defeated him. Chesterfield and half a dozen more were dismissed from Court posts and sinecures. The Duke of Bolton and

Lord Cobham even lost the command of regiments which they had purchased and therefore considered as private property.

But if Walpole's enemies thought they had him on the run, they were much mistaken. The general election of 1734 was hotly fought, with more contested seats than those of 1715 and 1727. Henry Pelham reported to his brother, Newcastle, 'the whole county almost is poisoned, very little regard for the King or Royal Family, less for the Ministry, in short it is personal interest must carry the election'. Walpole and Newcastle rose nobly to the occasion, rewarding the faithful, threatening or cajoling backsliders, purchasing anyone who would be bought. Treasury funds were lavished on the press; journals surporting the Government were distributed free by the Post Office and hawked round by Government officials – while the Opposition's propaganda always seemed to be lost, delayed or misdirected in the post. They won a resounding victory. Walpole's power had been shaken, but he was still the master.[21]

The tempest over Walpole's unlucky Excise Bill was followed by a teacup storm. The King had a genuine love of music, particularly the music of Handel. The Prince was also musical but, purely to tease his parents, sneered at Handel and set up a rival opera company under a musician, Buononcini, whose work has passed into well-merited oblivion. Attendance at one or other opera house now became the touchstone of a man's politics: the Opposition crowded into the opera house in Lincoln's Inn Fields to listen to Italian nonsense, while the King, Queen, Princess Royal and an ever-dwindling band of Handelites frequented the freezing and half-empty Haymarket Opera House. Chesterfield claimed that he had gone once to the German opera but, finding Their Majesties alone, assumed they had gone to talk business and tactfully left them to it. The Princess Royal said she expected in a little while to see half the House of Lords playing in Buononcini's orchestra in their robes and coronets. But His Majesty saw no humour in the situation and, with an angry eye on his son, exclaimed that he did not think setting oneself at the head of a faction of fiddlers a very honourable occupation for a person of quality.[22]

The Prince's open opposition to Walpole's pet project, the Excise Bill, his mischievous patronage of Buononcini and his feud with Hervey ended whatever hope there might otherwise have been of a reconciliation with his parents.

Even his horticultural tasks the King found objectionable, for Frederick laid out his town garden according to the fashionable notions of Mr Kent, 'without either level or line'. The result was most agreeable and diversified, an improved simulacrum of nature. Her Majesty, too, believed in 'helping nature, not losing it in art'. Her favourite creation, Merlin's Cave, designed by Kent, was approached through a maze with close alleys and clipped hedges; but the edifice itself was a thatched, rustic hut with allegorical figures of Merlin with his magical and mathematical instruments, Merlin's secretary, a witch and others. *The Craftsman* described this royal masterpiece of landscape gardening as a haystack thatched over, and the King observed, 'It is the first time I ever knew the scoundrel in the right.'[23]

However, quarrel as they might, the Prince's financial dependence on his father forced him to live in St James's Palace, though his mother seldom spoke to him and his father, never. When they happened to be in the same room, 'it put one in mind of stories of ghosts that appear to part of a company and are invisible to the rest ... wherever the Prince stood though the King passed him ever so often and ever so near, it always seemed as if the King thought the place the Prince filled a void space'.[24]

It was not, indeed, a happy family. Anne, the Princess Royal, was bored to desperation with home life and constantly complained to Hervey about her father's vanity, his tedious military reminiscences, his boasting of his success with women, his bullying the Queen, 'his insisting upon people's conversation who were to entertain him being always new, and his own being always the same things over and over again'. She conceded that major misfortunes he bore tolerably well, 'but when he is in his worst humours, and the devil to everybody that comes near him, it is always because one of his pages has powdered his periwig ill, or a housemaid set a chair where it does not use to stand, or something of that kind'. She disliked her brother Frederick almost as much.[25] The second sister, Amelia (or Emily), an evil-tongued shrew 'glad of any back to lash, lively, false and a great liar', occasionally sided with her brother, but only to make trouble. The third sister, Caroline, pretty but much too fat, was completely under the thumb of Hervey, for whom she nursed a passion requited only by a patronizing, avuncular semi-flirtation.[26]

The Prince's perennial resentment was at his father's parsimony. Parliament, it will be recalled, had voted the King £800,000 a year for his Civil List on the understanding that he make the Prince an annual allowance of £100,000. But the King angrily refused, preferring to keep the Prince in dependence by paying and engaging his staff and giving him only £24,000 a year as pocket-money.[27]

The Opposition blew on the coals of this quarrel, until Walpole and even Hervey were alarmed by its effects. 'People who make their fortunes under a Prince will submit to being snubbed and ill-used; and people who are caressed by a Prince, cajoled with good words and treated with kindness, will serve him without great hire.' But George Augustus, with neither the personality to win friends nor the liberality to buy them, was far from popular; and, always in the background, was the danger of a Jacobite revival. What on earth, Walpole and Hervey asked one another, was the point in both paying the Prince's 'family' and driving them into opposition? The King would then be put to the double expense of paying them to vote against him and others to vote against them.[28]

Hervey, despite his enmity for the Prince, took it on himself to advise the Queen that it would be in the King's own interests to give the Prince a regular allowance with which to maintain his own establishment. 'By God!' she exclaimed, 'that people will always be judging and deciding upon what they know nothing of.'[29]

In 1733 George Augustus decided to marry off his eldest daughter, Anne. His choice fell on William, Prince of Orange, on whose defects Hervey dwelt in loving detail. 'Besides being almost a dwarf, he was as much deformed as it was possible for a human creature to be; his face was not bad, his countenance was sensible, but his breath was more offensive than it is possible for those who have not been offended by it to imagine.' Events, however, showed him to be well endowed with courage and good sense. The Princess Royal, though somewhat overweight, had the assets of youth and 'an excellent warm animate constitution', which made of her 'now and then remember she was a woman'. But she made the best of a bad job, vowing she would marry him 'if he were a baboon'.

'Well, then,' replied her father, 'there is baboon enough for you.'

He arrived in London, promptly succumbed to a fever and retired to recoup his strength at Bath. ''Tis certain,' remarked Egmont, 'a man in his weak condition has little business to undertake the getting of maidenheads.'[30]

The wedding took place on his return, the King, for once, sparing no expense. However he insisted that Princess Anne was marrying far beneath her: 'What is the Prince of Orange until he has married my daughter?' The bridegroom did not cut too bad a figure. A long peruque concealed his humpback, and his face was really not too bad, the expression lively and sensible. Clearly he at least had made terms with his deformity. The King had planned, when the couple were bedded, that the bridegroom should be behind a curtain, to emphasize his lowly status (or perhaps indeed for kinder reasons) and only the bride exposed to the spectators. But this insult too was evaded, so all were privileged to behold the extraordinary spectacle of the Prince in a nightcap and long brocaded nightgown, looking from 'behind as if he had no head and from before as if he had no neck and no legs'.

'*Ah! Mon Dieu!*' confided the Queen to Hervey, '*Quand je voyais entrer ce monstre pour coucher avec ma fille, j'ai pensé m'évanouir.*'

'Lord! Madam,' replied Hervey, 'in half a year all persons are alike. The figure of the body one is married to, like the prospect of the place one lives in, grows so familiar to one's eye, that one looks at it mechanically, without regarding either the beauties or deformities that strike a stranger.'

But the bride behaved as though her husband were a positive Adonis, addressing everything she said to him, and applauding everything he said to anybody else.[31]

Oddly enough the Prince of Orange was very popular with Londoners who huzzaed him whenever he went out and used the occasion as a heavensent opportunity to tease the Court by loyal addresses recalling the Glorious Revolution, and hinting, as plainly as they dared, that this young man might serve his father-in-law as a previous Prince of Orange had done.

> Most gracious Sire, behold before you
> Your prostrate subjects that adore you,
> The Mayor and Citizens of London,
> By loss of trade and taxes undone,
> Who come with gratulation hearty
> (Altho' they're of the Country Party),
> To wish your Majesty much cheer
> On Anna's marriage with Myn'heer.
> Our hearts presage, from the alliance,
> The fairest hopes, the brightest triumphs ;
> For if one Revolution glorious
> Has made us wealthy and victorious,
> Another, by just consequence,
> Must double both our power and pence.[32]

The year of the Princess Royal's marriage, 1734, saw also the King's final break with Mrs Howard (or Lady Suffolk as she should properly be called after her husband's accession to the earldom). The King was tired of her and vexed by her friendship with Bolingbroke, Pulteney and particularly Pope, whose vitriolic verse was much resented in St James's. At the end of the summer, having for so long endured his snubs, boring conversation and irascibility, this patient and goodhumoured lady asked for permission to go for six weeks to Bath where Bolingbroke happened to be staying. Princess Amelia eagerly inflated their occasional meetings into a scandal, George Augustus duly erupted and, on her return, no longer visited her apartments. When Hervey expressed anxiety lest the King pick up someone who would be politically more troublesome, Princess Anne, on a visit from the Hague, remarked with filial candour, 'I wish with all my heart that he would take someone else. Then Mama might be a little relieved from the ennui of seeing him in her room.'[33]

A fortnight after her return from Bath Lady Suffolk had an extraordinary interview with the Queen, who on the whole would have preferred her to stay, in which she begged leave to retire because of the King's unkindness.

'I don't believe the King is angry,' replied Caroline sharply. 'Child, you dream.' She insisted, rather strangely in the circumstances, that this middle-aged woman of the world did not know a Court.

'He has been dearer to me than my own brother, so, madam, I feel resentment at being ill-treated . . . I wish I knew what I was accused of, for I know my conscience. But, madam, I know it must be some horrid crime.'

'Oh, fie! You commit a crime? Do not talk so.'

'His Majesty's public neglect could not escape any bystander . . . '

'Well, child, you know that the King leaves it to me. I will answer for it that all will be as well with you as any of the ladies, and I'm sure you can't leave my service then.'

'Really, madam, I do not know how it is possible to continue in it . . . '

'For God's sake consider your character! You leave me because the King will not be more particular to you than the others.'

'As to my character the world must have settled that long ago, whether just or unjust; but, madam, I think I have never been thought to betray His Majesty, and I cannot and will not submit to anything that may make that believed of me.'

'Oh, fie, Lady Suffolk! Upon my word, that is a very fine notion out of Celia or some other romance. Pray consider, be calm . . . Stay a week longer, will not you? Stay this week at my request, and give me your word not to read any romances in that time.'

'Yes, madam, I will obey you, but as I am under His Majesty's displeasure, Your Majesty will not expect my attendance.'

'Harkee, Lady Suffolk, you will come up as you used to do.'

She did so, for just one week, during which the wife interceded for the mistress and got snubbed for her pains. 'What the devil did you mean by trying to make an old, dull, deaf, peevish beast stay and plague me when I had so good an opportunity of getting rid of her!'[34]

Then Lady Suffolk shook the dust of St James's forever from her neat little feet and a few months later, her husband having providentially died, remarried. The King was in Hanover when he heard, from the Queen, the surprising news that 'my old mistress has married that old rake George Berkeley, and I am very glad of it', he wrote rather unchivalrously to Caroline. 'I would not make such a gift to my friends, and when my enemies rob me, please God it will always be in this manner.' But the amiable Mrs Howard lived happily ever after.

In this year, Hervey was readmitted to a half share in Miss Vane's favours, enjoyed somewhat precariously in the love-nest in Soho which the Prince had provided for her. It was from her that he learned the news of Bubb Dodington's replacement, as Frederick's principal adviser, by Sir George Lyttelton, a nephew of Lord Cobham, whose youthful relatives, known as the Cobham Cubs, were the most intransigent members of the Opposition. Lyttelton, tall, gawky, ugly and pompous, was hardly the sort of person the Prince usually attracted. He was addicted to the interminable repetition, in a lulling monotone, of the most trite and commonplace Opposition truisms. But he was both honest and economical, to the point of returning, with a thousand thanks, a banknote which Frederick forced into his hands; and he did his best to curb the Prince's extravagance.[35]

The strain on Walpole of these unending feuds in the Royal Family, and the difficulties which were made by the Prince going into open opposition, were aggravated by personal troubles. His charming and beloved mistress, Moll Skerrett, was dangerously ill with pleurisy. The Queen could not comprehend how she could put up with his dirty mouth and great belly, or how he could be fond of a woman who only lived with him for the money. 'She must be a clever gentlewoman to have made him believe she cares for him on any other score . . . and that poor man – *avec ce gros corps, ces jambes enflées et ce vilain ventre* – believes her. My God! What is human nature!'[36]

The trials of living in close proximity to His Majesty had been markedly increased in 1733 by the outbreak of the War of the Polish Succession, in which the Emperor looked for British support. Walpole knew that the House of Commons would turn against him if he asked for money for a war which seemed to be more the concern of Hanover than of Britain, and was determined to remain neutral. George Augustus, on the other hand, was put in an agony of frustrated martial ardour. Much as he disliked the Emperor

Charles VI, his electoral duty and his francophobia alike aligned him passionately on the Empire's side. 'His love of armies, his contempt for civil affairs and the great capacity he thought he possessed for military exploits inclined him with still greater violence to be meddling.' He longed to 'pull the laurels from the brows of the French generals and bind them on to his own temples'. Action and war, he ranted on to an unimpressed Walpole, were his sole pleasure, it was with his sword that he must preserve the balance of power in Europe. Besides, he was growing old and this might be his last chance of glory. While his booby brother-in-law, the brutal and cowardly King of Prussia, was commanding armies, he, the hero of Oudenarde, must busy himself with letters and bills and dispatches. Chesterfield, in *Fog's Journal*, made the disrespectful suggestion that he be given an army of wax soldiers, moved by clockwork, which would be cheap and harmless.[37]

The King may well have been right. He knew a good deal more than Walpole about European affairs, and could see that France was likely to defeat the Empire and establish the hegemony in Europe that William III and Marlborough had fought to destroy. The Queen, moreover, agreed with him, so Walpole was under strong pressure. But war, he knew, meant higher taxes for which he would bear the odium; war meant excitement, turmoil, the emergence of new Ministers and of military commanders who would be his rivals for power. He listened politely to the arguments of the Emperor's emissaries, but declined to be moved by them.

It was in vain that the fiery little George Augustus, and his wife, belaboured Walpole with their arguments. Bulky, placid and immovable, he reminded Her Majesty that 50,000 men had been slain in Europe that year – but not one Englishman.

The war came to an end in 1738 and Britain, having taken no part in the war, had no hand in the peace settlement.

In 1734 Prince Frederick petitioned the King for permission to serve with the Imperial forces against the French on the Rhine, for a regular and sufficient income and for a suitable marriage. The first request was refused, the second ignored and the third met at first by the offer of Princess Charlotte Aurelia of Denmark, who was deformed and mentally retarded. This match the Prince refused, and the House of Commons backed him up. The royal choice fell eventually on Princess Augusta of Saxe-Gotha, whom George Augustus inspected in 1735 on his visit to Hanover.[38]

In preparation for his marriage the Prince was obliged to dismiss Miss Vane. Egmont says that he performed this embarrassing task with tact and generosity. Hervey says he did so clumsily and brutally, so that she fell into a fit of convulsions which Hervey endeavoured to cure by cramming cordials and gold powder down her throat. She retired to Bath, solaced by the parting gift from the Prince of a house in Grosvenor Square and £1600 a year for life, adequate remuneration for what was, after all, only part-time employment. She died soon afterwards, a trivial, tragic little trull.[39]

During his visit to Hanover in the spring of 1735 George Augustus fell in love with Amelia Sophia von Walmoden, an attractive young married woman of the first fashion, whom he acquired at a bargain price of 1000 ducats, a tribute more to his economy than his ardour. As a niece of the younger Madame von Platen she was, so to speak, bred for the profession. A bizarre feature of his courtship was that at every stage, in letters of forty or fifty pages, he consulted his wife and, through her, his Prime Minister in whose judgement, as a man of the world, he placed infinite confidence. '*Montrez ceci*,' he would write at some crisis of his wooing, '*et consultez là-dessus le gros homme*. ... I know you will love Madame Walmoden, because she loves me.'

It is hardly credible that in the middle of his pursuit of Madame Walmoden, he should have sought his wife's assistance in making another conquest. The Princess of Modena, a daughter of his old enemy, the Regent Orléans, was, he had heard, pretty free of her person. Could not Caroline arrange for her to visit England next winter so that he could there pay her his addresses. '*Un plaisir que je suis sûr, ma chère Caroline, vous serez bien aise de me procurer, quand je vous dis combien je souhaite [son père]*.'[40] But perhaps it was a clumsy joke.

No less extraordinary than the letters to his wife was the fact that she showed most of them to Hervey, through whom they became common knowledge at St James's. She was hurt, thought Hervey, more in her pride than in her marital affection. But why, in that case, should she broadcast her shame? None of these letters has survived: Hervey is the only witness to their contents and, once again, a shadow of doubt is cast over his veracity.

George Augustus returned with manifest reluctance in October, arriving just before dinner as the Queen came out of chapel. After affectionate embraces – for she was always his favourite woman – and her repeatedly 'glueing her mouth to his hand', he made himself almost civil to the company for fully half an hour.

Travelling day and night had brought on a painful attack of piles. The Court was not supposed to know of his embarrassing disorder, but all suffered from the consequent eruptions of his abominable temper. So far from being ashamed or resentful of his snubs, his courtiers bragged about them. Those whom he had 'rumped', that is to say on whom he had deliberately and rudely turned his back, formed themselves into a Rumpsteak Club.

'*Quoi?*' he exploded when he heard of this. '*Ils osent se moquer de moi!*'[41]

Long ago he used to boast that he had not a drop of blood which was not English. Now he never ceased to compare unfavourably his adopted country with his fatherland.

No English or even French cook could dress a dinner; no English confectioner set out a dessert; no English player could act; no English coachman could drive, or English jockey ride, nor were there any English horses fit to be drove or fit to be ridden; no Englishman knew how to come into a room, nor any Englishwoman how to dress herself, nor were there any diversions in England, public or private, nor any man or woman in England whose conversation was to be borne – the one, as he said, talked of nothing but their dull politics, the other of nothing but their dull clothes. Whereas at Hanover all these things were in the utmost perfection. The men were patterns of politeness, bravery and gallantry; the women of beauty, wit and entertainment; his troops there were the bravest in the world, his counsellors the wisest, his manufacturers the most ingenious, his subjects the happiest; and at Hanover, in short, plenty reigned, magnificence resided, arts flourished, diversions abounded, riches flowed, and everything was in the utmost perfection that contributes to make a prince great or a people blessed.[42]

He condemned all the English as king-killers and republicans, and complained that while in Hanover he could distribute his royal favours as a reward for faithful service, in England he simply enriched people for not being rascals and bribed them not to cut his throat. It was the English parliamentary system, and the restrictions on the English monarchy, that he particularly resented – so different from the benevolent, paternal despotism he exercised over his dear fatherland. The bishops too, with their political pretensions, aroused the royal ire. 'I am sick to death of all this foolish stuff,' he exploded, 'and wish with all my heart that the devil may take all your bishops, and the devil take your Minister, and the devil take your Parliament, and the devil take the whole island, provided I can get out of it and go to Hanover.'[43]

On one occasion – but Hervey admits to hearing the story only at third hand – the Queen lost her temper and hit back at him. 'I see no reason that made your coming to England necessary; you might have continued there, without coming to torment yourself and us, since your pleasure did not call you; I am sure your business did not, for we could have done that just as well without you as you could have pleased yourself without us.' Upon which the King, in a great huff and shaking with rage, stamped out of the room.[44]

But all this pining for absolute power was, Walpole opined, mere bluff and brag.

> He thinks he is devilish stout, and never gives up his will or his opinion; but he never acts in anything material according to either of them but when I have a mind he should . . . [He] wishes himself absolute, and fancies he has courage enough to attempt making himself so; but . . . he is, with all his personal bravery, as great a political coward as ever wore a crown, and as much afraid to lose it.

The Queen too was irked by party politics and complained to Hervey, 'This is always the way of your nasty Whigs, though they themselves are supported by the Crown, they are always lukewarm in returning that support . . . and grudge [your King] even the power of doing you good.' Hervey reminded her that when William III, feeling a similar resentment, had threatened to form a Ministry of Tories because their principles were more favourable to kingship, the Earl of Sunderland had replied, 'That is very true, Sir, but you are not their King.'[45]

It was on this truth, or half-truth, implicitly believed by the

King and Queen, that Walpole's power was based, and he played on it adroitly, insisting that all Tories were Jacobites at heart. The only way Hanoverian Tories could display at once their loyalty to the Protestant succession and their abhorrence of the Prime Minister was by aligning themselves with the Prince of Wales, whose opposition thereby served a useful purpose.[46]

Walpole told the Queen frankly that at fifty-three she could hardly expect to rely on her physical charms to retain her influence over a vain and vigorous husband. He advised her to bring to Court Lady Tankerville, a good-looking, good-natured, simple sort of woman whom George Augustus had once fancied. She would at least be preferable to Lady Deloraine, who with her pretty face, lying tongue and false heart would be a far more dangerous rival, and with whom His Majesty, like many others, bragged of having lain last winter.[47]

Caroline put a brave face on it, and could still be amused at his 'gift' to her of a team of Hanover coach horses – a gift in the sense that she paid for their keep, while he continued to use them.[48]

The only member of the family who escaped the King's explosive temper was Prince Frederick, who prudently kept out of range. But his father had plenty to say about, if not to him. Of one excellent man who had an unsatisfactory son, His Majesty observed judicially,

The father might be a very worthy man, though his son is a puppy. One often sees fathers and sons very little alike; a wise father has very often a fool for his son. One sees the father a brave man and his son a scoundrel; a father very honest, and his son a great knave; a father a man of truth, and his son a great liar; in short, a father that has all sorts of good qualities, and a son that is good for nothing.

The Queen and Hervey caught each other's eye and could hardly refrain from laughing, at which the King added hastily that sometimes it was just the reverse, and disagreeable fathers had very agreeable sons – presumably thinking of his own father and himself.[49]

After seeing a performance of Henry IV, he remarked on the excellence of the actor who had played the Prince of Wales: 'I never saw so awkward a fellow or so mean a scoundrel in my life.'

Giving his observations a personal application, all the courtiers present took them up and poured abuse on the theatrical Prince of Wales.

But the puppy's marriage could hardly be postponed much longer, for George Augustus had promised Madame Walmoden that he would be back in Hanover for her next birthday, 29 May 1736. Moreover the promise was generally known for she had at dinner, on his last night at Herrenhausen, in a mixture of tears and smiles, toasted that felicitous date. His appetite to return was whetted by numerous pictures of festivities at Hanover which he hung in the Queen's dressing room. From these and from his detailed descriptions of her charms, Caroline could easily have painted an accurate portrait of the lady. What clinched his determination to go to Hanover in May in defiance of his Minister's advice was the birth during the spring of a son, which he naturally took as proof of his own, rather than Herr von Walmoden's, potency.[50]

So Princess Augusta was sent for from Saxe-Gotha, arrived on 25 April at Greenwich and two days later in London, to be married that very day. She was tall and quite good-looking, but somewhat marked by smallpox, gawky and awkward in her movements. At seventeen she had led a very sheltered life: she knew little French and no English, her mother having assumed that since the Hanoverians had been for over twenty years on the throne, surely everyone in England would by now speak German. But most people (excluding, of course, Lord Hervey) were impressed by her quiet and modest good sense.[51]

The Prince was delighted with his bride. He met her at Greenwich, dined and supped with her and did not leave her until two in the morning. The following day he took her for a trip on the Thames in his barge with musical accompaniment. On being introduced to her future father- and mother-in-law she prostrated herself at their feet, a civility which was well received. The Queen strongly advised the Princess to 'avoid jealousy and to be easy in regard to amours', a practice to which she attributed her happy marriage.[52]

The wedding ceremony was performed at nine o'clock that night, and at the wedding supper the bridegroom made himself painfully conspicuous by eating several helpings of jelly (believed to be an aphrodisiac), every time laughing and winking at his servants. At the bedding ceremony George Augustus steeled himself for the odious task of dressing his son in a nightshirt and a cap higher than any grenadier's. The bride was undressed by the Princesses and the Quality were admitted to see them sitting in bed surrounded by their loving relatives. The Queen, who would never believe that her eldest son was not impotent, later remarked that the bride looked extremely tired on her wedding night but quite refreshed next morning, which suggested that she had enjoyed an undisturbed night's sleep. As to the jelly and the nightcap, the one, she said, made her sick and the other made her laugh.[53]

The King, on his departure for Hanover, sent a gracious message to the Prince to the effect that wherever his mother resided, there would always be a home for him and his young wife: but this the young man interpreted as meaning there would always be a prison. There was a row because the Queen refused to make Lady Archibald Hamilton a Lady of the Princess's Bedchamber, a customary appointment for one who had access to the Prince's; and another row because she refused a similar job to the wife of William Townshend, an Opposition M.P. whom His Majesty condemned as the most impertinent puppy in the Prince's whole family, and was determined not to reward for being so. The Prince's allowance was raised to £50,000 a year, which he said was robbing him of £50,000. (He received also the revenues of the Duchy of Cornwall, amounting to £8–9000 a year.) Egmont believed that the King refused to pay the bridegroom's bachelor debts lest the Prince become too popular.[54]

One of 'Cobham's Cubs', William Pitt, an active and articulate member of the Opposition, whose observations on Walpole and the Excise Bill had made him *persona non grata* to His Majesty, was broke* for his insolent speech on the Prince's marriage. He dwelt on the filial piety of the Prince, his goodness in acceding to the wishes of his people in getting married. 'The merit of the King in granting the request [to be married] occupied a less prominent position' in Cornet Pitt's oration. More was to be heard of this 'terrible Cornet of Horse'.[55]

* i.e. deprived of his commission in the Army.

So off went the King, in high spirits, to Hanover. Before his departure he left strict instructions that the Prince and Princess of Wales were not to dine in public or attempt any 'progress' through the country; and he appointed the Queen 'Protector of the Realm'. He did, however, uncharacteristically send his son a present of £1000.[1]

His ecstatic reunion with his lady love was somewhat marred, a few weeks later, by the fortuitous discovery of a ladder leading to her bedroom window and a young officer hiding behind an espalier in the garden. Madame Walmoden hastened to the King to get in first with her story of a plot to ruin her, but the King could not entirely quieten his suspicions that her conduct may not have been altogether prudent. As usual in a difficulty, he sought the advice of his wife and his Prime Minister. '*Consultez le gros homme,*' he wrote to her, '*qui a plus d'expérience, ma chère Caroline, que vous dans ces affairs, et moins de préjugé que moi dans celle-ci.*' However, like most elderly lovers in a similar situation, he decided that half a loaf was better than no bread, and gave the lady the benefit of the doubt.[2]

In London, according to Hervey, Frederick egged his wife on to various discourtesies which the Queen bore with exemplary patience. 'Poor creature, if she were to spit in my face, I should only pity her for being under such a fool's direction, and wipe it off.' She found their company tedious, and complained that an afternoon with them made her as tired as though she had carried them round the garden on her back.[3]

She bore with fortitude her husband's absence, but was cross when he proposed to prolong it beyond his birthday (30 October), which she considered a deliberate slight. Again and again, Walpole besought her, if she wanted to retain her power over her husband, to put up with his amours, even to allow him to bring his mistress to England where she would be far less dangerous than in Hanover, and, Hervey added, would soon be to the King everything Lady Suffolk was, except deaf. Caroline wrote, accordingly, a most submissive letter suggesting 'that, as nothing was agreeable to him in England, he had better bring over that person who would make it so'. She assured Hervey that only girls and fools resented conjugal infidelities. How she regretted the departure of Lady Suffolk! She received in return a tender missive in which the King accepted with rapture her suggestion and favoured her with the fullest description of Madame Walmoden's physical and intellectual perfections. It was rumoured that Horatio Walpole advised the lady, if she came to England, to keep out of politics. 'This put the King in such a passion that he kicked him.' No one loved poor Horatio, and the Queen complained often of his 'dirty, sweaty body offending her nose'.[4]

Walpole had some difficulty in holding the Queen to her resolution since, as he complained to Hervey, 'those bitches Lady Pomfret and Lady Sundon were always . . . making their court to the Queen by saying they hoped never to see this saucy whore brought under Her Majesty's nose.' The lady, too, was apprehensive of a confrontation with a wronged wife, and aware perhaps that absence makes the heart grow fonder. So nothing was definitely decided.[5]

The King's prolonged absence, and the reason for it, was gold-dust to the Opposition. A wreck of an old horse, with broken saddle and pillion, was turned out into the London streets bearing a placard: 'Let nobody stop me – I am the King's Hanover equipage going to fetch His Majesty and his whore to England.' In the Stock Exchange it was announced that His Hanoverian Majesty planned to visit his British dominions for three months in the spring.[6]

More extravagant rumours ran that the lady had cost His Majesty £50,000 for herself, another £50,000 for her husband; and that having paid those exorbitant sums for the exclusive use of the merchandise, 'the King found him in bed with her and was much incensed . . . Others say that she had poxt him.' Why, if His Majesty required a whore, did he not take an English one and stay at home? 'There are enough of them to be had and cheaper.' It was even asserted, *horribile dictu*, that she was a Papist, and he was building a Papist chapel for her in London.[7] It was 'a common speech of the vulgar that the King had done what his predecessors could never do – made all men of one mind'. It was whispered that the Young Pretender was a fine, upstanding boy.[8]

Parliament seldom condescended to social legislation, being more concerned with the great questions of liberty, the standing army, property and foreign policy to bother much about the people's welfare. But in September 1736 it passed the Gin Act, to control and restrict the sale of rot-gut spirit which made one 'drunk for a penny, dead-drunk for tuppence'. Its main result was to produce a crop of informers and hawkers selling on the streets bottles labelled 'Cuckold's Comfort', 'Makeshift' or 'Ladies Delight'. But it was, naturally, much resented by the people whom it was supposed to benefit. They rioted round the Queen's coach yelling, 'No Gin! No King!' With great self-possession she leaned out of the window to assure them that, if they would only be patient, they would have their gin and their King too. Meanwhile the Prince grew more popular every day. He made a great show of downing his noggin of gin in common taverns: of chatting to the vulgar; of picking up an old woman's oranges upset by his coach. He let it be known that he had actually gone without dinner rather than keep an opera audience waiting. 'Huzza for the Prince!' shouted the mob, and he replied 'Huzza for Liberty and Property'.[9] The City granted him its Freedom in a gold box and made him a member of the Worshipful Company of Saddlers. 'Here was a saddler to mend old Oliver's gear and make use of it.' The Queen was not amused, and His Majesty used to refer sourly to his son as 'the Saddler'.[10]

There was in the Prince's party a revival of the plan to divide Britain and Hanover, the Electorate going, at the King's death, to Prince William. It would indeed be a popular move, 'A message from Heaven', as the Speaker said. It was to be linked with the increase of the Prince's allowance to £100,000, a price which he thought his parents would willingly pay for the sake of William. The Queen was in two minds about it. 'The mean fool! The poor-spirited beast! . . . If the Pretender offered him £500,000 for the reversion of the Crown, he would say, "Give me the money!"' If, however, her worthless elder son cared to pluck out one of his eyes and give it to her dear William, she would not refuse it. 'For though I had as lief go and live upon a dunghill as to go to Hanover, for William it would be a very good morsel.' However, the scheme came to nothing, though Frederick in his will recommended it because 'from that moment Jacobitism will be rooted out.'[11]

On St James's gate an advertisement was pasted:

Lost or strayed out of this house, a man who has left a wife and six children on the parish; whoever will give any tidings of them to the churchwardens of St James's Parish, so as he may be got again, shall receive four shillings and sixpence reward. N.B. This reward will not be increased, no one judging him to be worth a crown.

The King was not at all concerned at the possibility that he might be unpopular: he simply refused to believe it. The Queen, *à propos* Walmoden, remarked that she was sorry for the scandal it gave others; but for herself, she minded it less than his going to the close-stool. Archbishop Blackburn congratulated her on being 'so sensible a woman as to like her husband should divert himself'.[12]

Frederick was constantly dropping hints that his wife was breeding, a notion she encouraged by her habit of playing with, dressing and undressing a large doll. Her Majesty expressed open doubts as to the marriage having even been consummated, and consulted Hervey on this question. He assured her that Miss Vane had described the Prince, in these matters, as 'ignorant to a degree inconceivable, but not impotent'. The Queen was not convinced. 'He has told me that he has often got nasty distempers from women, *dont je ne crois pas un mot.*' She begged Hervey to seek accurate information from Lady Dudley. 'You know that woman has lain with half the town as well as Fretz, and consequently must know whether he is like other men or not.'

She speculated as to the possibility of her son arranging for an-other man to lie with his wife without her knowing it, and

15. 'The Stature of a Great Man or the English Colossus': Sir Robert Walpole 1740; all allusions refer to his inactivity and reluctance to engage in war in the face of the aggressions of Spain and France

16. 'The Vulture': Lord Chancellor Hardwicke 1756;
the French fleurs-de-lys on the medallion round his
neck refer to the alleged subservience to France of
Hardwicke and the Newcastle administration

17. 'The treacherous patriot unmask'd', 12 March
1742: William Pulteney holding a mask of a
good and open countenance

Hervey thought this would be quite possible. 'For a month before and after I would advise the Prince to go to bed several hours after his wife, and to pretend to get up for a flux several times in the night, and to perfume himself always with some predominant smell, and by the help of these tricks it would be very easy to put the change of any man near his own size upon her that he pleased.'

'I love you mightily, my dear Lord Hervey, but if I thought you would get a little Hervey by the Princess of Saxe-Gotha to disinherit my dear William, I could not bear it.'

He assured his 'dear, good and amiable Queen' that he was the very last man her son would employ for that purpose. But she insisted that Fretz might well, in his frantic wish to be thought capable of fatherhood, employ a *locum tenens*. 'Altogether, it makes me very uneasy.' Princess Caroline entered eagerly into these fascinating discussions, and shared her mother's apprehension.[13]

On the night of the 7–8 December the King at last disengaged himself from the arms of Madame Walmoden and set out for home. But at Helvoetsluys, where the royal yacht awaited him, he was met by a terrific westerly gale. No one in London knew whether or not he had embarked: the Queen was beside herself with anxiety, and the Prince with pleasurable anticipation.

Walpole was in unrelieved gloom at the prospect of the Queen's and his own fall from power.

A poor, weak, irresolute, false, lying, dishonest, contemptible wretch, that nobody loves, that nobody believes, that nobody will trust, and will trust everybody by turns, and that everybody by turns will impose upon, betray, mislead and plunder. And then what will become of this divided family, and this divided country, is too melancholy a prospect to admit conjecture to paint it.

Hervey argued that the Queen would have a powerful influence over her son. 'Zounds, my lord, he would tear the flesh off her bones with hot irons!'[14] But Walpole was wrong in maintaining that Poor Fred was universally despised and hated. On the contrary. 'My God!' exclaimed the Queen, 'popularity always makes me sick, but Fretz's popularity makes me vomit. I hear that yesterday they talked of the King's being cast away with the same sang-froid as you would talk of a coach being overturned, and that my good son strutted about as if he had already been King.' Hervey suggested that, if he came to the throne, the Queen would govern him as she did his father. 'Jesus!' interrupted Princess Caroline, 'he hates Mama!'[15]

To the Queen's vast relief a vessel from Holland reached Yarmouth, by a miracle, in the teeth of the gale, with the news that the King was still ashore.[16] That, however, was not the end of it. There were more false alarms, more rumours and conjecture that the royal yacht had put out from Helvoetsluys, had returned there, had been sunk with all hands. In fact the King had had a terrific row with Admiral Wager, insisting that he sail while the Admiral insisted that he should not.

'Let the weather be what it will, I am not afraid.'

'If you are not,' retorted this sea-dog, 'I am.'

'I would rather be twelve hours in a storm than twenty-four more at Helvoetsluys.'

'Sir, you need not wish for twelve. Four will do your business.'

'I positively order you to sail.'

'Sir, you can oblige me to go, but I can make you come back again.' Which was precisely what happened – the royal yacht put out into the tempestuous seas and then returned to port.

By his own account, related repeatedly to Hervey and others, he braved the tempest firm and undaunted. He rallied his pale and trembling page, '*Comment? Tu as peur?*' To which the poltroon replied, '*Oui, Sire, vraiment, et je crois qu'il n'y a que Votre Majesté dans le vaisseau qui ne l'a pas.*' The cabin boy, seeing His Majesty at his prayers, said, 'The King is coaxing the Almighty, but, by God, he will be doomed for all that.'[17]

The King's danger did not in the least soften the Opposition's distaste. Wits repeated that the wind, like the nation, was against him. A fellow in an alehouse lifted his tankard to some soldiers: 'I suppose you are all brave English boys, and so conclude that you will pledge me, "Damnation to your master!"'

When the City Sheriffs, who were politically of some importance, were due to be 'pricked', that is chosen by lot from a panel of

names, Pulteney improved the occasion with some characteristic
verse:

> 'What shall we do,' quoth Walpole to the Queen,
>   'Unless the wind turn quick?
> The Sheriffs in all times have been
>   Still chosen by a prick.'
>   Answer: Queen
> 'The instrument that does the job
>   The King he has about him.
> But can't you help me, good Sir Bob,
>   To do the thing without him?'

The Prince really did distinguish himself in fighting a great fire
at the temple, setting a fine example to the troops and firemen.
The mob shouted, 'Crown him! Crown him!' – or so the Opposition averred.[18]

Whether or not this was true, there were plenty of people who
thought the time ripe for the Prince to 'think right and act
accordingly' – in other words to attempt a coup. But he held back
from the brink. 'Believing the King had perished, the Chiefs of the
Opposition waited on the Prince to assure him of their service – to
which he made a prudent and proper reply, that he hoped His
Majesty safe and could not bear the thought of it otherwise.'[19]

Meanwhile the Queen sent her husband a long, tender letter,
and he replied with one of thirty pages, which might have been
written by some young sailor of twenty, to his first mistress. He
wrote 'in a style that would have made one believe him the rival of
Hercules for vigour, and her of Venus's beauty, her person being
mentioned in the most exalted strains of rapture, and his own
eagerness to feed, after those weeks' abstinence, in the warmest
phrases'. And the Queen, apparently, showed it proudly to Walpole
and Hervey.[20]

At last, after five weeks of crisis, news arrived that His Majesty
had arrived safely at Lowestoft. On 15 January 1737 he arrived in
London in a mood as sunny as it had been black on his previous
arrival. He kissed all his family, even his eldest son, complimented
the Queen, complimented Sir Robert, and took her swiftly up to
bed.

Next morning Walpole and Hervey happened to meet within

hearing of a sentry. '*Optime, optime, omnia rident,*' quoth the Prime Minister. 'Excellent, excellent, everything going splendidly.' Hervey knew his Horace and replied with equal felicity,

> '*Prisca redit Venus*
> *Diductosque jugo cogit aëneo.*
> *Flava excutitur Chloe*
> *Rejectaeque patet janua Lydiae.*'

> (Their former passion has returned
> And bound them with a chain of bronze.
> Goldenhaired Chloe has been dislodged
> And the door lies open to once-rejected Lydia.)

Walpole continued in an ingenious adaptation: '*Dixit ad uxorem,* "*Quamquam sidere pulchrior illa est tecum vivere amen tecum obeam libens.*"' ('He said to his wife, "Although that girl is lovelier than a star, it is with you that I want to live, with you I would gladly die"').* He added, as he heaved his bulk into his sedan-chair, 'I do not believe Mr *Bis* has been upstairs, notwithstanding all his rant.' Hervey replied, 'If Mr *Semel* was there, I believe it was better company than Her Majesty had last year on a similar occasion.'[21] †

Chesterfield's vitriolic pen did not allow the occasion to pass without comment.

> Great George, escaped from narrow seas and storms,
> Now rides at large in Carolina's arms.
> Bold Jonah, thus, as holy writ will tell ye,
> A whale received at once into her belly.

And, on the same theme,

> What, just escaped from Cleopatra's charms
> To souse at once into your Fulvia's arms?
> With equal evidence of haste to run
> From blooming twenty to fat fifty-one.
> So travelled Hotentot, refined in vain,
> Returns with rapture to his Guts again.

---

* Quotation and adaptation from Horace, Odes III, ix, 14–24.
† *Semel*, once: *bis*, twice.

On the summoning of Parliament, Pulteney again resorted to verse.

> The King this summer having spent
>   *Amoribus in teneris* (In pleasant love-making)
> Appoints his loving Parliament
>   To meet him *Die Veneris*[22] *

The Queen was unwise enough to brag of the many proofs His Majesty had given of his affection. 'Madam,' replied Walpole, 'do not flatter yourself. For pleasure of the body there must be youth on one side; and, believe me, marriage is never so properly called one flesh as after twenty years' marriage, for no husband then knows his wife's from his own.' The King's kindness, he insisted, was no more than compensation for the sins of the summer.[23]

Moreover His Majesty again suffered from his distressing and painful complaint, the piles. Worse still, he had a fistula in the same region. He could not bear the thought that anyone knew of it, and promptly dismissed one of the Lords of the Bedchamber who incautiously inquired after his health. It was one of his foibles that he would never admit to being ill, and much resented other people's illnesses. Choking with a sore throat and in a high fever, he would still insist on dressing to attend a levée. Not even Prince William, his favourite, dared stay away from Court on the excuse of illness.[24]

In February 1737 the Prince of Wales and his friends, determined on a straight trial of strength, laid before Parliament his claims for £100,000 a year. The King had submitted to the agonizing operation of being cut for the piles, and was in a high fever and very feeble health: they were not without hope that their measure would put him in such a passion as to kill him. Calculations of voting strengths seemed to show that the Opposition would carry their point by a majority of about forty. The King took it better than was expected. To silence rumours, he appeared at a levée, was less grumpy than usual and from that day began to get better.[25]

The whole family was furious with Fretz. A hundred times a day they wished him dead of an apoplexy, his mother cursing the day he was born and his sister Caroline grudging every hour he continued to breathe: the nauseous beast, she said, cared for

* The day of Venus, 1 April, All Fools' Day.

189

nobody but his nauseous self, and for nothing but money, was the greatest liar that ever spoke and would not scruple to put one arm round a person's neck to kiss him and with the other arm stab him for five guineas.

Walpole, who feared that the Commons vote would bring him down, proposed making terms with the Prince: a jointure for his wife, and for himself the conversion into a fixed settlement of his present precarious allowance of £50,000 a year. To Walpole's formal offer of these concessions, conveyed by the Lords of the Council, the Prince returned a curt verbal reply that the matter was now out of his hands. 'Indeed, my lords, it is in other hands, I am sorry for it.'[26]

The King and Queen were furious, both at Walpole for persuading them to offer a concession, and at their son – 'the lowest, stinking coward in the world' – for so contemptuously rejecting it. 'I know if I was asleep he is capable of shooting me through the head or stabbing me in the back . . . But if I saw him and held up this pin . . . he would tremble and cry and fall at my feet'. Her Majesty espied her son walking across the court. 'Look! There he goes – that wretch! That villain! – I wish the ground would open this moment and sink the monster to the lowest hole in hell.'[27]

Walpole put it about that the question was not really about the Prince's allowance, but whether he or his father should be King. This point, together with his adroit parliamentary management, carried the day. The Tories abstained and the Opposition motion was defeated by thirty votes. The Prince continued to live at St James's, dined at the same table as his parents, attended their levées; but the Queen never said a word to him, and the King never seemed to know he was in the same room.[28]

Walpole had some difficulty in persuading the King that, despite the Prince's attitude, it would be politic to make the jointure and the settlement of £50,000. Why, His Majesty asked, should he do anything for a silly puppy, an undutiful insolent scoundrel? Eventually, with a very ill grace, he gave way. 'I see my affairs are upon that footing that I must yield in everything.'[29]

He seemed to have lost interest in Madame Walmoden, and the son whom he claimed by her had died. Loose, empty, baby-faced

Lady Deloraine,* whose current husband was a Mr Wyndham, now engrossed the royal favour and boasted about it freely. When Walpole said of the child she carried in her arms, 'That's a very pretty boy, Lady Deloraine: who got it?' her ladyship replied, 'Mr Wyndham, upon honour. But I will not promise whose the next shall be.' The country, she said, was under a great obligation to her, for it was solely owing to her that the King did not go to Hanover in 1737. She used to ask Princess Caroline for advice on coping with the King's urgent desire, and the Princess used to reply, 'Ah, my dear Fly,† you really must know your own affairs better than I.'[30]

Walpole wished His Majesty had taken somebody less mischievous than that lying bitch, but Hervey replied: 'If she got the ear of anyone in power, it might be of very bad consequence, but since 'tis only the King, I think it is of no great signification.' The Prime Minister capped this by assuring the Queen that as Lady Deloraine only went to bed with His Majesty, lying *with* him or *to* him was much the same as lying *to* or *with* Mr Wyndham.[31]

The Princess of Wales was indeed breeding, though the Queen refused to see it. Augusta would not give her mother-in-law the specific details which she suspiciously demanded.

'When are you like to lie in?' asked the Queen.

'I don't know.'

'Are you yet quick?'

'I don't know.'

'Is it, then, the beginning of your being with child?'

'I don't know.'[32]

Her husband wished her to lie in in London, Their Majesties were consequently resolved that she should remain at Hampton Court, where they could witness the event. Said Her Majesty, 'I cannot help it, but at her labour I positively will be, let her lie in where she will; for she cannot be brought to bed as quick as one could blow one's nose, and I will be sure it is her child. For my part, I do not see she is big; you all say you see it, and therefore I suppose it is so, and I am blind.' She wished the King's order to be

---

* She still seems to have been called Lady Deloraine. Perhaps she changed partners so often that people could not be bothered to remember her name.

† Lady Deloraine's nickname at Court.

sent at once. 'Sir Robert, we shall be catched: he will remove her [from Hampton Court] before he receives any order.' Walpole procrastinated. There was no hurry, he insisted; the baby was not due until October – or so the Prince said, though it was not until 5 July that he gave his parents proper notice of this.[33]

But the Queen's apprehensions proved well founded. After two false alarms, on 31 July Augusta's labour pains started. Immediately her husband, assisted by Dunoyer, the dancing-master, and one of his equerries, lugged her downstairs. Accompanied by Lady Archibald Hamilton, two other ladies and the Prince's valet who had some pretensions to being a man midwife, they drove post-haste to London. 'The tortures of the miserable patient were expressed by dolorous screaming and pinching her attendants, and the coach was plentifully stained with her excessive floodings.' Her husband, with all the cheerfulness of a toothdrawer or an executioner, assured that it would soon be over, plied handkerchiefs under her petticoats and extinguished the lights so that passersby should not see. They reached St James's just in time, and hurried round borrowing napkins, warming pans and two tablecloths to serve as sheets. At a quarter to eleven she was 'delivered of a little rat of a girl, about the bigness of a good, large toothpick-case', none of the Lords of the Council being present except Wilmington and Lord Godolphin.[34]

The Prince's motive for this extraordinary conduct was a mystery. The King's friends said that Augusta, terrified and already in labour, pleaded to be allowed to stay at Hampton Court, but the Prince insisted on moving her, rallying her with cries of 'Come, it will soon be over', and 'Courage, courage! Ah, quelle sottise.'[35] On the other hand it has been conjectured, with no supporting evidence, that it was she who insisted on being moved, because she simply did not feel safe in her in-laws' house, and feared they would do away with her baby in order that their favourite son, William, should succeed to the throne.[36] The Prince's case was that he 'acted a wise and tender part in hastening her away', for there was neither midwife, nurse nor arrangements for an accouchement at Hampton Court.[37] To this one can only retort, 'If not, why not?' With false alarms a few days before, there was ample warning of a premature birth – if, indeed, it was premature.

If, as is quite possible, his intention was simply to tease his parents, he abundantly succeeded. They went to bed at eleven without hearing a word about the Princess's state. At half past one a courier brought to Hampton Court the news of her being in labour. A woman of the Bedchamber aroused the King and Queen, who asked if the palace was on fire. She replied that the Princess was in labour.

'My God!' cried Her Majesty. 'My nightgown! I'll go to her this moment.'

'Your coaches, too,' Mrs Titchburne replied. 'The Princess is at St James's.'

'Are you mad, or are you asleep, my good Titchburne? You dream.'

When they were at last convinced of the truth, the King lost his temper and characteristically blamed his wife. 'This is all your fault. There is a false child will be put on us, and how will you answer it to all your children? This has been a fine care and fine management for your son, William; he is mightily obliged to you.'

The Queen was at St James's by four o'clock. She refused a cup of chocolate, winking at Hervey and saying, 'You need not fear my tasting anything in this side of the house.'

The Prince gave her the good news, and swore he had sent her immediate word of it. This she did not believe, but she congratulated her daughter-in-law and added, '*Apparemment, madame, vous avez horriblement souffert.*'

'*Point de tout,*' replied Augusta. '*Ce n'est rien.*'

The Queen kissed the child and said, '*Le bon Dieu vous bénisse, pauvre petite créature. Vous voilà arrivée dans un desagréable monde.*'[38]

The Prince made copious excuses, but the Queen ignored him, and merely reproached Lady Archibald Hamilton for allowing this to happen. Lady Archibald, who had tried to dissuade the Prince from his intention, merely said, 'You see, Sir' – which placed the blame exactly where it should lie. After warning her son that she could not answer for the consequences if he insisted on seeing his father for several days, she returned to Hampton. She said that she no longer doubted it being the Princess's child. 'If, instead of this poor, ugly little she-mouse, there had been a large, fat, jolly boy, I should not have been cured of my suspicions.'[39]

Nine days later she paid a second visit to St James's where the Prince spoke not a single word to her in private, but in public, handing her into her coach, knelt down and kissed her hand. After this she went no more, and His Majesty observed that she was well enough served for thrusting her nose where it had been shit on already.[40]

His first comment on the birth of a granddaughter was, 'So the saddler's wife is brought to bed.' But when he learned the full enormity of his son's conduct, he sent Lord Essex with word that 'it was looked upon by the King to be such a deliberate insult to himself and to the Queen, that he has commanded me to acquaint Your Royal Highness that he resents it in the highest degree'.

Princess Caroline sent Dunoyer, the dancing master, to tell the Prince that, 'saving the respect I owe you, Your Royal Highness deserves to be hanged'. Fretz spat in the fire and observed, 'Ah, you know Caroline. She is always like that.'[41]

A man more eventempered than George Augustus might be forgiven his displeasure on such an occasion. He and the Queen stood as godparents to their granddaughter and then resolved to send the Prince packing, but not to deprive him (as he himself had been deprived) of the custody of his child, 'lest any accident might happen to the royal little animal, and the world in that case accuses the King and Queen of having murdered it, for the sake of the Duke'.[42] *

The Cabinet Council agreed with this decision, and the Queen at breakfast next day exclaimed, 'I hope in God that I shall never see that monster's face again ... I was fond of that monster, I looked upon him as one that would make the happiness of my life, and now I wish he had never been born.'

'Pray, mama,' said Princess Caroline, 'wish that he may die, and that we may all go about with smiling faces, glad hearts, and crêpe and hoods for him.'

The King observed, 'I am weary of the puppy's name, but at least I shall not be plagued any more with seeing his nasty face ... I never loved the puppy well enough to have him ungrateful to me, but to you he is a monster.'

* Prince William, Duke of Cumberland.

194

He expatiated on the trouble to which he had been put in finding his son a bride. It was quite untrue, he said, to call the Princess of Denmark old, ugly, crooked and a dwarf. She was not, indeed, handsome, and was low, but well-shaped and only twenty-seven. 'Besides, for Protestant princesses there is not great choice of matches. The Princess of Denmark he would not have. The Princesses of Prussia have a madman for their father, and I did not think engrafting my half-witted coxcomb on a madwoman would mend the breed.' As for the Würtemberg royal family, the grandmother had had the madness of not letting her husband lie with her after their first child for fear of spoiling her shape, and the greatgrandmother the madness of letting anybody lie with her that pleased.[43]

After much drafting and redrafting by Hervey, Walpole and others, the King's orders to his son were finally signed and despatched on 10 September.

The profession you have lately made, in your letters, of your particular regard for me, are so contradictory to all your actions, that I cannot suffer myself to be impos'd upon by them.

You know very well, you did not give the least intimation to me or to the Queen, that the Princess was with child, or breeding, until within less than a month of the birth of the young Princess.

You remov'd the Princess twice, in the week immediately preceding the day of her delivery, from the place of my residence, in expectation, as you have voluntarily declared, of her labour, and both times, upon your return, you industriously conceal'd from me, and the Queen every circumstance of this important affair and you at last without giving any notice to me or the Queen, precipitately hurried the Princess from Hampton Court in a condition not fit to be named. After having thus, in execution of your determined measures, exposed the Princess and her child to the greatest perils, you now plead surprise and your tenderness for the Princess as the only motives which occasioned these repeated indignities offered to me and to the Queen, your mother.

This extravagant and undutiful behaviour in so essential a point as the birth of an heir to my Crown is such an evidence of your premeditated defiance of me, and such contempt for my authority and of the natural right belonging to your parents, as cannot be excused by the pretended innocence of your intentions, nor palliated or disguised by specious words only.

The whole tenour of your conduct for a considerable time, has been so entirely void of all real duty to me, that I have long had reason to be highly offended with you.

And until you withdraw your regard and confidence from those, by whose instigation, and advice you are directed, and encouraged in your unwarrantable behaviour to me, and to the Queen; and until you return to your duty, you shall not reside in my palace, which I will not suffer to be made the resort of them, who under the appearance of an attachment to you, foment the division which you have made in my family.

In the meantime, it is my pleasure, that you leave St James's, with all your family, when it can be done without prejudice or inconvenience to the Princess.

I shall for the present leave to the Princess the care of my grand-daughter, until a proper times calls on me to consider of her education.[44]

'I hope in God,' the Queen kept repeating, 'I shall never see him again', and the King thanked the Almighty that by next day the puppy would be out of his house. The Prince's advisers were all, without exception, half-witted coxcombs, boobies, lunatics or stuttering puppies.

Foreign ministers, peers and Privy Councillors were told – as they had been told in 1717 – that whoever went to the Prince's Court would not be admitted to the King's. Handel was forbidden to give a concert for the Prince, the Prince's physicians forbidden to attend his birthday dinner and his servants forbidden to collect ice in St James's Park. The Prince was deprived of his guard, and the very furniture of his apartments. Hervey suggested that really their Royal Highnesses could not be expected to carry away all their clothes and possessions like dirty linen in a basket. 'Why not?' snapped His Majesty. 'A basket is good enough for them.' He was, nevertheless, less vindictive than his father had been in somewhat similar circumstances: he did not separate the child from his parents, nor did he specifically order the Prince's servants to quit his service.[45]

On 12 September the Prince, Princess and their whole household migrated to Kew. Many of the onlookers were in tears and cried 'God bless you!' The sentry at St James's, having received positive orders not to salute the Prince, said he would have done so if his Captain had not been watching him. City magnates, the 'independents' and Tories flocked to the rival Court.[46] The King opined that they would soon be tired of the puppy's fiddlefaddle nonsense. He had often, he said, asked the Queen if the beast was his son. 'I fancy he is what in German we call a *Wechselbag* . . . a child put in the cradle instead of another.'

'A changeling,' suggested Hervey, and the King was pleased with this translation.

Her Majesty summed up the argument. 'My dear first-born is the greatest ass, and the greatest liar, and the greatest canaille, and the greatest beast, in the whole world, and I most heartily wish he was out of it.'[47]

The Prince sent his father a verbal reply which was a model of dutiful submission, and then held, as the eighteenth-century equivalent of a press conference, an audience for the Lord Mayor and aldermen, Carteret, Chesterfield and his principal advisers, at which he told his side of the story and distributed copies of the King's message. 'You see, gentlemen,' said Carteret, 'how the Prince is threatened if he does not dismiss us. But we are here still, for all that. He is a rock. You may depend upon him. He is firm.'[48]

For a long time the Queen had known, but kept secret from everyone except her husband, that she had an umbilical rupture, a result of the difficult birth of her last born child. On 9 November 1737 she fell ill with colic, frightful stomach pains and vomiting. Snakeroot and brandy, usquebaugh, Sir Walter Raleigh's Cordial, Daffy's Elixir and mint-water were tried in vain: the purgings and vomitings continued, and Dr Ranby bled her twelve ounces. A glister came out of her just as it went in and even Dr Ward's Pills failed to relieve her. On the 10th she was bled again, and knew she was dying.[1]

Two more physicians were called in: purges, blistering and glisters were applied in quick succession. All they did was to stop her bowels working at all, and redouble her vomiting. It was rumoured that the Prince would call to inquire after his mother's health. If the puppy called, ordered the King, he should be told his mother was in no condition to see him act his false, whining, cringing tricks, nor was his father in a mood to hear his impertinences. On receiving a dutiful message from his son, the King flew into a passion. 'I always hated the rascal, and now I hate him worse than ever. He wants to come and insult his poor, dying mother, but she shall not see him . . . No, no! He shall not come and act any of his silly plays here, false, lying, cowardly, nauseous puppy! . . . I will be plagued with no more messages.' So the Prince was forbidden to see his mother or even come to St James's. The Queen wondered that 'the Griff' had not come to plague her and for the pleasure of seeing her die. 'At least I shall have one comfort in having my eyes eternally closed. I shall never see that monster again.'[2]

On 11 November the King insisted on telling Ranby, the surgeon, what was really the matter. Still the Queen tried to conceal the rupture of which she was so ashamed, but Ranby found it, and said he must operate. At this the Queen wept for the first and last time. Three surgeons argued over what to do. Should they cut a hole in her navel big enough to thrust the gut back, or simply lance the swelling and hope for the best? They tried the latter course, letting out 'a great deal of stinking stuff', but by 15 November it was plain that the wound was mortifying, and nothing could save her.[3]

She expressed her last wishes for her children and desired that her husband should remarry. With heartbroken sobs he managed to reply, '*Non – j'aurai – des – maîtresses.*'

'*Ah, mon Dieu!*' she sighed. '*Cela n'empêche pas.*'[4]

As the mortification did not spread, the surgeons began to have faint hopes of recovery, and cut off what had mortified, she bearing the agony with unflinching fortitude.

Walpole was allowed in. 'My good Sir Robert,' she said, 'you see me in a very indifferent situation. I . . . recommend the King, my children and the kingdom to your care.' The King complained crossly that there were so many visitors one could hardly move in the antechamber. So the room was cleared of all but those who had business there. For the next two days she seemed to be holding her own.[5]

'Oh, my Lord,' said Walpole, anxious as never before for his own future, 'if this woman should die, what a scene of confusion will there be! Who can tell into whose hands the King will fall?'

'He will cry for her for a fortnight,' replied Hervey, 'forget her in a month, have two or three women to lie with now and then and to make people believe he lies with them day and night; but whilst they have most of his time . . . you will have more power than ever you have.' The King, he added, was less suspicious and penetrating than the Queen.

Walpole replied moodily, 'You do not know how often he refuses to hear me when it is on a subject he does not like; but by the

Queen I can with time fetch him round to those subjects again; she can make him do the same thing in another shape, and when I give her the lesson, can make him propose the very thing as his own opinion which a week before he had rejected as mine.'[6]

On the 17th, eight days after she was first taken ill, the vomitings increased and a gut burst so that all the contents of her belly soaked through the sheets and over the floor. Some foolish people who thought it a natural evacuation congratulated her and told her it would do her good. She, who knew the truth, replied with great calmness that she hoped so too. Pope, implacable, referred to her plight in an infamous couplet.

> Here lies, wrapt in forty thousand towels
> The only proof that Caroline had bowels.

Every day the surgeons were forced to make a new incision, and each one, asking the King for his consent, she bore with the most indomitable fortitude, though she knew it was of no use. Patiently she suffered them to cut and probe as deeply as they saw fit. Nor did her mordant sense of humour desert her, for she asked Ranby if he would not enjoy doing this to his cross old wife whom he hated so. When a candle set alight the wig of another surgeon assisting in the operation, she begged Danby to stay his hand so that she could laugh. If ever a groan escaped her under the knife, she would apologize for her silly complaints, when she knew they were doing all they could to help her.[7]

To forestall impertinent criticism by the pious, Walpole suggested that the Archbishop of Canterbury be sent for. Princess Amelia demurred, but he insisted. 'Pray, madam, let this farce be played. The Archbishop will act it very well. You may bid him be as short as you will. It will do the Queen no hurt, any more than any good; and it will satisfy all the wise and good fools who will call us atheists if we don't pretend to be as great fools as they are.' So Dr Potter, who was as near an atheist as an Archbishop can be, came morning and evening, and left, evading questions on whether she had taken the Sacrament by the non committal statement that she was in a 'heavenly disposition'.[8]

The King was frantic with grief and anxiety, and bored his

daughters, Hervey, the physicians and surgeons hour after hour with eulogies of the most wonderful wife that ever man had, incapable of any thought, let alone any word or deed that fell short of perfection – the best wife, the best mother, the best companion, the best friend and the best woman that ever was born; never out of temper, always assiduous to please him, of more use to him as a minister than any minister to any prince; with a patience, of which he was not master, to suffer the babbling of impertinent fools and puppies. Joined to the softness and delicacy of her sex, she was blessed with all the courage and firmness of a man. '*Comme elle soutenait son dignité avec grâce, avec politesse, avec douceur.*'[9]

Yet this adoration, which was not in the least counterfeit or insincere, did not prevent him constantly snubbing her. If, from pain, she shifted around, he would ask how the devil could she expect to sleep if she would never lie still. If he had bullied her into eating what she immediately threw up, he would say roughly, 'My God! If you do not like a thing, why call for it? And if you do like it, why give it away?' Lying awake with her eyes open she reminded him, he said, of a calf '*à qui on vient de couper la gorge*'. Perhaps, if he had not behaved in his normal manner, she would have missed the snubs and the bullying.[10]

His praise of the Queen was not unmixed with anecdotes illustrating his own firmness and resolution. 'Is he gone?' asked Princess Amelia as he left the room after one of the monologues in praise of the departing. 'Jesus, how tiresome he is! . . . I am sick to death of hearing of his great courage.'[11]

On the 20th the Queen asked one of the physicians how long she was likely to last. '*Je crois*,' he replied, '*que Votre Majesté sera bientôt soulagée.*'

'*Tant mieux*,' she said calmly.

She took leave of the King and thanked him for all his goodness to her. Her last words were, 'I believe I have now got an asthma . . . Open the window . . . Pray.'[12]

George Augustus's grief, as even Hervey admitted, was tender and unaffected. It was combined with a strange, superstitious fear of her spirit returning to haunt him, to guard against which he desired a page to keep watch beside his bed for several nights after her death. He gave instructions that when he died, his coffin should be placed beside hers with the sides removed, so that their dust be mingled. He spoke incessantly about the Queen, weeping the whole time. He even took over the payment of all her private salaries, pensions and charities amounting to £13,000 a year, declaring that no one should be the poorer for her death. Her portrait he had placed on a chair at the foot of his bed, telling the page, 'Wait outside till I ring the bell.' Two hours later, calm and dry-eyed, he told the page. 'Take that picture away, I never yet saw a woman fit to buckle her shoe.' Those who knew him best were astonished. 'Is it,' wrote a Lady of the Bedchamber, 'to be believed of a man who has been called false to her, fickle in his friendships and avaricious?'[13]

The first sign of his recovering was when he came into the room half laughing, half in tears at poor Horatio Walpole, who *'pleure de si mauvaise grâce, qu'au milieu de mes larmes, il m'a fait rire'*. A week later he went to look over a new consignment of fine Arab horses, and cynics said he would soon be looking over some fine women.[14]

The great question which agitated the politicians was, who would now control him? Newcastle was sure it would be Princess Amelia, but the Prime Minister knew better. 'Does she design to commit incest? Will she go to bed with her father? If not, do not tell me the King intends to make a vow of chastity, or that those that lie with him won't have the best interest with him. I am for Madame Walmoden. I'll bring her over.' Meanwhile Lady Deloraine would do as a stopgap, 'for people must wear old gloves till they can get new'. His Majesty declared that Lady Deloraine stank so of Spanish wine that of late he could not bear her. However, while waiting for Madame Walmoden, he from time to time sent for her as a man might send casually for a girl from a tavern.[15]

His violent dislike for his son somewhat abated, and the Prince's advisers, notably Chesterfield, urged Frederick to act with great circumspection, showing the utmost personal respect to His Majesty. The Prince was not, however, too pleased when a curate read innocently, at the beginning of Morning Prayer, 'I will arise and go to my Father and will say to him, "Father, I have sinned against Heaven and before Thee, and am no more worthy to be called Thy son.'''[16]

The Opposition were confident that Walpole could not survive the death of his friend and protectress, but they underestimated his powers of survival, and the King continued to lean on him as much as ever. Early in the new year, freed at last by the death of a wife he detested, he married Moll Skerrett. She was a pleasant, decent woman: his family approved of the marriage, and she made him happy for a few months before she died.

The Queen's death did not in the least abate the King's unpopularity, and the epitaph-writers made the most of their opportunity. One was found pasted up in the Royal Exchange.

> Oh death, where is thy sting?
> To take the Queen, and leave the King?

Another was handed about in broadsheets, concluding

> She to her offspring, pardon asked, denied,
> And unforgiving, unforgiven died.

On Kensington Gate someone posted yet another attack on the Monarch:

> Here lives a man of fifty-four
> Whose royal father's will he tore,
> And thrust his children out of door
> Then killed his wife and took a whore.[17]

But Madame Walmoden, when she arrived, behaved with discretion, and gave no cause for complaint except for her comparatively harmless habit of selling peerages, including among her customers, the grandson of a footman and the son of a Barbados pedlar. It was not for some years that she became a force to be reckoned with in politics.[18]

13

George II reigned for twenty-three years after his wife's death, but our picture of him during those years is less clearcut. Perhaps, however, it is less distorted. For the early years of his reign the biographer must draw much of his material from Hervey's memoirs, and Hervey hated the King. Indeed he hated almost everyone but the Queen and Princess Caroline. Soon after the Queen's death Hervey left the Court. Thereafter we have no more detailed, intimate description of the King at home and in his family, pompous, opiniated and irascible; but the information we have is more objective. Some diarists found George Augustus almost amiable.

His unfeigned grief at Caroline's death was soon assuaged not only by the arrival of Madame Walmoden, but by the heady prospect of war with Spain. The quarrel had its roots in the Assiento of 1713, a treaty which gave Britain a thirty-one-year monopoly of the slave trade with the Spanish Main, and the right to send there each year one general trading ship of 500 tons. It had long been customary for British merchants to trade *indirectly* with the Main via Spain, though they resented the profits accruing to Spanish middlemen. They would much rather trade direct with the Main, and did so. Far more than one trading ship a year sailed for Spanish America, and the Caribbean swarmed with British interlopers and smugglers, some barely distinguished from pirates. The Spanish coastguards, rewarded by a commission on every ship they seized, were tough and determined. It was they, the British sea-dogs angrily argued, who behaved like pirates. Had they not, between 1713 and 1731, pillaged 180 English ships? Even when the Courts of Madrid and St James's were on good terms, conditions in the Caribbean were reminiscent of the days of Drake and Hawkins.

At home the British people were bored with twenty-five years of peace and eager for war against Spain, which had so often proved lucrative. The King shared this view, as did the Prince of Wales and the Opposition. Only the Ministry were for conciliation, partly because Walpole was constitutionally a man of peace, and partly because they feared the costs of war and the unpopularity which would accrue to a government which increased taxes.

The dilatory negotiations – the Court at Madrid was never very good at answering letters – dragged on month after month, and early in 1738 the Opposition produced a sea-captain named Jenkins who, exhibiting his severed ear to the House of Commons, claimed that it had been barbarously hacked off by a Spanish coastguard eight years previously. News came, moreover, that 'seventy of our brave sailors are now in chains in Spain. Our countrymen in chains and slaves to Spaniards! Is not this enough to fire the coldest?'[1] It did indeed rouse the British people. 'I commended', Captain Jenkins told the Commons, 'my soul to God and my cause to my country' – doubtless an expurgated version of his observations on that occasion. Although some tiresome people alleged that he had in fact lost his ear in the pillory or in a tavern brawl, while others even denied that the shrivelled object was an ear at all, his words struck a chord in every Patriot heart.[2]

Certainly the warmongers had a case when they spoke of the freedom of the seas. It was monstrous that the Spaniards should continue to regard the Caribbean as their private lake and seize foreign ships on the mere suspicion of smuggling or illegal trade. The Patriots were not impressed by Walpole's patient attempts to obtain compensation by peaceful means: what they wanted was a war of plunder.[3]

'The right of search', cried Lyttelton, 'is the root of all our grievances.' Why should *Spaniards*, of all people, search British

205

ships sailing the high seas? 'Is this', thundered Pitt, 'any longer a nation?'[4]

The pressure on Walpole was irresistible: even Newcastle was for a fight; and the summer of 1734 saw leisurely preparations for war. British merchants in Spanish ports were warned to withdraw 'without delay but with as much secrecy as possible'. J.P.s were ordered to press seafaring men for the navy. In August the Ambassador, after sending an intelligence report on Spanish ports, fortifications and shipping, left Madrid, gratified by the King's praise for his good work. In August too the fire-eating Admiral Vernon was despatched with a squadron,

to annoy and distress the Spaniards in the most effectual manner you are able. His Majesty doubts not that you will make use of the ships under your command . . . you will not only take, sink, burn or otherwise destroy all Spanish ships and vessels, but commit all destruction upon that coast that you may think practicable and particularly destroying any of their towns and settlements in the West Indies.

In September the military authorities began to bestir themselves. Cavalry reviews were ordered, though the horses were still at grass. 'I wish,' said the Colonel of the Enniskillen Dragoons, 'that we are not catched napping, like the foolish virgins with no oil in our lamps.'[5]

Finally, on 26 October, when Vernon was well on his way to the West Indies, war against Spain was declared. 'The people were transported with joy. The Prince of Wales drank success to the war at Temple Bar. The King was delighted, imagining himself a heavenborn commander. Nothing was talked of but humbling the pride of Spain.' In serene confidence of easy pickings in the South Seas, prices on Change Alley rocketed. A new song, *Rule Britannia*, expressed the country's aspirations and church bells were set a-ringing. Walpole's sour comment has been often quoted. 'Aye, they will ring their bells now, but they'll wring their hands ere long.'[6]

Unfortunately, although the country was spoiling for a fight, the armed forces were by no means fit for it. This was especially so of the Army, despite the King's keen personal interest. The fault was due partly to Walpole who could never bring himself to regard it as useful for anything more than an aid to the civil power. Far more was it the fault of the Opposition politicians who insisted day in and day out that 'there was no danger but in a standing army'. Pitt, who had made a study of the military profession and should have known better, clamoured for cuts in the standing army at the very time he was clamouring for war against Spain.[7] There was always the Irish Establishment over which the Westminster Patriots had no control, but in times of stress His Majesty's Government was reduced to the humiliating expedient of hiring Dutch and German troops to defend the soil of Great Britain.

The British troops, including those on the Irish Establishment, in peacetime numbered between 16,000 and 17,000 but internal security, which included precautions against a Jacobite rising, absorbed most of these in garrison duties. During the long war which was just beginning, the strength rose to 74,000 which would seem to be an expansion likely to overstrain the Army's resources of trained officers and N.C.O.s, equipment and administration. Normally only volunteers were enlisted, and for life, so there were no trained reserves. The pay* and conditions did not attract recruits of good quality, and too many 'volunteers' were debtors and convicted criminals released from prison on condition that they enlisted. In time of war volunteers of better quality were encouraged to join up on three- or four-year engagements.

There were few barracks, for it was thought that soldiers living together, isolated from the civilian population, would be politically dangerous. Instead they were 'quartered' on reluctant householders. A company might be spread over several villages which was hardly conducive to good training and discipline. Discipline, such as it was, depended on the lash or on other punishments hardly less barbarous; but this should, of course, be judged in the context of a penal code under which civilians could be flogged or hanged for quite trivial offences.

The Secretary of State was responsible for strategic planning; the Secretary at War for administration and supplies; the Board of

* For instance a private of the line was paid 3s 6d a week, but compulsory stoppages reduced this to 6d a week. A dragoon trooper was paid 9s 11d a week, out of which he had to feed and shoe his horse, leaving him 1s 2d a week.

Ordnance for engineer and artillery stores; and the Paymaster for pay and allowances. Coordination between these departments was poor.

In its close order battle drill – of the utmost importance when they were armed only with muzzle-loading muskets – the infantry had not kept pace with the methods being developed in the Prussian Army. Indeed battle-drill was not even standardized, but varied widely between regiments.[8] This made the British infantry ponderous and slow-moving on the battlefield. The cavalry, on the other hand, was addicted to moving much too fast, in unpredictable directions and under very little control.

Few officers made any attempt to study their profession, confident that on the field of battle courage would compensate for ignorance and defects in training. Worst of all were cavalry officers. The Earl of Pembroke, a Colonel of the Royals and a serious soldier, condemned even their horsemanship as a disgrace to themselves and the animals they rode.

The poor quality of the officers was due to the long years of peace and to the system of promotion by purchase and political patronage. George I, George II and the Duke of Cumberland* all disliked the purchase system, but custom and political pressures were too strong for them. The best George II could do was to stop the grant of commissions to infants and to lay down a regular tariff for promotion. In wartime, however, he tended to make important appointments and promotions himself, on military rather than political grounds, a practice which the Ministry deplored.[9]

From these defects the Royal Regiment of Artillery, founded in 1727, was notably free. There was no purchase, and from 1741 Woolwich Academy produced a steady supply of gentleman cadets grounded in the rudiments of their profession.

Apart from the professional expertise of the artillery, the British Army's sole virtue was the dogged, obstinate courage of the infantry and its murderous close-range volleys. The latter was achieved partly by training in musketry which was never wholly abandoned, partly by the nature of the British musket, already known as Brown Bess. This fired a heavier ball than continental muskets,

* The Duke became Captain-General in 1745.

but the ball was slightly smaller than the bore, and this facilitated rapid loading. It was less accurate, it is true, but at the range at which battles were fought, this was not of great importance. The target was a solid block of men, shoulder to shoulder, usually less than sixty yards away. It was speed in loading and fire-discipline that won battles, and the British infantry's platoon volleys were devastating.

The Royal Navy was in better shape, largely because even Tories were proud of it, did not consider it a political danger and were not so grudging in their votes. The East and West Indian merchants valued the Navy's services in policing the sea lanes against pirates. Pay (unchanged since 1653), conditions at sea and rations were just as poor as in the Army, discipline was as savagely enforced. But naval officers were professionals. Going to sea at twelve to fourteen, serving six or seven years as able-bodied seamen* or midshipmen before taking a stiff examination to promotion to commissioned rank, they knew their job inside out. Moreover even in peacetime the King's ships were at sea, and thousands of what we should regard as reservists, manning the merchant and fishing fleets, were constantly practised in seamanship and navigation. British ships were not as fast or as heavily gunned as the first products of French and Spanish dockyards, but there was nothing much wrong with British crews. The principal weaknesses of the Navy were the *Fighting Instructions* which laid too much stress on keeping in line and thereby discouraged individual initiative, and ignored the senility of some senior officers. Norris, for instance, commanding the Channel Fleet at the start of the war, was seventy-nine.

The war started off with a bang, just as everyone expected. In November 1739, with only six ships, Admiral Vernon seized the great Spanish American base and treasure depot of Porto Bello. The nation – or at least the Opposition – was delirious with joy: if such a victory crowned the first four months of war, what more triumphs were in store? The Ministry's rejoicings were more restrained, for Vernon was politically unsound. Unfortunately, the

---

* Those of superior social status were sheltered against the worse rigours of service below the deck by employment as captains' and admirals' servants.

effect of his naval *coup de main* was limited, for the Ministry had omitted to send with him any troops. When an expeditionary force of 10,000 men was eventually assembled and despatched in 1741 to follow up Vernon's victory by the capture of Cartagena, it was too little and too late. The force achieved nothing, was decimated by yellow fever, and had to be withdrawn the following year.[10]

Vernon had from the beginning insisted that troops were unnecessary in the Caribbean. Provided he had the ships, 'let who will possess the country, our Royal Master will command the wealth of it'. On his return to England, he reiterated the argument in a long interview with the King: 'Security', he told His Majesty, 'lay in being master of the sea, and when he ceased to be so, his land army could not preserve him.' George Augustus was not pleased, answering that soldiers were necessary.[11] It is a recurrent argument in British strategy, and our history seems to support the King's view. Though the Navy was our sure shield, a continental power could not be defeated save on land. But the coordination of fleets and armies is an art which escaped the comprehension of the Duke of Newcastle.

So by the end of 1740 the nation was disappointed and disillusioned, and naturally blamed Walpole for failure. When the King returned in the autumn from a six months' visit to Hanover, he found ministerial morale low and Ministers at variance with one another. Pointedly he told Newcastle that he feared not the Opposition so long as the Cabinet was united, and Newcastle charged Walpole with tale-bearing. 'This war is yours,' was Walpole's sour reply. 'You have the conduct of it – I wish you joy of it.' [12]

Meanwhile the war of plunder had merged into a far more serious conflict, the War of the Austrian Succession. It will be recalled that the Emperor Charles VI, having no legitimate son, had prevailed upon most of the powers of Europe, including Britain, France, Hanover, Prussia and Spain, to accede to the Pragmatic Sanctions which guaranteed that on his death his dominions should pass intact to his daughter, Maria Theresa, even though she, as a woman, was debarred by the Salic Law from the Imperial title. The idea was that her husband, Francis of Lorraine, now Duke of

Tuscany, would be elected Emperor, but this was not specifically written into the sanctions.

Charles VI died in October 1740, soon after the young King Frederick of Prussia had inherited a full treasury and a formidable army. Promptly and with characteristic turpitude, Frederick invaded Silesia, and then suggested that Maria Theresa cede this to him in return for his support against other marauders, an offer which the spirited young woman refused. The Court of Versailles, delighted to see the Empire in trouble, and the Court of Madrid eager for pickings in Italy, found pretexts for evading their treaty obligations to go to her aid; the Electors of Saxony and Bavaria declared their support for Prussia and for the former, Charles Albert, to be elected Emperor. It seemed a golden opportunity to dismember the debilitated Empire. The hyenas gathered round.

Maria Theresa called on Britain to honour her word. Walpole naturally did not want another war. If only, he thought, this tiresome woman were left to her own resources she would have to give up Silesia, and everyone would be saved so much trouble and expense. But George II knew well his nephew Frederick's restless ambitions. He saw great danger in a Franco–Prussian alliance, and public opinion chivalrously rallied to the intrepid 'Queen of Hungary', now beset by so many foes. Walpole, than whom there was never a more costive and reluctant St George, came to her rescue with a subsidy of £300,000 and 12,000 Hessian and Danish mercenaries.[13] Nevertheless in June a Franco–Prussian alliance was formed, and it was clear that the country was faced with the third round of its terrible struggle against France. Few people could see Walpole as the organizer of victory.

Although the King of England was spoiling for a fight, the Elector of Hanover soon found he had bitten off more than he could chew. One French army captured Prague, and another was poised to invade his beloved Electorate, though neither Britain nor Hanover were at war with France. As Elector he secured, in September 1741, a French promise to respect Hanover's neutrality, in exchange for his promise to vote for Charles Albert of Bavaria, whose candidature the French supported. Finally he retained to protect Hanover the 12,000 mercenaries whom Parliament had hired to assist the Queen of Hungary. This transaction, carried out without consulting his English Ministers, may have been the only way to spare his native country the horrors of a French invasion, but it was not one which his admirers could contemplate with pride, or the Opposition pass over in silence. In October Walpole persuaded Maria Theresa to buy off Frederick by the cession of Silesia.[14]

There had been a general election in April 1741, in which the Prince of Wales and the Duke of Argyll had thrown their whole weight against Walpole. That autumn Newcastle, acknowledged expert in such matters, calculated that in the new Parliament the Ministry would have a majority of only fourteen, which would soon be eroded by desertions. So in the new year of 1742 it was agreed to buy off the Prince of Wales with a further £50,000 a year, the payment of his debts amounting to £200,000, and an entry for his friends to the Court of St James's. In return he must acknowledge his manifold sins and wickednesses. The Prince, confident that his friends would soon be in power and in a position to recompense his services even more generously (and, of course, *vice versa*), replied, 'I have all the duty imaginable for my father, but I cannot approach him while Sir Robert Walpole continues about him, nor never will.' At this the King, who was firm in his support of a friend and Prime Minister in adversity, flew into 'great passions', flinging down his wig and upsetting Newcastle as he ran from the room. (But Egmont thought this 'an idle report . . . you see how ready people are to make stories of the King.')[15]

For Walpole it really seemed a choice of Downing Street or the Tower. It was to be a straight, or almost straight, trial of strength and Walpole could plausibly be depicted as the sole obstacle to a royal reconciliation. Party feeling ran high. 'It was a shocking sight to see the sick and dead brought in on both sides! Men on crutches, and Sir William Gordon from his bed with a blister on his hand and flannel hanging out from under his wig . . . [looking] like Lazarus at his resurrection.' Zealous Patriots even blocked keyholes with sand to prevent ministerial invalids being carried into the House by side-doors to vote.[16]

In the event Walpole was defeated over the trumpery issue of the Chippenham election. On the morning of 1st February he presented his resignation to the King, kissing hands for the last time as Minister. George Augustus was genuinely moved; he 'fell on Sir Robert's neck, wept and kissed him and begged to see him frequently'. It was a dismal end to a long and not ignoble partnership, and he saw nothing but trouble ahead.[17]

Caroline had gone, Walpole had gone. The King was on his own now and, accurately assessing the limits of his residual powers, used these with a sagacity that might not have been expected of him. He displayed a sound judgement of men when he selected his Ministers, and his favourite expressions such as 'Stuff and nonsense!' and 'puppies', so far from reflecting merely an irascible temper, were not infrequently a shrewd assessment of policies and politicians. He had no desire to see his son's friends in office, but clearly the Ministry must be reinforced from the ranks of its enemies. Should it be with Argyll's group, of which the most prominent members were Chesterfield, Cobham and Bubb Dodington? Or with 'New Whigs' such as Pulteney and Carteret? At the same time the 'Old Corps' of Newcastle and Hardwicke must not be offended. George Augustus had no difficulty in deciding. Argyll and his brother, Lord Isla, had betrayed him in Scotland. He despised Bubb, disliked Chesterfield and loathed Cobham and his 'Cubs', the Boy Patriots. But for Lord Carteret he had considerable admiration. Carteret was, indeed, far too able to prosper under Walpole. His only rival among the New Whigs, Pulteney, had so often said that he would never accept office that he could now be fobbed off with the Earldom of Bath. This allowed Carteret to go to the Northern Department, where his knowledge of German and Germany would be invaluable. Lesser offices could be divided between the lesser New Whigs and the Old Corps. The Argylls, friends of the Prince, would be left in sulky impotent opposition. It was a neat piece of work by George II in which some professed to see the hand of Walpole, now ennobled as Earl of Oxford; but of this there is no evidence, only speculation. A modest niche in the new Ministry was found even for Hervey, who had the face to assure the King, 'I have no attachment but to your service; no connection but with your interests and inclination; belong to you and no other.'[18]

213

In February both the Prince and Princess of Wales were persuaded to attend the King's Court, which brought tears of loyalty to many eyes. But all George Augustus would say to his son was, 'How does the Princess do? I hope she is well.'[19]

Even some Tories put in an appearance.

> The King was surprised to see such a number of new faces of gentlemen and lords of great property and interest in their counties, and expressed himself troubled that (as he had heard), some said they would come but once. To which Mr Pulteney replied that it was not for want of respect to His Majesty, but fear of being troublesome to him in applying for appointments.[20]

It must almost have seemed as though Nature had created in Carteret the perfect Secretary of State. He was a glutton for work, an adroit diplomat. He spoke fluently French, German, Swedish and Spanish, and had a thorough knowledge of the tangled politics of the Holy Roman Empire. The King had the highest regard for his capability. But he had two fatal weaknesses: he had no parliamentary base, and he could not, he did not try to, get on with the House of Commons. 'Give any man the Crown on his side,' said Carteret, 'and he can defy anything.' So why bother with the Commons? He treated them with patrician disdain. 'I never dine in taverns', he replied when colleagues invited him to a political dinner at *The Feathers*, a slight which was not forgotten. 'What is it to me who is judge and who is bishop?' he asked. 'It is my business to make Kings and Emperors.' He treated foreign potentates no less cavalierly than he treated M.P.s, but this the country gentlemen did not realize. But while he was busy with his grandiose plans, at Westminster his enemies were undermining him like moles.[21]

When Carteret accepted the seals of office in 1742 Europe was
still in a state of confusion. Frederick of Prussia was again at war
with Maria Theresa, Queen of Hungary, and was being backed by
France. Britain, although not at war with France, supported Maria
Theresa. George II as King of England backed one claimant for
the Empire, as the Elector of Hanover another. Carteret recognized
that France was the real enemy, and that Austria must be kept
in being as a counterweight. He must therefore restore the old
system of an alliance between Britain, Austria and Holland against
France, Bavaria and Spain. But first he must straighten out the
position of Hanover, which was undeniably exposed to a joint
invasion by French and Prussian armies. What, the Opposition
asked, did that matter? Hanover was a mere encumbrance and, as
Chesterfield quipped, if they wanted to destroy the Pretender's
chance of becoming King of England, they had only to make him
Elector of Hanover.[1] But so long as Hanover was in danger, George
Augustus could give his mind to nothing else. So Frederick must
again be bought off, and Maria Theresa, whose army was thrashed
by Frederick at Chotusitz in May, must reconcile herself to the loss
of Silesia. In June 1742 this was achieved: the Preliminaries of
Breslau detached Prussia from the Franco–Bavarian camp, and the
King of England could be persuaded that the Elector of Hanover need
no longer take refuge in ignoble neutrality. At this the Commons,
which had resented paying for a German war in which Hanover
remained neutral, increased to £500,000 the subsidy paid to

Britain's allies. Hanover was further safeguarded by an Anglo–Prussian defensive alliance in November and an Anglo–Russian pact in December 1742.

Unfortunately, as fast as his fears for Hanover were set at rest, so his parsimonious instincts reasserted themselves. Although Hanover was committed to Maria Theresa's aid, he decided to economize by reducing the Hanoverian forces. This upset the injured Queen. Carteret saw nothing for it but to persuade Parliament to take the Hanoverians and Hessians on to the British payroll.[2] Although the money was voted in the end, the suggestion was ill-received, Pitt remarking in a speech which George II never forgave, that England was now a province to a despicable electorate.[3] Indeed throughout the year Pitt lost no opportunity of making himself obnoxious.

> The troops of Hanover [he said], whom we are now expected to pay . . . marched to the place most distant from the enemy, least in danger of attack and most strongly fortified had an attack been designed. They have, therefore, no other claim to be paid than that they left their own country for a place of greater security. I shall not be surprised . . . to be told that the money of this nation cannot be more properly employed than in hiring Hanoverians to eat and sleep.

He was sceptical of intervention on the land mass of Europe, suggesting that His Majesty would never have sent troops, who might be better employed in colonial conquests, to help the Austrians, 'had not the temptation of greater profit been laid industriously before him'.[4]

Carteret's year of remarkable diplomatic achievement was not crowned by much in the way of military success. A Pragmatic Army of British, Hanoverian and Hessian troops assembled in June 1742 in the Low Countries, under command of Marlborough's old officer, Lord Stair, until a greater than he should come. The French armies in Bohemia, their rear threatened, were extricated in some haste, but for a whole year the Pragmatic Army made no move. Stair's bold plan to attack the French base at Dunkirk and thence advance on Paris was rejected by the King in one of his cautious moods. Unwilling to provoke Louis XV, with whom he was not at war, he thought it too risky to make a direct attack on

The Right Honourable
HENRY PELHAM

18. Henry Pelham

19. George Bubb Dodington

20. *Above left* John Carteret, Earl Granville: *portrait from the studio of William Hoare c. 1750*

21. *Above right* Philip, Earl of Chesterfield *by Allan Ramsay* 1765

22. *Left* Lord Hervey of Ickworth: *portrait from the studio of J. B. van Loo c. 1740–41*

French territory.[5] It was not until the spring of 1743 that a Dutch contingent, and one from Hanover, joined Stair's polyglot force. Then at last the Pragmatic Army began to move slowly into Germany. Its progress was somewhat delayed by the absence of so many officers whose leave, Stair acidly remarked, he had found it hard to refuse when they pleaded that their promotion depended on their friends at Court: 'They had no notion that it depended on their exertions here.'[6]

British, Hanoverians, Hessians, Austrians and Dutch – well might Marshal Noailles tremble when he saw the host arranged against him, commanded moreover by the King of England in person. For on 8 June 1743 George Augustus took the field for the first time since that glorious day of Oudenarde. He was insured – some might say overinsured – against the rigours of campaigning by a personal baggage train of 662 horses, 13 Berlin carriages, 35 wagons and 54 carts. Certainly his equipment was on a generous scale: with 900 dozen napkins, for instance, he could hardly run short of these essential items of military equipment. The heavy burdens which he laid on the Army's supply system did not pass unnoticed, but he evidently thought that if a sixty-one-year-old King was prepared to die like any private soldier, there was no obligation for him to live like one. He was accompanied by his favourite son, William, Duke of Cumberland, a beefy young man of twenty-two whom he had already marked as a chip off the old block, destined for a career of military glory. Stair, seventy years old but still active and efficient, remained to keep a professional eye on his royal master whose unenterprising instructions sent from Hanover had already, Stair thought, prevented him from winning a decisive victory.[7]

The Army of which King George on 8* June assumed command was encamped on the right bank of the Main, which here flows in a north-westerly direction, at Aschaffenburg. There it remained a week, as though not sure what to do next. The King was in high spirits, 'always booted – rides out to several of the most material posts twice a day'. Not so his soldiers, who committed 'great disorders' in search of food which was scarcer every day.[8] The King's

* By the English calendar. According to the Gregorian calendar, in use on the continent, it was the 19th.

stern measures suppressed these, but Noailles, a competent commander, was bridging the Main and methodically moving to surround the allies and cut them off from their base at Hanau, some twenty miles downstream. He posted his second-in-command, Count Gramont, with 28,000 men in a strong position near the village of Dettingen, covering the bridge where the high road to Hanau crossed a narrow ravine through which flowed a boggy little tributary of the Main.

By the 15th it was clear that the Pragmatic Army must retire on Hanau or starve, and orders were issued for a move next day. As they broke camp, Noailles moved upstream to cross the river behind them and threaten their rear. With Gramont waiting for them in front, the Main to their left and thick forest to their right, it did not seem as though King George's army could escape, and Noailles exulted that he had them in a mouse-trap.[9]

They had to pass by a single narrow road through the village of Klein Ostheim; and Noailles, anticipating this, had posted batteries on the opposite bank of the river, ready to fire into the allied column as it debouched from the village. The British cavalry passed through this dangerous defile first and then formed a line to the left, covering that exposed flank while the infantry and baggage sorted themselves out and moved slowly down the road. The fire was heavy and the cavalry could do nothing but endure it. Behind them the slow-moving infantry columns and the jam-packed baggage train was a target no gunner could miss.

George Augustus, exhilarated by danger, rushed about in great excitement and sent officer after officer for the artillery which, however, was far in the rear and could not force its way through the crowded village. For a whole hour the cavalry and infantry had to endure a destructive fire to which they could make no reply. 'Our men', wrote an officer in Pier's regiment of foot, 'were eager to come to action, and did not at all like the long bullets (as they termed them) for indeed they swept off ranks and file.'

It was a horrible ordeal, endured with courage and discipline. 'The French fired at His Majesty from a battery of twelve cannon, but levelled too high. I saw the balls go within half a yard of his head. The Duc d'Aremburg* desired him to go out of danger.

* Commanding the Austrian contingent.

He answered, "Don't tell me of danger. I'll be even with them!"
He is certainly the boldest man I ever saw,' wrote Mr Kendal of
Lord Albemarle's troop.

Unwisely, Gramont now left his strong position and moved forward, crossing the stream. While the British infantry and an
Austrian brigade deployed in a long line of which the left was
within a furlong of the river, the French seemed to be working
through the wood round their right flank. The King, having been
dissuaded from posting himself directly opposite the French
batteries shooting across the river, was now on the right of the
line. Drawing his sword, he ordered up some Hanoverian and
British infantry to clear the wood. Riding about 'like a lion', he
drew up the line himself, ordered up a six-gun battery and directed
their fire onto the enemy flank. 'He stood by till they fired, and did
great execution, killing thirty or forty at a shot. Then he went
to the foot and ordered them not to fire till the French came close,
which were a hundred yards distant; then the French fired on us
directly, and the shot flew thick as hail.'

Now that the high command had done its worst, all depended
on the dogged, enduring courage of the British infantry. The King,
red-faced and angry, was well to the fore and, in the acid words
of his nephew, the King of Prussia, 'putting himself in the posture
of a fencing master and flourishing his sword'. His soldiers appreciated the way he exposed himself recklessly to fire, now at the
head of one battalion, now another. But animating as his example
was, it did little to clear the fog of war or to preserve the exact
alignment which was essential in days of muzzle-loaders. There was
confusion, and the right of the line was somewhat in advance of the
left which had to toil through thick mud. The line was halted to
close up and dress, and an irregular cheer was raised for the King
which Stair thought at this juncture to be untimely and unpro-
fessional. The advance was resumed, much harassed by the en-
filade fire from the enemy batteries across the Main, and some men,
nervous and ill-disciplined, fired at far too long a range to produce
any effect.

At this, to his fury, the King's horse took the bit between his
teeth and bolted to the rear. He did not get far: His Majesty was a
good horseman and sawing with both hands at his mouth, soon

brought him round; but dismounted now, observing that he could trust his own legs not to run away. The line was again halted, to allow those who had fired to reload. They then marched in close order 'as firm as a wall' to within sixty paces of the enemy. Now, at last, they were within range of the enemy, now was the moment for those murderous short-range volleys for which the British infantry was famed and feared.

'Now, boys!' shouted George Augustus, 'Now for the honour of England! Fire, and behave brave, and the French will run!'

'Then the foot gave a huzza and fired very fast.' Having reloaded, they continued to advance. 'The smoke blew off a little. Instead of being among the living, we found the dead in heaps about us.'

The continuous, annihilating drum-fire of rolling platoon volleys was deadly: no French officer, wrote Noailles afterwards, had ever seen the like. The French infantry retired in disorder behind their horse. 'What preserved us', wrote the officer of Colonel Pier's regiment, 'was our keeping close order and advancing near the enemy ere we fired. Several that popped at 100 paces lost more of their men and did less execution.'

That was almost the end of the infantry battle. There followed a fierce cavalry fight, mainly on the river-flank, charge and counter-charge with the Third Dragoons, who had suffered so severely from the French artillery across the river, charging again and again until almost decimated. At one time the Blues and the First and Seventh Dragoons were repulsed by the French Household Cavalry who, flushed with success, broke into the ranks of the 21st and 23rd Foot; but the Gendarmes were all shot down by terrible British volleys, and at last the allies were masters of the field.

Stair urged a vigorous pursuit, but the King, on foot till ten at night, felt they had come well out of it and should tempt Providence no further. It was characteristic of him that having behaved all day like a hero, if not a consummate tactician, he lacked the resolution now to press on to the enemy's destruction.

He had other work to do. Elated by the victory and by his own conduct, he decided to revive the ancient practice of making knights banneret on the field. George Augustus was a snob. He hated creating new peers because it diluted the aristocracy. He once said, 'I cannot bear when women of quality marry one don't know whom.'[10] But valour in the face of the enemy transcended, in his opinion, all deficiencies of birth and breeding. The first man to be knighted by the King on the field of Dettingen was Lord Stair. The last was Trooper Thomas Brown, of the Third Dragoons.

The British Army had escaped from a trap as dangerous as any it had ever been in, and hastened on to Hanau. It was delighted with its own and the King's performance, as indeed was His Majesty himself. As for young William, wounded in the leg, 'he should do well if they can but keep him quiet; but his spirits are so high and his tongue runs so fast that he will talk himself into a fever'.[11]

Newcastle wrote exultantly of the 'general satisfaction and joy . . . What particularly affects all honest men is the share the King has personally had in this great action; which I verily believe will be of lasting service to him, and make impressions in his favour which falsehood and malice will not be able hereafter to efface.'[12]

Falsehood and malice were soon doing their best. The King was unquestionably partial to Hanover. He refused (not surprisingly, considering the amateur character of British cavalry officers) to put the Hanoverian horse under the Duke of Richmond. Moreover he had worn a yellow Hanoverian sash on the day of battle, a *faux pas* which Lyttelton compared to that of Alexander disgusting his faithful Greeks by wearing Persian robes.[13] The rumours multiplied when Lord Stair resigned because the King consistently ignored his advice and consulted only Hanoverian generals. It was said that 'there is not a general nor a common soldier in the whole army that is not in some degree discontented'. Hanoverian regiments, it was alleged, were issued with four days' bread ration while British regiments received only two. When a soldier let off his musket accidentally, a Hanoverian officer reported that the culprit was English and the King said his English soldiers were under no discipline.[14]

Soon the poets and pamphleteers took a hand. A ministerial writer praised the King in psalmic form:

The Glory of England is exalted, and the honour of Britain's is lifted up, and fear is fallen upon our enemies.

221

For from the blood of the slain, from the fat of the mighty, the bow of William turned not back, and the sword of George returned not empty.

George and William were lovely and pleasant in peace, and in war they were not divided. They were swifter than eagles, more watchful than hawks, stronger than lions.[15]

Opposition bards had their answer pat, in a ditty sung to the tune of *Lilliburlero* and entitled *H—r Beshit*.

> The bold English called out, 'Who can now be afraid?'
> What a question to Ilton,* now quaking with fear,
> Who behind a great tree was then running with speed
> Letting fly as he went a discharge from his rear
> By the H—r, H—r all are undone.
>
> Ilton's sash and his breeches were all of one hue,
> The H—r colour and truly his own.
> Nor one step would he stir while the foe were in view,
> So away all our shitten auxiliaries run.
> By H—r, H—r all are undone.
>
> Now bold Stair whose proud soul valued Death not a fart
> For his fighting's disgraced and sent empty away.
> While the humble and meek and the lowly of heart
> Yellow Ilton's exalted for sh—tting that day
> By H—r, H—r all are undone.
>
> Yet though England prevails in her conquering red
> By the H—r yellow herself is undone.
> We for H—r only at Dettingen bled
> Who o'er us triumphed most, when their yellow tails run
> By H—r, H—r all are undone.[16]

There was obviously some truth in these damaging rumours, but they were grossly exaggerated. It was not, for instance, true, wrote the Duke of Richmond (one of the loudest complainants) that the King had put himself at the head only of a Hanover regiment; 'He was sometimes at the head of them, but indeed often at the head of Pulteney's and sometimes at the head of Onslow's brigade, so if you hear him accused of that, you may say I vouched the contrary.' It is noteworthy that the vicious rumours of Hanoverian misbehaviour and the King's partiality did not really gain ground

* A Hanoverian general put in command of a British brigade.

until two or three weeks after the battle. On the day the British soldiers were proud of their King – even if British generals were less satisfied. It was, after all, wrote Richmond, 'the King of England and not the Elector of Hanover who beat the French that day'. It may be no coincidence that for some time before Stair departed in a huff, George Augustus was 'very much out of order', suffering from his old enemy, the piles, from stoppages and violent purges, from painful and swollen eyes – none of them complaints conducive to evenness of temper.[17]

His critics were on surer ground when they criticized his handling of the army after his victory. Lord Derby judged it 'not so complete as a good Englishman would wish, or else the French would not have been suffered to pass the Main so easily'. 'Our inaction', wrote Richmond, 'must surprise all those who are not in the secrets of the Closet.' Newcastle himself complained that he was totally unacquainted with schemes for carrying on the war, or with steps that might be taken for bringing about a peace.[18]

In November, the campaigning season at an end, the King returned home to a triumphal welcome. Pall Mall was all lit up, for fear that if any window was left dark, it would be broken by a mob hired to shout 'Long Live King George'. 'The tallow candle makers and glaziers excite them on to this scandalous business.' But it hardly seems as though a hired mob was needed. According to Horace Walpole, no admirer of the King's,

We were in great fear of his coming through the City, after the treason that has been publishing for these two months; but it was incredible how well his reception was; beyond what it had ever been before; in short, you would have thought it had not been a week after the victory of Dettingen. They almost carried him into the palace on their shoulders; and at night the whole town was illuminated and bonfired. He looks much better than he has these five years and is in great spirits.[19]

So, despite all the carping criticism, George Augustus was accepted by his people as a gallant little man, the victor of Dettingen; and he is remembered principally as the last King of England to lead his troops into battle. It is the distinction that, above all others, he would have valued.

15

The King returned to a scene of strife far less congenial to him than the field of Dettingen. Pitt's volleys were now aimed at Carteret, 'who seemed to have drunk of the potion described in poetic fiction which made men forget their country'. He even impugned the King's conduct in battle, hinting that 'His Majesty was exposed to few or no dangers abroad but those to which he is daily liable at home, such as the overturning of his coach or the stumbling of his horse'. Why, he asked, did we continue fighting, save for the satisfaction of bestowing four or five hundred thousand pounds on Hanover?[1] He castigated Carteret as a Hanoverian troop-minister, a flagitious taskmaster with a party composed of 16,000 Hanoverians.

At the Treasury now was Henry Pelham, Newcastle's brother, whose talents and family patronage made him almost as formidable a Commons man as Walpole. The Ministry was heavily weighted with Pelham influence, and Carteret, though still retaining the confidence of the King, was isolated in the Cabinet; his schemes for acquiring new allies against the French were condemned by his own colleagues as too ingenious and too expensive. The Pelhams were beginning to feel that he was a burden rather than an asset to the Ministry, though they were not ready to discard him until there was some one put in his place.

When they did act they chose an indirect method of attack. The Chancellor, Lord Hardwicke, Newcastle's close friend, drafted a memorandum recommending that the Dutch be pressed to fulfil their obligations under the Anglo–Dutch Treaty of 1678 and declare war on France. But Carteret, fearing that the Dutch would make a similar demand of Hanover, rejected this policy. On 1 November, they delivered a joint memorandum to the King, positively demanding Carteret's dismissal, failing which all the 'Old Corps' would resign. It was an ultimatum.[2]

'The effect produced was sullenness, ill-humour, fear and a disposition to acquiesce' if this could be done with Carteret's agreement. The King liked and respected Carteret, as the only Minister who had a proper grasp of foreign affairs and understood his feeling for Hanover. He despised Newcastle's bumbling incompetence, and considered Pelham a mere party hack. 'Lord Carteret has served me very well,' he told them. 'You will make a bad peace, as your friends did in 1712, the nation will cry out against you and I will join in.' To Hardwicke he added, 'You would persuade me to abandon my allies; but that shall never be the reproach of my reign, as it was of Queen Anne's.' Bitterly he complained that he was a king 'in toils'.[3]

But he had learned the art of politics under a master. Much as he might rail at it, he knew, if Carteret did not, that the King's support was not enough to sustain a Minister who was obnoxious both to the Commons and to his own colleagues. Reluctantly George II came to the unwelcome conclusion that Carteret would have to go. On 23 November 1744 Lord Carteret (or, rather, Lord Granville, since he had recently inherited that title from his mother) resigned the seals of the Northern Department and was replaced by Lord Harrington.[4]

The Prince of Wales had been, of course, the figurehead and paymaster of the Opposition. Now, with Carteret ousted, he expected something better than a Pelhamite in charge of the Northern Department. He had, indeed, while the changes were still pending, tried to warn Harrington off. 'Remember, my lord, that the King is sixty-one, and I am twenty-seven.'[5] But the Pelhams were determined, while broadening their parliamentary support, to reserve the freshest loaves and the plumpest fishes for Old Whigs on whom they could rely. Lyttelton and George Grenville, two of the noisier Patriots, were found junior places in the Treasury and the Admiralty. Chesterfield was fobbed off with Dublin, though when his name was first mentioned, the King fairly exploded; 'He shall have nothing! I command you to trouble me no more with such nonsense!'[6] Even four Tories were accommodated on the payroll, though two proved unreliable and two soon became indistinguishable from Whigs. Only Pitt, ablest of all, was left out: he had made himself too obnoxious to His Majesty for Pelham to dare put his name forward.

The Administration was further strengthened by the appointment of Anson to the Board of Admiralty. Captain Anson had recently returned from a three-and-a-half-years' buccaneering voyage round the world, during which he had captured a Spanish galleon with treasure worth £1½ million. In addition to this, his charting and surveying was of great value, and he had given his countrymen, in the doldrums of a dismal year, something to be proud of. What was more important, he gave a number of young officers priceless professional training: many of the most successful naval officers of long wars which lay ahead had sailed with Anson. His personal exertions in the circumnavigation, the example he set, made him a hero on his return, and deservedly so. Another point in his favour was that he was Hardwicke's son-in-law.

Although he yielded to the Pelhams, George Augustus did so with a very bad grace.

'I have done all you asked me,' he grumbled to Hardwicke. 'I have put all the power into your hands, and I suppose you will make the most of it.'

'The disposition of places,' replied the Lord Chancellor, 'is not enough if Your Majesty takes pains to show the world that you disapprove of your own work.'

'My work!' the King exploded. 'I was forced, I was threatened!'

'I am sorry to hear Your Majesty use those expressions. I know of no force. I know of no threats. No means were employed but what have been used in all times, the humble advice of your servants, supported by such reasons as convince them that the measures were necessary for your service.'[7]

The fact was that Walpole in his long years of power had always been able to retain the confidence of both the King and the Commons. The question, King or Commons? had never arisen. But as soon as it did arise, it became clear that although the King had the right to appoint to office anyone he chose, he could not keep him there without support in the lower House. Normally the King provided such support: but in this case he could not do so, because Carteret's own colleagues, who controlled the ministerial patronage, had turned against him. Those who could see nothing good in George II ascribed his dropping of Carteret to political cowardice. It would be more correct to ascribe it to a realistic appraisal of the limitations on a constitutional monarch. He bitterly resented them but he accepted them.

The new Ministry was in its early months concerned mainly with the prosecution of the war. There were two immediate, interlocking problems – command of the Pragmatic Army and the war effort of the reluctant, costive Dutch. The King would probably have liked to take command himself, but among Britain's allies there was no discernible enthusiasm for this arrangement. The choice seemed to lie between Marshal Königsegg, on loan from Maria Theresa, who was old and frail, and the Duke of Cumberland, who was young and inexperienced. In the event it was decided to appoint both. Cumberland, in March 1745, two months before his twenty-fourth birthday, was made Commander-in-Chief of the Pragmatic Army, with the aged Königsegg as his second-in-command.

There have been many worse soldiers than the Duke of Cumberland. He was a painstaking and competent administrator, with a care for his troops' health and welfare; despite his stern disciplinary methods, they rather liked their 'Billy'. He had sound ideas on strategy. It was in the field of battle that he failed. Not that he lacked courage, but in the face of the enemy he was hesitant, slow in decision, sluggish and unimaginative in movement, incapable of grasping, let alone creating, the fleeting opportunity. Unfortunately he was faced by Marshal Saxe, a master of war.

To bring the Dutch up to scratch, Chesterfield, before his immurement in Dublin, was sent on a special mission to the Hague and eventually negotiated an agreement on the Dutch contribution and the subsidies to be paid them.

In January 1745 the Emperor Charles VII (Charles Albert of Lorraine) died, so to the complex negotiations about the Pragmatic

227

Army and the Dutch war effort were added the complexities of electing a new Emperor. In these matters George Augustus, both as King and Elector, was concerned and interested. He was for the Grand Duke Francis of Tuscany, Maria Theresa's husband, largely because of his aversion to his nephew of Prussia; as indeed were the Pelhams, for 'it is in the general interest that the imperial dignity should be established in the House of Austria, for experience has showed that a weak emperor will sooner or later be a French emperor'.[8] The French candidate was Augustus III, King of Poland and Elector of Saxony. Frederick of Prussia was prepared to put his vote up for auction, but on the whole seemed likely to support Augustus. 'This', wrote Newcastle to Chesterfield, 'will go down very hardly [with the King] and to be sure great objection will be made to it. And the difficulty of any dependence on a prince who has acted as [Frederick] has will add great weight to the objection.'

But [wrote Newcastle] here I must own freely that whatever we say relating to the election of an emperor makes but little impression. We are always being told that His Majesty understands that best himself, that he must go his own way, and that that, being the business of the Electors, must be left to them; and neither the interposition of England or Holland is at all tasted . . . Most of the material foreign ministers [i.e. of the allied powers] are much attached to a certain person [Granville] and act as much in concert with him as formerly. And, what is worse, I am afraid this is not only known but approved, and done in concert with somebody else [the King] . . . The King's servants must be his Ministers, exclusive of all others, or they cannot remain his servants.[10]

George Augustus did, in fact, promise his vote for the Grand Duke Francis, unknown to his English Ministers, though they would not have disagreed if they had known. With the aid of his vote, the Grand Duke was elected. The Newcastle–Chesterfield correspondence had to be conducted secretly because of the odium in which the King held Chesterfield. It is quoted at some length not because it influenced this decision, but because it showed clearly in the spring of 1745 how the King was far from being 'in toils', and how the constitutional position in Britain was confused by the connection with Hanover.

'This declaration [to vote for the Grand Duke],' Chesterfield warned, 'is not the first and will not be by many the last that will be signed without the privity of the King's servants, unless they take care to make themselves his Ministers too.'[11] Chesterfield was deeply suspicious of the King, and would not face the fact that, in the matter of the imperial election, King and Ministry were, in fact agreed. 'Your Grace says,' he upbraided Newcastle,

and very truly, that the King's servants must be his Ministers, or they cannot remain his servants. But give me leave to say that, if you do not bring the matter to a decision before Parliament meets, you will certainly be neither after it is up. Your strength is in Parliament, and you must use it while you have it. The unanimity you have procured there, far from recommending you in the Closet, is used as an argument against you there, and somebody [i.e. the King] is told [i.e. by Granville], *since they can do what they will there, make 'em do what you will.*[12]

It is, perhaps, just as well for Newcastle and Chesterfield that their letters were sent by a sure hand so that the King did not see them. But on occasion the Post Office letter-openers served a useful purpose. 'Pray take care', wrote Chesterfield, 'to have [those] letters opened and read in a proper place, because I have taken care to have *certain doses* administered in that way.'[13]

These events and intrigues did nothing to sweeten the royal temper. Newcastle scribbled in a note to Hardwicke in April: 'The King has been worse than ever. He had been promised that Parliament should rise in a fortnight. "Damn *it* and *you*!" (he replied). "I shall be obliged to strike a strong stroke." My brother replied very properly desiring him to do it, to which no answer.'

Any dramatic reversal of policy would have fundamentally divided the Broad-Bottomed Administration. The ties with Hanover could not, in fact, be loosened, and Maria Theresa was not to be left to her fate. They would continue to 'carry on the war with vigour in order to obtain a peace'. But there was a change of emphasis: the British army would be employed in Flanders against the French, rather than in Germany in support of Hanover, which Pitt approved.[14]

The Pelhams' expert management, every scrap of patronage bestowed where it would most strengthen the Ministry, quite as though Walpole were still in charge, had indeed produced a remarkably docile Parliament. 'If Your Majesty looks round the House of Commons,' Hardwicke told the King in January 1745, 'you will find no man of business, nor even of weight, left capable of conducting an opposition.'

Except, of course, Pitt. But Pitt, financially refreshed by a legacy of £10,000 from the ancient Duchess of Marlborough, although himself left out in the cold, lent his powerful aid to the Ministry which included George Grenville and Lyttelton, his two closest friends, and seemed to share the view that the war against France was the only one that mattered.

This loyalty was sorely strained when Pelham solved the problem of the Hanoverian troops by transferring them to Maria Theresa's service and increasing her subsidy so that she could pay them. 'On such occasions it is well not to hesitate or refine.' Tortured by gout, Pitt was carried down to the House 'with the mien and apparatus of an invalid'. There, leaning on his crutches, he gave stentorian support to a blatant fiddle. 'I verily believe that a dawn of salvation to this country has broke out . . . I am the greatest dupe in the world if those now at the helm do not mean the honour of their master and the good of the nation.'[15]

Whatever the Ministry's intentions, there would be no salvation unless the French were beaten. The King had visited his army in the spring, hoping no doubt to smell powder again. He took no Minister with him, 'a precaution he always takes', noted Chesterfield, 'when he meditates a sudden turn'.[16] Whatever he had meditated, he made no sudden turn, but proceeded to Hanover. A few weeks later, on 11 May 1745, the Pragmatic Army, some 44,000 strong, was led by the Duke of Cumberland in a frontal attack on 76,000 Frenchmen entrenched in an impregnable position at Fontenoy. Despite their desperate valour the British infantry were finally halted, and then repulsed by a brilliant charge of the Jacobite Irish Brigade. Saxe proceeded to overrun most of Flanders, even capturing the British base of Ostend.

The battle of Fontenoy and the spectacular success of the Irish exiles against the best British regiments stimulated Jacobite hopes. Their best chance had been a year earlier, when Saxe had been poised with an army at Dunkirk. But now Prince Charles Edward, the Young Pretender, determined to succeed with his native resources, French aid being limited to modest financial assistance and a shipload of arms. He was himself the Jacobites' best advertisement: young, handsome, adventurous and brave, he had an extraordinary capacity to win over to his opinion, which was often erroneous, more prudent and sensible men. Certainly he was a more inspiring leader than his father. But he lacked a balanced judgement, and given a choice of advisers could almost be guaranteed to choose the worst. Like his father, he was damned in the eyes of thousands of Tory squires by the fact that he was a Papist.

On 27 June* 1745 he sailed from Nantes with two ships, one carrying arms and one carrying himself and seven followers – three Irishmen, three Highlanders and an English Jacobite. The arms ship was intercepted by an English frigate, badly mauled and forced back to France – his first and perhaps his most serious setback. Prince Charles Edward himself, with the 'Seven Men' landed at Eriskay Island, off the west coast of Scotland, on 21 July, and at Moidart on the mainland two days later. The first Highlanders he met viewed his arrival with dismay, and advised him to go back: but by 19 August his army had grown from seven to about 900, mainly Camerons, Stuarts and Macdonalds; and he was on his way to Edinburgh.

The Government had not been taken by surprise. The King was in Hanover, but had sent orders strengthening the Channel squadron and warning Cumberland to be ready to take troops over from Holland. He had even offered to cut short his Hanover holiday, and Newcastle had begged him 'not to defer putting these gracious intentions into execution'.

But it was the middle of August before news of the actual landing reached London. In the King's absence the Council of Regency did nothing very decisive. They offered a reward of £30,000 for the Pretender's apprehension, and the Pretender offered the same sum for the apprehension of the Elector of Hanover. In Scotland the pillars of the Administration were the Duke of Argyll and Duncan Forbes of Culloden, President of the Court of Session. The former, noted Horace Walpole, promptly posted to London: 'The King was to see that he was not in rebellion, the rebels that he was not in

* By the English calendar.

arms.' The regular troops in Scotland numbered only 3750, in scattered garrisons under Sir John Cope. There was a bustle to raise new regiments on both sides of the Border, and Duncan Forbes did good work rallying the Munroes and other anti-Jacobite clans. For the rest, wrote Newcastle, 'when the King comes everything will and must unveil itself'.[17]

The King's absence made everything very difficult: no one, it seemed, could take a decision. As Lord Bath quipped,

> Pray consider, my lords, how disastrous a thing
> To have two Prince of Wales's, but never a king.

Pelham was 'not so apprehensive of the strength and zeal of the enemy, as fearful of the inability and languidness of our friends'.[18]

The King did not return until the end of August; when he did he refused to be rattled. 'He came over', wrote Newcastle to Chesterfield, 'in good humour; but not so affected with the miscarriage of this campaign or so sensible of the difficulties of continuing the war as one would have imagined.'[19] Miscarriages there were in plenty. With an army which increased every day, the Chevalier captured Perth and, on 17 September, marched into Edinburgh. He proclaimed his father King, held court at Holyrood and had the whole city save the castle in his possession. On the 21st the Highlanders, 'fighting like enraged furies', in one charge routed Sir John Cope's small force of regulars at Prestonpans. By the end of October the Pretender had a force of 400 horse and 4500 foot, wonderful fighting material and burning with zeal for his cause, but not too well armed or disciplined. With these he invaded England, capturing Carlisle on 17 November.

London was in a panic, the stocks falling fast. The King, wrote an unfriendly pen, was 'obstinate, angry, determined impracticability throughout'. But, unlike some, he was not scared. He was sceptical of the value of the newly raised regiments, and in no hurry to arm the numerous retainers of the Scottish peers: when William arrived with the Fontenoy veterans, all would come right. It was a pity he could not sack the dithering Newcastle and recall Granville, but that was clearly impracticable.[20]

The Prince of Wales, according to Horace Walpole, occupied himself with bombarding with sugar-plums a model of Carlisle

Castle. A few weeks later he was 'much dissatisfied that he is not suffered to go to command in Scotland'. Since he had done not a day's soldiering, it was a ludicrous proposal, put forward, one suspects, to embarrass his father rather than in any hope of acceptance. But it was ungenerous of the King not to let Fretz serve in any capacity: the puppy should not share William's glory.[21]

The London mob was violently anti-Jacobite, and almost tore to pieces two rebel prisoners, Lord Derwentwater and his son, who reckoned themselves lucky to reach the Tower alive. There was no lack of fighting spirit in the Flanders veterans, who 'adore the Duke, and are in the highest spirits'. The Guards, shortly before Hogarth drew his unflattering picture of them, vowed neither to give nor to receive quarter of the rebels.[22]

Horace Walpole, surprisingly enough, was able to visualize the other side's difficulties, writing when they seemed in full flush of victory, 'The rebels are certainly in a very difficult situation. They dare not meet Wade;* and if they had waited for him, their troops would have deserted. Unless they meet with great risings in their favour in Lancashire, I do not see what they can hope, except from a combination of our neglect.' General Lord Ligonier, a stout-hearted and capable Huguenot, advised his friends on 28 November that this was the time to buy shares.[23]

With this judgement, which to most Londoners would have seemed irresponsibly sanguine, George II agreed. He had all the military reports laid regularly before him, and made sensible suggestions. He ordered special reconnaissances where necessary, but viewed alarmist reports with scepticism. 'I believe there must be some mistake in this intelligence, except the rebels shall have divided their forces, which is not probable.' In a long talk with Lord Marchmont he showed himself remarkably well in-formed on Scotland – the loyalty of the Presbyterians and the Lowlands in general, except perhaps Edinburgh, which had not benefited from the Union; the zeal of Lowlanders to enlist. But he would not have any general arming of the people, preferring to leave the job to the regulars. The only enemies, he believed, were the 'Camerons, the Stuarts of Appin and the Athole men'. But he

* With 18,000 men at Newcastle.

resisted the temptation to peer over his son's shoulder and interfere in military operations, 'not doubting that he will make the greatest expedition possible'. In short he set an example of cool common-sense, not a quality usually associated with George II, which his capital and Government might well have imitated. When his Ministers seemed to overestimate the emergency, 'Pho!' he exclaimed, 'Don't talk to me of that stuff!'[24]

The King was right. Already the Pretender was in difficulties. As he moved away from the Highlands, his army lost more in deserters than it gained in recruits. English Jacobites, willing enough to drink to 'the King over the Water', would not risk their necks for him, especially when his son arrived in command of a savage Highland horde, as alien to decent country squires as a war party of Iroquois. The towns were emptied on the Highlanders' approach and the people hid, burying all their valuables, even their pewter.[25] While panic mounted in London (outside St James's Palace) the tide, with ever diminishing strength, reached Derby on 4 December, and then receded. What would have happened if the Pretender had pressed on as he wished none can now tell. But a superior force of regular troops under Cumberland and Ligonier blocked his advance at Lichfield, and Wade was positioned to take the Highland army in the rear. Probably the advice the Chevalier received from his commander-in-chief, Lord George Murray, was sound: he must go back to Scotland and hold at least the Highlands for King James.

With the rebels in retreat from Derby, the Pelhams felt free to tackle the problem of Pitt, who had for some time been showing signs of disenchantment with the Broad-Bottomed Administration. In October he had proposed in the House that all British troops be withdrawn from Flanders, and lost by only twelve votes. In November, being

ravenous for the place of Secretary of War . . . he insists on a declaration of having nothing to do with the continent . . . The motion was to augment our naval force, which, Pitt said, was the only method of putting an end to the rebellion. Ships built a year hence to suppress an army of Highlanders, now marching through England!

By 20 November Pitt had reduced his demands: he was prepared to settle for a contingent of not more than 10,000 men on the continent to help the Dutch, and a full naval effort. Newcastle badly needed Pitt in the Ministry, mainly because he was such a nuisance outside it – but not on these terms, which the King would never accept.[26]

Pitt had derided his policies, insulted his native country and impugned his personal courage. No gentleman could forgive such conduct. He utterly rejected the idea of making him Secretary of War; he would 'use him ill if he had it' and 'not allow him into his presence to do the business of it'. Bath stoked up the royal resentment and reproached the Pelhams for 'forcing him to take a disagreeable man into a particular office, and thereby dishonouring His Majesty'. The King being 'extremely irritated, loudly complaining of our conduct' and making private approaches to Granville, the Pelham Ministry took the unprecedented step of collective resignation.[27]

Delighted to see them go, the King directed Bath and Granville to form a Ministry, a task which they cheerfully undertook. Within two days, however, it was obvious that against the full weight of Pelham patronage, allied to the Opposition and the Patriots, they could not secure a parliamentary majority without seeking aid from the Prince's party and the Tories. Such a step was unthinkable in the very turmoil of a Jacobite rebellion. So 'bounce went all the project in shivers'. For the second time in a year George II had to bow to political realities and accept the limitation on a constitutional monarch. He recalled the Pelhams.[28]

They agreed to resume office, but on terms. There must be a wholesale purge of Granville's men, and Pitt must be admitted to 'some honourable office'. But Pitt said, 'in many pretty words of which he had plenty, that he would not go into the Closet against the King's will'. This ruled out the War Office, but the office of Vice-Treasurer for Ireland seemed sufficiently honourable for Pitt and sufficiently remote to satisfy the royal aversion. Later he was given the lucrative post of Paymaster to the Forces, which did not necessitate personal contact with the King. He had, however, to be admitted to the Closet to take the Privy Councillor's oath. The King wept as his triumphant enemy knelt humbly before him.[29]

Thereafter, wrote Newcastle to Chesterfield, 'we rub on. We meet with no great obstacles and few encouragements [from His

Majesty]. We have no reason to complain, and as little to feel elated.' Chesterfield, speaking as a professed man of pleasure, recommended that Lady Yarmouth be counted as the key to royal favour, 'for even the wisest man, like the chameleon, takes without knowing it more or less the hue of what he is often *upon*'.[30]

Meanwhile the rebels, although no longer a danger to the dynasty, had been doing rather well in Scotland. Glasgow and Dumfries, Presbyterian and stoutly Whig, had been compelled to make large contributions to the Pretender's treasure chest. Aberdeen, Inverness, Fort Augustus and most of the Highlands were in rebel hands. But Cumberland, though no thunderbolt of war, had taken the rebels' measure and methodically closed on them. The regulars were confident of the outcome. They were far superior in cavalry and artillery, which the clansmen feared, and they had devised a method of bayonet fighting which they believed was the answer to the Highlanders' fearful charge with targe and claymore: each soldier, instead of thrusting with his bayonet at the man in front, who could catch the point in the bull's hide targe and then cut him down, would thrust at the clansman to his right front, at the unprotected side.[31] These tactics were tried for the first and last time on the open moor at Culloden against a Jacobite army inferior in numbers, hungry and exhausted by fruitless marching and countermarching the previous night. Artillery, crashing volleys of musketry and the new bayonet drill broke the Camerons' and Stuarts' wild charge, and the Macdonalds, sulky from an unintended slight, did no justice to a great warrior tradition. The rebellion was smashed, and Cumberland exacted a terrible vengeance on the Highlands. Not only were the rebel wounded and prisoners bayoneted and hanged without mercy, but the English and Lowland troops, with little interference from the higher command, burnt, looted and raped at will for months in the rebel clans' country. When, some months later, it was proposed that Cumberland be given the freedom of some City Company, an Alderman suggested, 'Then let it be the Butchers!' The King himself later admitted that he 'believed William had been rough with them', but he had not, after all, 'gone there to please them'.[32]

The tale of Prince Charles Edward's escape to France is one of the great epics of the Highlands. His gallantry, gaiety and endurance, the defeated clansmen's steadfast refusal to betray him, have cast an evening glory over an ill-judged and mismanaged adventure. Some eighty of his followers were less fortunate: spared summary execution by rope, bayonet or firing squad, they were taken to Edinburgh and London, for the ordeal of a trial with a foregone conclusion and the hideous penalties for treason.

The Jacobite peers naturally aroused more sympathy than mere clansmen whose hanging, drawing and quartering provided Londoners with an agreeable holiday spectacle. The hero of the trials in the summer of 1746 was Lord Balmerino, the most natural, brave old fellow Horace Walpole ever saw.

At the bar he behaved like a soldier and a man; in the intervals of form, with carelessness and humour. He pressed extremely to have his wife, his pretty Peggy, with him in the Tower. But the instant she came, he stripped her and went to bed. . . . When they were to be brought from the Tower in separate coaches, there was some dispute in which the axe must go – old Balmerino cried, 'Come, come, put it with me.' At the bar, he plays with his fingers upon the axe, while he talks to the gentleman-gaoler; and one day somebody coming up to listen, he took the blade and held it like a fan between their faces. During the trial, a little boy was near him, but not tall enough to see; he made room for the child and placed him near himself.

After being found guilty and condemned by his peers, 'old Balmerino keeps up his spirits in the same pitch of gaiety. In the cell at Westminster he showed Lord Kilmarnock how he must lay his head; bid him not wince, lest the stroke should cut his skull or his shoulders, and advised him to bite his lips. As they were to return, he begged they might have another bottle together, as they should never meet any more till – , and then pointed to his neck. At getting into the coach, he said to the gaoler, 'Take care, or you will break my shins with this damned axe.'[33]

The final responsibility for the executions lay, of course, on the King who was 'inclined to some mercy; but the Duke is for the utmost severity'. There was, however, no real reason for sparing rebel officers. Many lesser rebels did receive the royal pardon, to the annoyance of the London mob. Lady Cromartie personally begged the King to pardon her husband. He was 'very civil to her, but would not at all give her any hopes'. Cromartie was eventually pardoned, but Balmerino's was a bad case, for he had deserted to the rebels, and been pardoned, in 1715. It was important that he should not escape, and His Majesty ordered the sensible precaution of repeatedly changing the officers who guarded him. Once sentence had been passed, His Majesty was 'entirely of the Lord Chamberlain's opinion that execution should not be put off. Whenever criminals are reprieved, it always looks like a hardship if they are executed afterwards.'[34]

Balmerino and Kilmarnock suffered on the same day. After Kilmarnock had been beheaded,

the scaffold was immediately new-strewed with sawdust, the block new-covered, the executioner new-dressed, and a new axe brought. Then came old Balmerino, treading with the air of a general. As soon as he mounted the scaffold he read the inscription on his coffin, as he did again afterwards: he then surveyed the spectators, who were in amazing numbers, even upon masts of ships in the river; and pulling out his spectacles read a treasonable speech, which he delivered to the Sheriff, and said the young Pretender was so sweet a Prince, that flesh and blood could not resist following him; and lying down to try the block, he said, 'If I had a thousand lives, I would lay them all down here in the same cause.' He said, if he had not taken the sacrament the day before, he would have knocked down Williamson, the Lieutenant of the Tower, for his ill usage of him. He took the axe and felt it, and asked the headsman how many blows he had given Lord Kilmarnock; and gave him three guineas. Two clergymen, who attended him, coming up, he said, 'No, gentlemen, I believe you have already done me all the service you can.' Then he went to the corner of the scaffold, and called very loud for the warder, to give him his perriwig, which he took off, and put on a night-cap of Scotch plaid, and then pulled off his coat and waistcoat and lay down; but being told he was on the wrong side, vaulted round, and immediately gave the sign by tossing up his arm, as if he were giving the signal for battle. He received three blows, but the first certainly took away all sensation.[35]

'I am very glad,' minuted the King, 'this tedious affair is over, and everything that is done to show humanity, without preventing justice is very proper.'[36]

Actually, it was not quite all over. The following year Lord Lovat was executed, but he was a double-dyed traitor to both King

George and King James, with a murky history which included rape and brutalities to his own clansmen. No one was very sorry for him. Two months later the King granted a general pardon to all rebels who returned to their allegiance.[37]

The war dragged on, with varying fortunes. The Cabinet was divided: Pelham, Chesterfield and Harrington were for peace at almost any price, but Newcastle and Hardwicke believed that a great effort in 1747 might produce a better peace. So, of course, did the King, who approved a raid on the French coast and ordered that arrangements for the next year's campaign be put in train. 'My opinion,' he said, 'is to see the French coming and not propose ourselves, till the situation is such that we may heighten our demands.'[1]

In 1747 Britain's naval investment at last paid dividends. Anson had gone to sea again, and his blockading squadrons took, sank, burnt or destroyed scores of French merchantmen and escorts. Remorselessly the blockade tightened, impressing on France and Spain the advantages of peace. In May 1748 the preliminaries of a peace treaty were signed at Aix-la-Chapelle, and prolonged negotiations opened for a definitive treaty.

Forthwith His Majesty departed for Hanover, followed reluctantly by Newcastle, who was terrified of the sea. In Hanover the disparate pair got on quite well, and the royal temper survived even an accident in which his chaise overturned and, if the horses had stirred in the least, the King's legs must have been 'broke to pieces'.[2]

The principal obstacle to a peace was the stubbornness of Maria Theresa, who expected Europe to remain at war until her wrongs were righted. But George II, who could no longer tolerate her inordinate claims, was quite prepared, if she proved obdurate, to

make peace without her.[3] So in October 1748 the definitive treaty
of Aix-la-Chapelle was signed. It was a peace which, like the war,
was unintelligible even to those who made it – except, of course, to
Frederick of Prussia, who had made war or peace just as it suited
him and finished with his first plunder still in his knapsack. That
Britain gained little or nothing from nine years of more or less
successful war was due mainly to lack of any definite objective, save
Spanish plunder. George II and Granville had a clear understanding of Europe, but of little outside it. They saw the need to maintain Austria as a counter to France, and they saw the looming
Prussian menace, but they saw it largely as though from Hanover.
Newcastle and the Old Whigs saw the war as a renewal of the
Grand Alliance's struggle against Louis XIV; their strategy was
essentially that of Marlborough, but implemented, alas, by the
Duke of Cumberland. Only Pitt saw dimly that the real issue was
maritime supremacy and control of the New World, and he was as
yet in no position to impose his ideas on his colleagues.

A bizarre feature of the treaty, characteristic rather of the Middle
Ages than of the Age of Enlightenment, was the stipulation that
France and Britain should exchange distinguished hostages as
security for the implementation of the peace terms. The Ministry
were indignant that the hostages should be English peers: 'What
a flame it would raise in the House of Lords.' Hardwicke, by a
happy inspiration, suggested that Scottish peers would serve the
purpose; but eventually two gentlemen, eager for the delights of
Paris at His Majesty's expense, positively insisted on offering themselves for this exotic duty.[4]

The King's favourite complaint was that he was 'in toils', but
this is hardly confirmed by the grave embarrassment of his
Ministry at his long sojourn in Hanover. 'How', asked Pelham in
September, preparing for the opening of the new Parliament, 'can
anyone form a speech without receiving His Majesty's particular
commands?' When Newcastle plucked up courage and pressed him
to return, 'he said a great many things I need not repeat'.

Having made peace, the Pelhams turned their attention to re-
trenchment and, less convincingly, reform. The first cuts were, of
course, in the standing Army. Even before the definitive treaty was

241

signed, Cumberland had gone to Hanover to plan with his father the reduction from 50,000 to 18,850. (There was some unpleasantness about his desire to save his own regiment of dragoons at the expense of regiments which were senior in the Army List.) The Navy was reduced from 51,550 to 8000 over three years. Then, owing mainly to Pitt's vigorous protests, it was fixed at a reasonable peace establishment of 10,000. These and lesser economies made possible dramatic cuts in the budget, from £10 million in 1747–8 to £2·6 million four years later. By a rather tricky conversion, interest on the national debt was reduced to $3\frac{1}{2}$ per cent, and a multitude of Government stocks were consolidated in 3 per cent 'Consols'. It was all very laudable and Walpolean, but does not seem to have met with any marked expression of royal approval, for George II was generally more impressed by the dangers of the European jungle than by the need to keep the Commons sweet.

The Pelham reforms were more modest. In 1752, against a good deal of ignorant prejudice, they brought Britain into line with the rest of Europe by adopting the Gregorian Calendar at the cost of eleven days struck off (the mob believed) from their lives. The evils of uninhibited gin-selling, irregular marriages, the brutality of the lower orders, highwaymen and smuggling they sought to amend by legislation. A Bill was passed for the naturalization of Jews, but then repealed in response to outraged public opinion.

In Scotland Cumberland's harsh repression of the Highlands was followed by more constructive measures. Disarmament, and the more questionable prohibition of the Highland dress, drew the teeth of the Jacobite clans. The hereditary jurisdiction of the chieftains over their clans, plainly anachronistic and inimical to the royal authority, was abolished in 1746, with proper compensation. Estates forfeited for rebellion were leased out in small farms to industrious loyalists who undertook to reside on and cultivate them: the income from the estates was spent by the Crown on 'civilizing the inhabitants, in diffusing among them Protestant principles, and in training them to arts and manufactures'.[5] These measures, together with roadbuilding, had their effect in bringing the Highlands into the modern world, increasing the prosperity of Scotland as a whole and smothering the spirit of rebellion. Within a few years Pitt was to judge it safe to raise new regiments from the Jacobite clans to fight for King George II.

The Pelhams' benevolent measures were hardly to the King's taste, though he took an interest in the pacification of the Highlands. What concerned him more was the re-entry into active politics of the Prince of Wales, who had been unnaturally quiescent for several years. Having been caught napping by the general election of 1747, defeated by the power of the Pelhams, 'Walpole's rump, and my poor father's money', Frederick issued in February 1748 a manifesto listing the traditional demands of the country party and undertaking to grant them as soon as he came to the throne. He would, of course, 'abolish for the future all distinction of party', and any gentleman (even, by implication, a Tory) paying £300 a year in land tax might in that golden age be a justice of the peace. The militia would be strengthened, and regular officers below the rank of colonel or rear-admiral would be debarred from sitting in the Commons. There would be an immediate inquiry into 'the great number of abuses in office', and he himself would accept for his Civil List no more than £800,000 a year. All this was promised, and heaven too, 'when we shall have the misfortune to lose his Majesty'. As a pledge of better things to come, the salaries of the Prince's 'family' rose from £21,195 in 1742 to £38,892 in 1749. These egregious sentiments gratified the Opposition, and Lyttelton observed that the Prince's party of Whigs out of office and Tories, advised and inspired by Bolingbroke, was again formidable as a result of money spent freely on elections and, above all, the prospects of Frederick's speedy succession to the throne. For the King was now sixty-five and in poor health, suffering from recurrent agues which he treated with Jesuits' bark, as well as his painful and intimate complaint.[6]

In his political testament, drawn up in the form of a letter to his eldest son and heir, the Prince expressed all the usual sentiments of those in Opposition. Economy in Government expenditure, he wrote, and the reduction of the National Debt should be his son's greatest pride. He should call upon the monied men 'to ease the land of the vast burden it is loaded with . . . If you can do without war, let not your ambition draw you into it . . . Unsteady measures, you see, my son, have sullied and hurt the reign of your grandfather. Let your steadiness retrieve the glory of the throne.' Prince George should be first and foremost an Englishman, not a Hanoverian; and should seek to promote George I's plan for separating England and Hanover: 'from that moment, Jacobitism will be in a manner rooted out'.[7]

There was, it will be noted, nothing in this political testament to support the theory that Frederick imparted to his son the political theories expressed in Bolingbroke's *Patriot King*. The latter put the case for enlightened despotism – for a King ruling with the interests of all his people at heart, consulting Ministers whom he appointed irrespective of party, noted for their ability and disinterested devotion to the common weal.

Whatever the purity of the Prince's intentions, his political judgement may be assessed from his decision in March 1748 to rebuild his power on the unsure foundation of George Bubb Dodington, who had defected to the King's party for the lucrative post of Treasurer to the Navy. Messages and compliments were exchanged, promises were made; and Bubb, estimating the King's expectation of life and the advantage of paying court to the rising sun, came to the conclusion that he 'had long thought the country in a most dangerous and irretrievable state of decline ... I thought it became me to retire and not stand loaded with emoluments without the power of doing any real service either to the country or my friends'. He therefore resigned his post, a loss which His Majesty bore with fortitude, and hastened to Leicester House, there to learn that the Prince wished him 'to come into his service upon any terms and by any title I pleased; he meant to put the principal direction of his affairs into my hands; and what he could not do for me in his present situation must be made up to me in futurity'. Frederick thought that Bubb 'might as well be called Treasurer of the Chamber, as any other name', at a salary of £2000 a year, with the reversion of a peerage, the management of the House of Lords, and the seals of the Southern Department, 'upon the word and honour of a Prince ... and I give you leave to kiss my hands upon it now, by way of acceptance'.[8]

The Prince and his shadow cabinet – Bubb, Egmont and Dr George Lee – discussed the intoxicating subject of the steps to be

taken on the King's demise, which surely could not long be delayed. Parliament, they agreed, should immediately be dissolved,
writs issued for a general election, and a clean sweep made of all
the King's servants. 'His Royal Highness came heartily into it,
gave us his hand and made us take hands with each other to stand
by and support it.'[9]

The Prince of Wales was not the King's only worry. He was also
concerned that his two Secretaries of State were an ill-matched
team. The Duke of Newcastle, though immensely diligent, was
ineffective, fussy and constantly immersed in pettifogging detail.
Bitterly he resented the indolence of his colleague, the Duke of
Bedford, who totally neglected the voluminous correspondence of
his Department and thought his duty well done if, every fortnight
or so, he rode post from Woburn to Westminster, conducted a few
hours' business and rode post back again. He was all 'jollity,
boyishness and vanity'. Reconciled now to the Pelhams, the King
considered that they and their close friend Lord Chancellor
Hardwicke were the only Ministers: 'the others are for show'.
Idleness was a fault which His Majesty found unbearable, and he
'could not forbear brusquing' Bedford, who did not 'trouble much
about business'.[10]

But though idle, Bedford could be obstinate and singularly unimpressed by Newcastle's sagacity and seniority. He had collected
round him a party known as the Bloomsbury Gang, small in
numbers, but rich in influence through its connections with the
royal family. Its most able member was the Earl of Sandwich, a
witty *bon viveur* devoted to sport, catch-singing and the dubious
pleasures of the Hellfire Club.* Closely associated with him was
Henry Fox, notoriously venal but an adroit debater and an expert in
parliamentary management. Between them they drew into the
Bedford party the Duke of Cumberland and his sister, Princess
Amelia.

Convinced that Bedford was supplanting him in the King's
favour, Newcastle was eaten up with suspicion and jealousy. He
even threatened to resign unless His Majesty shunted Bedford off to
some honorific post for which indolence was no great drawback,
and appointed in his place a Secretary of State 'who has a proper

* More properly known as the Knights of St Francis of Wycombe.

deference for one who has been in that office above six-and-twenty years'.

The King, although basically in agreement with Newcastle, had upset him by commending some of Bedford's party. 'They are not like those puppies who are always changing their minds. Those are your Pitts and your Grenvilles whom you have always cried up to me so much. You know I never liked them.'[11]

Newcastle's unbalanced jealousy made him see even the King as a departmental rival, and Hardwicke took it on himself to remonstrate with his old friend.

Your Grace owns that he does what you wish and propose, both as to English and foreign affairs. His reserve and want of good humour, now and then, may proceed from different causes. May it not have proceeded now from his illness? Pain – apprehension of such a distemper as the gout returning, and giving him frequent vexations. Your Grace knows the King much better than I do; but I should think him of a make likely to be affected by such incidents.[12]

The ideal solution, first proposed by Lady Yarmouth, was to make Bedford Master-of-Horse in place of the Duke of Richmond who had recently died, to the King's great grief ('I couldn't have lost anybody more affectionate, and a more sincere friend'). The duties of that office were light, the emoluments generous: but the King could not accept in it one who was personally repugnant to him, and Bedford could never replace 'the poor man that is gone . . . the dear Duke of Richmond'. Yet the King saw very plainly 'how lamely things go on'. Perhaps Bedford would do for Lord President: the job had, thought His Majesty, 'business enough, but not too much: and it was four thousand a year'.[13] The problem of how to get rid of Bedford without a reverberating row remained unsolved. The debate was still continuing when a sudden shake of the kaleidoscope changed the whole pattern of politics.

The Prince of Wales had been ill of a pleurisy. He was blistered, had a plentiful evacuation and seemed out of all danger. But two days later a black thrush appeared in his mouth and throat.

On Wednesday night between nine and ten o'clock, Wilmot and Hawkins* were with him; he had a fit of coughing. Wilmot said, 'Sir,

---

* The Court Physician and Surgeon.

you have brought up all the phlegm; I hope this will be over in a quarter of an hour, and that your Royal Highness will have a good night.' Hawkins went out of the room, and said, 'Here is something I don't like.' The cough continued; the Prince laid his hand upon his stomach, and said, '*Je sens la mort.*' His favourite German valet-de-chambre, who was holding him up, felt him shiver, and cried, 'Good God, the Prince is going!' The Princess, who was at the foot of the bed, snatched up a candle, but before she got to him, he was dead! An imposthume had broken, which, on his body being opened, the Physicians were of opinion had been occasioned by a blow from a tennis-ball three years before.[14]

The King acted – indeed somewhat overacted – the part of a sorrowing father. To the Princess Augusta, whom he had always rather liked, he sent messages worded 'in the tenderest terms'. Nay, more, he paid her a personal visit, embraced her, sat with her on a sofa and wept with her. His grandsons, he said, 'must be brave boys, obedient to their mother, and deserve the fortune to which they were born'. He arranged for the most solemn obsequies, and for the deceased's bowels, after examination by the physicians and surgeons, to be carried in a box covered in red velvet for a special interment in Henry VIII's chapel.[15]

The fact that Frederick, Prince of Wales, was so savagely handled by Hervey and Horace Walpole, and so unkindly treated by his parents, impels one to seek in him some redeeming features. He was, after all, popular in London and in the country as a whole, especially at times when his father was disliked. So one pleads his gaiety and generosity, his cultural and artistic tastes. The state of politics during his lifetime put him in a very difficult situation: it was inevitable that he should become, if not the leader, at least the figurehead of the Opposition, with his shadow cabinet held together by reversions. But the irony was that his followers, by courting the Prime Minister or exploiting their nuisance value, might attain office, but he could never do so, he was in permanent opposition. To retain his dignity and balance for twenty years of frustration and political impotence required a stronger character, more 'bottom' than Providence had granted Prince Frederick. 'Bottom' was the quality he most conspicuously lacked. He was not a monster of depravity, mendacity or extravagance, but he was a lightweight, he never matured. He frequently expressed the most becomingly enlightened and liberal views, but anyone can be enlightened and liberal while in opposition. His erratic and at times irresponsible behaviour does not suggest that he would have been a successful monarch. He seems to have treated politics as an exciting game, inviting Bubb, Lyttelton and even the formidable Pitt to play with him.

> Here lies Fred
> Who was alive and is dead:
> Had it been his father,
> I had much rather;
> Had it been his brother,
> Still better than another;
> Had it been his sister,
> No one would have missed her;
> Had it been the whole generation,
> Still better for the nation:
> But since 'tis only Fred,
> Who was alive and is dead,
> There's no more to be said.[16]

The well-known anonymous epitaph, while certainly unkind, is hardly unfair to Poor Fred. Londoners showed him some measure of affection at least to the extent of lamenting, 'Oh, that it was but the Butcher.'[17]

For 'the Duke', as Cumberland was usually called, was at this time in general disrepute. His manners were atrocious. As Captain General he attracted to himself all the distaste and distrust felt by Englishmen for the standing army. This, in his case, was enhanced by his efforts to improve its discipline and make it more of a profession: the gentry resented his attempt to abolish promotion by purchase: the people grumbled at his increasing the powers of courts martial and at his treatment of English soldiers as though they were Hessian mercenaries. The Prince had financed a newspaper dedicated to denigrating him. The Pelhams abhorred him for caballing with Bedford, and the Opposition for being the King's favourite son and a chip off the old block. Not only Leicester House, but Pitt, the Grenvilles and even the Speaker of the House of Commons believed, or affected to believe, that he might take

23. George II on the field of Dettingen 1743 *by John Wootton*

24. A Jacobite satire on 'Butcher' Cumberland 1746: the Young Pretender, Cumberland and between them Britannia in whose scales Mercy outweighs Butchery

advantage of his position as Captain General and stage a *coup d'état*, usurping the throne from his elder brother or nephew.[18]

There is not the smallest evidence to justify these suspicions, and the King thought them the product of a monstrous campaign of calumny. 'It was the lies they told,' he said 'against my son for the service he did this country, which had raised this clamour against him.'[19] Nevertheless the unpopularity of the Duke had to be taken into account in considering a Regency which would be needed if the King should die before his grandson, now aged nearly thirteen, came of age. Bedford's faction in the Ministry urged the claims of Cumberland to be Regent with full powers. This was the course towards which the King's natural affections inclined him, but he yielded to the arguments of Pelham, Hardwicke, Newcastle and Pitt that, because of the Duke's unpopularity, Princess Augusta should be Regent, assisted by a Council of twelve, with Cumberland as president. Her powers would, however, be restricted: she would not be able to change any of the Ministers left by her father-in-law save on the advice of a majority in the Council, or an address by both Houses of Parliament. Since at least seven, probably nine or ten, of the Council would in fact be Ministers, it seems that the Pelhams had adequately safeguarded themselves against misfortune.[20]

After this Regency Act was passed, the King asked Henry Fox, 'Whom would you have made Regent?'

Fox regretted it was not the Duke.

'My affection was there,' George replied. 'I have a good opinion of the Princess, but I don't quite know her. A Council was necessary for her, even in cases of treason: women are apt to pardon; I myself am always inclined to mercy; it is better to have somebody to refuse for her. As to the power of peace and war, I never would declare either without consulting others. And as to the objection of the Council being irremovable, who knows it will be composed of the present people? It will be the Ministers I shall leave: had you rather have those I shall leave, or have the Princess at liberty to go and put in Lord Cobham or Lord Egmont? What did you say against the Bill – do you like it? tell me honestly.'

'If you ask me, Sir – no . . . It was against the Duke.'

'I thank you for that,' replied the King. 'My affection is with my son: I assure you, Mr Fox, I like you better for wishing well to him. The English nation is so changeable! I don't know why they dislike him. It is brought about by the Scotch, the Jacobites, and the English that don't love discipline; and by all this not being enough discouraged by the Ministry.'[21]

Cumberland gave way, with an ill-grace, and bore a grudge thereafter against Pitt and the Pelhams.

Except for William, whom no one else liked, George II's children gave him very little satisfaction. Anne, to be sure, had done her duty by marrying the Prince of Orange, but she nagged her father, magnified his faults and defied his wishes. Princess Amelia, deaf and peevish, fat Caroline pining for her dead lover, Lord Hervey, and dull Mary were a trio of querulous old maids. Louisa, the youngest, pretty and vivacious, had married the King of Denmark, but had then been imprisoned for adultery with a court physician. She and the Prince of Orange, whom George respected, died in the same year, 1751, as Frederick. 'This has been a fatal year for my family,' said the King. 'I lost my eldest son – but I am glad of it. Then the Prince of Orange died, and left everything in confusion. Poor little Edward* has been cut open (for an imposthume in his side.) Now the Queen of Denmark is gone. I know I did not love my children when they were young: I hated to have them running into my room; but now I love them as well as most fathers.'[22]

However, he probably gained some satisfaction from his refusal to pay Fretz's debts, and from the fact that the new Prince of Wales cost £30,000 a year less than his father.[23] Troublemakers made great play of the discovery that one or two of the Princes' tutors had, many years before, while Oxford undergraduates, flirted with Jacobitism. But the King was unimpressed. 'It is,' he remarked composedly, 'of very little importance to me what the parties accused may have said, or done, or thought, while they were little more than boys.' However, he ordered the investigation of the charges by a committee which found there was nothing in them.[24]

The death of Frederick had diverted attention from the problems of the Ministry. But in the summer of 1751 the Pelhams devised

* The Duke of York.

an ingenious plan, to which the King agreed, for getting rid of Bedford by dismissing Sandwich. They were banking on Bedford resigning, which he duly did. After this the three years following the death of Prince Frederick were quiet years for George Augustus and his Ministry. Although they had differed from time to time, particularly on foreign policy which the King understood far better than most of his Ministers, they rubbed along pretty well. But in March 1754 Henry Pelham died, after a short illness. He had not been a great Prime Minister. Solid and sensible rather than brilliant, consulting his experience rather than his intuition, too pliable in negotiation, more conscious of the trees than of the wood, he appears in popular history merely as filling a gap between Walpole and Pitt. But he had a proper care for his country's prosperity; he was scrupulously honest and, though a compulsive gambler with his own money, never wasted the state's. He made few enemies, and as a practical politician, a manager of majorities, he was nearly as able as his tutor, Walpole. George Augustus mourned, if not the man, the Minister. 'Now,' he said, 'I shall have no more peace.'[25]

It was one of the virtues of Henry Pelham that, unlike Walpole, he
attracted able men into his Ministry: indeed when he died most
of the country's political talent was serving under him. It should
not have been difficult to replace him. He had been First Lord of
the Treasury, Chancellor of the Exchequer and the Government's
leader in the House of Commons. His obvious successor at the
Treasury was his brother, the Duke of Newcastle. But Newcastle
was not the man to be Chancellor of the Exchequer, and could not
lead the Commons. If Newcastle went to the Treasury, where could
the King find men to replace him as Secretary of State, Pelham as
Chancellor of the Exchequer and to steer his business through the
Commons without arousing Newcastle's pathological jealousy?
Moreover the peace with France was looking more fragile every
day. Any Ministry now formed would probably have to fight a war.

There were two politicians of outstanding talent, both in the
Ministry, both avid for promotion – Pitt, the Paymaster, and Fox,
the Secretary at War. Pitt, at forty-five, was pastmaster of baroque
oratory, his voice flexible and sonorous, his gestures compelling
attention, his language fine and flowing. His tall, gaunt figure with
his fierce 'eagle profile . . . commanded reverence. His tongue
dripped venom'. Satire and polemic were his weapons, reasoned
argument one which he seldom unsheathed. Often his speeches
were rambling and obscure, but 'his eye and countenance would
have conveyed his feelings to the deaf; and his invectives were
terrible; he carried with him the strength of thunder and the

splendour of lightning'. According to his sister, Ann, he knew nothing accurately but Spenser's *Faerie Queene*.[1]

His manners were as a rule stiff and far from conciliatory, his conversation was affected and stilted. But he had considerable charm when he chose to exert it. A dissolute young admirer of his, John Wilkes, testified that 'on rare occasions his wit sparkled, and as a companion in festive moments, he was enchanting, able with his warm and sportive imagination to charm the whole day'.

He could kick any policy to death, and rejoiced in doing so. All the more remarkable was it that he had for eight years in the Ministry played the role of the industrious apprentice, labouring conscientously with the minutiae of business, loyally supporting the Pelhams in the House, a peacemaker in ministerial squabbles. He had a small but devoted following within Parliament, and a large one outside it, mainly among the merchants and mob of the City of London. The former approved his vigorous Francophobia and his outspoken preference for naval operations and expeditions to capture lucrative sugar islands, rather than sanguinary battles in the Continent to protect Hanover. The common folk were enchanted by his rugged radicalism, his antimonarchical postures. He had further entrenched himself in popular favour by his ostentatious rejection of the customary perquisites of the Paymaster's office, notably poundage on all foreign subsidies and the right to invest for his own profit the unexpended balances of any Army pay. He refused to touch a penny beyond the salary of his office, a £10,000 legacy from the ancient Duchess of Marlborough and £100 a year private income. He was not the first Paymaster to refuse these irregular but customary emoluments. Pelham had done so. But while Pelham's abstinence had passed without notice, Pitt saw – or his friends saw – that the public was well aware of his stoic rejection of wealth beyond dreams of avarice, wealth which had founded dukedoms and built palaces for Paymasters less sensitive to public opinion.

In sheer ability, in popularity and as a reward for loyal service, Pitt deserved the office of Secretary of State for the Southern Department, key post in a war against France. But he had three great drawbacks. Largely because of his abrasive character, his parliamentary following was small; he was always in bad health, suffering tortures from gout;[2] worst of all, his person and politics were alike abhorrent to the King.

It was the old problem of finding a Minister both acceptable to the King and able to manage the Commons. Newcastle would do for the King but not the Commons. Pitt would do for neither. What, then, of Henry Fox? The King liked him, because he was a friend and adherent of Cumberland. He was a genial, 'clubbable' person, more practical than Pitt, more a man of business, a debater who relied on reason rather than invective and satire. But he was a compulsive intriguer whose financial probity was not above suspicion. Unfortunately his association with Cumberland made him abhorrent to Pitt and to Leicester House; and he was also at variance with Hardwicke, whose Clandestine Marriage Act Fox – having himself eloped with the Duke of Richmond's daughter and lived happily ever after – regarded as a personal insult. (When he complained to the King about Hardwicke's enmity, His Majesty interrupted, 'Oh, Sir, I believe you have given him cause. It is now pretty even.')[3]

Fox lost not a moment in pressing his claims for preferment, to Newcastle (who was prostrate and almost hysterical in this crisis), to Hardwicke (on whom fell the burden of Ministry-making), and even to Pitt. The latter, 'totally unable to travel', was obliged to express his views in long letters to Newcastle and Hardwicke, and, more confidentially, to his allies – Sir George Lyttelton, Earl Temple,* and Temple's brother, George Grenville. Their object, he declared somewhat platitudinously on the day of Pelham's death, must be 'to support the King in quiet as long as he may have to live; and to strengthen the hands of the Princess of Wales, in order to maintain her power . . . in case of the misfortune of the King's demise'. In short, they must frustrate Cumberland's supposed ambitions. 'The King's inclination to Mr Fox' made it impossible to ignore him but Pitt thought he should have as little power as possible. In any case, he added, he was 'too odious to last for ever'.[4]

Through Lyttelton Pitt sent dutiful, pompous messages to Hardwicke, expressing every obligation and zeal for His Majesty's service, despite the unhappiness of knowing that he laboured under

* Cobham; he had recently inherited the title.

the royal disapprobation.[5] His real confidences were reserved for Earl Temple, whose

great possessions, turbulent and unscrupulous character, restless activity and skill in the most ignoble tactics of faction made him one of the most formidable enemies a Ministry could have . . . Those who knew his habits tracked him as men track a mole. It was his nature to grub underground. Whenever a heap of dirt was flung up, it might well be expected that he was at work in some foul, crooked labyrinth underneath.[6]

To Temple Pitt developed his secret plan for grasping at power:

to declare attachment to the King's government and the future plan under the Princess, neither to intend nor intimate the quitting of service . . . to look out and fish in troubled waters, and perhaps help trouble them in order to fish the better . . . To leave them (Newcastle, Hardwicke and Fox) under the impressions of their own fears and resentments, the only friends we shall ever have at Court, but not to say a syllable that shall scatter terrors or imply menaces . . . [To express resentment at] the foul play we have had offered us in the Closet: to wait the working of all these things.[7]

The threat of his wrath, if he did not receive an office to match his genius, would hang over the Government 'like a thundercloud, dark, silent, menacing, possibly to be dispelled, but ready and in an instant to pour destruction down'.[8]

But Pitt's application and Lyttelton's intercessions were all in vain. His Majesty's views on Pitt were such that Newcastle never even considered him for promotion.

Apart from barring Pitt and recommending Fox's claims, the King took little part in this cabinet-making. He had, he said, an open mind and would be guided by the cabinet's advice on who was the best man, though he hoped they would not recommend anyone who had flown in his face. This horrified Hardwicke: 'To poll in a Cabinet Council for his first minister, which should only be settled in the Closet, I could by no means digest.' So, by common consent, Newcastle went to the Treasury, though warned by the King that this did not imply being Prime Minister, an office which the constitution did not recognize. He chose Fox for the Southern Department, with management of the Commons. Newcastle, however, insisted on reserving to himself disposal of the secret service funds and the Government patronage. These once 'settled in safe hands, the office of Secretary of State would carry very little efficient power along with it'.[9]

For Fox this would not do at all. 'How,' he asked, 'shall I be able to talk to members when some have received gratifications and others not?'[10] He declined the offer, preferring to remain at the War Office. So the coveted Southern Department went to a man of whom not even Newcastle could be jealous, Sir Thomas Robinson, formerly ambassador at the Hague. Robinson was no fool; he was an able diplomat who had earned the King's praises for his negotiations at Aix-la-Chapelle. But he was a political nonentity, totally inexperienced in parliamentary debate, procedure and manoeuvres. Pitt and Fox could, if they wished, make mincemeat of him. Indeed the King, shrewd in such matters, was apprehensive about Robinson's probable fate. As for Pitt, he remained where he was in the Paymaster's office.

He was mortified. His friends had taken good care of themselves, but had totally neglected the pain-racked invalid at Bath. To Newcastle he wrote a letter in which elaborate compliments alternated with bitter complaints at being passed over in favour of political pygmies.

Let me entreat Your Grace (if you can divest your mind of the great disparity between us) to transport yourself for a moment into my place ... An indelible negative is fixed against my name ... How have mortifications been multiplied upon me ... I venture to appeal to Your Grace's candour and justice whether upon such feeble pretensions as twenty years use of Parliament may have given me, I have not cause to feel so many and visible humiliations.

He had, he explained with characteristic pomposity, trusted Newcastle 'to surmount in the royal mind the unfavourable impressions I have the unhappiness to be under'. Now comes the sting in the tail:

Indeed, my lord, the inside of the House must be considered in other respects besides merely numbers, or the reins of government will soon slip or be wrested out of any minister's hands.[11]

A few days later he returned to the charge.

I should have felt far less personally humiliated, had Mr Fox been placed by the King's favour at the head of the House of Commons ... My mortification arises not from silly pride, but from being evidently excluded by a negative personal to me (now and forever) flowing from a displeasure utterly irremovable.

To Hardwicke he complained, 'The weight of irremovable royal displeasure is a load too great to move under; it must crush any man; it has sunk and broken me.' So despondent was he that he talked of retirement. He even said that he was not fond of making speeches.[12]

The King was disappointed with Fox's refusal. 'It was a great place I designed for you,' he said. 'I thought I did much for you: many dukes have had it.'

'Sir,' Fox replied, 'Your Majesty has been told that I asked too much.'

'You did. The secret service money has never been in any other hands than the person's at the head of the Treasury.'

'I prefer serving Your Majesty as a private man, without seeing the Duke of Newcastle. He promised me his confidence. I can never believe him more. I am honest, he is not.'

'I know it cannot be made up,' concluded the King. 'You are not apt to depart from your resolution. It is a great office! But I have learned, *nemini obtrudere beneficium*.'[13]

His critics might have remarked that this was, indeed, an aphorism which had always guided His Majesty.

It was not a happy time for George Augustus. He was seventy-one, and feeling his age. When in a play, a young woman said to an elderly admirer, 'You are villainously old; you are sixty-six; you can't have the impudence to think of living above two years,' the King, in the stage-box, turned about in a passion, exclaiming, 'This is damned stuff!' He still admired a pretty woman, though he no longer aspired to a *droit de seigneur* over her. One of his favourites was Lady Betty Waldegrave. 'That woman,' he enthused to his daughter, Princess Caroline, 'has had three children and still looks like a virgin!' The Princess, who hadn't and didn't, was displeased. So enchanted was he with Lady Betty's company that he was once ten minutes late for his evening game of cards. But when she mentioned Vernon's celebrated walking-match, the King replied sadly, 'I could easily have done that, for I was once a very strong man, though now grown old and useless.'[14]

Another of his favourites was the famous beauty, Lady Coventry. Hearing that she had been insulted – perhaps merely whistled at – in the Park, George Augustus chivalrously ordered that a military guard be provided for her when she walked abroad. This was interpreted as an escort of two Guards sergeants with halberds marching before and twelve guardsmen with matchlocks marching behind. But the mob still whistled, till Fielding's men took up some of the more troublesome.[15]

He was still extremely irascible, although he denied any addiction to quarrelling: 'That is my rule, never to begin, but I love reprisals.' Even Horace Walpole admitted that 'often situated in humiliating circumstances, his resentments seldom operated when the power of revenge returned'.[16]

Politically, foreign and military affairs engrossed his interest, and on these he could hold his own with his Ministers. He still preferred the Hanoverian system 'where the government is military, as here it is legal'; but conceded that his family came to England 'to preserve the laws, and were therefore to retain them'.[17] On home affairs he usually remained silent and there is no evidence to show that he was aware of the new developments in agriculture, heavy industry, shipbuilding and transport. These expanding industries were the sinews of war which were to carry Britain to triumphs as great as those of Marlborough. Nor did he have any realization of the religious and moral revival initiated a few years earlier by the Wesley brothers, now just beginning to gather momentum. While his interests were concentrated in Europe, and more particularly in Germany, the most important developments were taking place in America.

There were fifteen separate British colonies in America, with a total white population of about 1·2 million. Each had its governor, appointed by the Crown, and a locally elected assembly. No one in 1754 questioned the right of the British Parliament to legislate for each colony, but local patriotism was strong, and it was never in fact possible for His Majesty's Government to impose any uniformity. The colonists were aggressive, restless and expansionist, and there was a constant westward movement of individual trappers, traders and farmers. This uncontrolled expansion had no efficient military backing; the only regular troops in the British colonies when Pelham died were a few officers seconded to train the local militias. The strongest unifying force was the French military presence, based on Canada in the north and Louisiana in the south. The French colonists were outnumbered by the English by, perhaps, twenty to one, but they were united, disciplined and obedient to an autocratic, centralized government which worked to a coherent imperial policy. The Court of Versailles, alarmed at the restless, unpredictable advance of Virginians, devised a master plan which would restrict the English to the Atlantic seaboard, reserving for French exploitation the remainder of the continent. Geography favoured the French plan, for the St Lawrence, Ohio and Mississippi valleys run roughly parallel to the coast: if the French could control these navigable rivers, those troublesome British colonists would be effectively contained. So after the Treaty of Aix-la-Chapelle, backed by a contingent of regular troops from France, the French constructed along these rivers a chain of forts, which served also as depots for trading with the Indian tribes. The British appealed for regular reinforcements. On military matters the King had more sagacity and mental flexibility than his Ministers: when he finally brought his mind to bear on American rather than European affairs, he saw that for fighting the French and their Indian allies in the depths of the American forests, regular troops trained for war in the Low Countries would not do. He wished to strengthen the colonial militia with munitions, officers and instructors, and let them do the job. But he allowed himself to be persuaded by Cumberland, 'who had no opinion but of regular troops', to send General Braddock, a sound conventional officer, with two regiments from the Irish establishment.[18] In July 1755 Braddock, moving on Fort Duquesne, marched straight into a French–Indian ambush. Despite their disciplined crashing volleys, fired in the general direction of an invisible foe, the entire force was massacred. Braddock had, said the King, neglected every rule of war, and should never have been sent.

While Britain and France had been fighting this undeclared war in America, the Secretary at War, Fox, and the Paymaster, Pitt, inveterate enemies but temporarily allied by the disappointment of

259

their hopes, had been absorbed in the amusing diversion of making life a misery for the leaders of the Ministry in which they served. Their favourite target – surely one unworthy of their skill – was the hapless Robinson. A large, unwieldy man, utterly at loss in parliamentary debate, he used to address the House in a peculiar stance with both arms outspread, looking like a signpost.

Pitt was in great form. In the autumn of 1754, to everyone's astonishment, he had fallen in love with and married Lady Hester Grenville, Temple's sister, a plain, sensible, middle-aged woman who adored him, put up with his moods and nursed him through his agonizing attacks of gout. It was in vain that Newcastle sought to placate his formidable subordinate by consulting him about the plans for Braddock's expedition. Pitt had the audacity to reply: 'Your Grace knows I have no capacity for such things.'[19] In November he raked with savage sarcasm his own colleague, the Solicitor-General, William Murray. 'Shall we go home now?' asked one member of another, when Murray had been reduced almost to tears. 'No,' was the reply, 'let us wait until he has made the little man vanish entirely.' Never, said the ebullient Wilkes, at Westminster School* had he felt greater terror when summoned for a flogging, never when let off a greater relief than on this occasion; terror when uncertain when the bolt would fall, relief when he found it was destined for another.[20]

Clearly the Ministry could not survive such mauling by two of its junior Ministers. 'The world expects to see these two commanders first unite to overturn all their antagonists, and then worry one another. They have mumbled poor Sir Thomas Robinson cruelly.'[21] Beset by these two, Newcastle resorted to the classic tactic of buying off the weakest and least intransigent. At the end of November the King sent for Fox and reproached him for worrying Sir Thomas. When Fox denied an alliance with Pitt to undermine the Ministry, the King asked straight out:

'Then will you stand up and carry on my measures in the House of Commons, as you can do, with spirit?'

Fox hedged. 'I must know, Sir, what means I shall have, or I cannot answer for what I cannot answer.'

* This, in contrast to many of the Patriot's statements, was literally true. He was never at Westminster School.

'It will be better for you,' replied the King. 'You shall have favour, advantage and confidence.'[22]

Indeed, on 26 April 1755, two days before his departure for Hanover, as a mark of the royal confidence, the King graciously informed Fox of his admission to the Cabinet and the Council of Regency.

Pitt was understandably cross. The day after his rival's promotion, Pitt asked Newcastle, 'with a peremptory demand for an explicit answer', if he would be made Secretary of State at the next vacancy. It was not in Newcastle's nature to give an explicit reply to any question, and Pitt, finding his answer unsatisfactory, made a formal break with Fox – though they were still colleagues in the same Ministry – a fortnight later. He then began to pay his court to Leicester House, playing the old game of reversions.[23]

Nothing would move George Augustus from his habit of visiting Hanover every other year. In 1753 the threatening attitude of the French, the defenceless state of his kingdom, the dubious faith of Frederick of Prussia, the King's age and his heir's youth all argued that he might for once forego his treat. 'But as His Majesty was never despotic save in the single point of leaving his kingdom, no arguments or representations had any weight with him.'[1] So off he went, accompanied by Newcastle, who was well satisfied that by enlisting Fox he had disarmed Pitt. This was all the more necessary because, in preparation for the war against France, with Hanover opposed to Prussian invasion, Hessians must be hired and subsidies paid to German allies – matters about which Pitt could make himself singularly unpleasant.

The King and Newcastle naturally favoured a return to 'the old system', an alliance with Austria and Holland against France and, perhaps, Prussia. Maria Theresa was burning to avenge the rape of Silesia, but regarded Prussia, not France, as the enemy; and George Augustus, much as he disliked his cousin Frederick, knew well how exposed Hanover was to the ravages of a Prussian army. There was an alternative policy, that of a Prussian alliance against France and, perhaps, Austria. Pitt's friend, Henry Legge, when Ambassador to the Court of Berlin, had urged this in 1748. But the King had then been sceptical though quite good-humoured on the subject: gaining Prussia might mean the loss of all Britain's other allies and, bearing in mind his nephew's record of perfidy and broken treaties, he had thought Legge too naive and credulous. When Newcastle gave lukewarm support to the plan, the King had said, 'Well, I am not against your trying it, but I shall laugh at Legge and you.' He was still sceptical, though he did open negotiations with Frederick for a promise not to attack Hanover. Rather than entrust his Electorate to the desperate hazard of his nephew's integrity, he preferred a subsidy treaty with Russia and the engagement of mercenaries. Pitt would countenance no such plan. To the Speech from the Throne, delivered by Fox, Pitt replied with one of his more famous polemics. Warships, he thundered, not subsidies, should defend these shores. The sole purpose of subsidies was to defend Hanover. The only proper *casus belli* was the long-injured, long-forgotten cause of the American colonists. His oratory was so offensive to His Majesty's Hanoverian susceptibilities that on 20 November Pitt and his friends, Legge and Grenville were dismissed from office. The blow was softened by Temple's offer, made that very day, of £1000 a year till better times. The man of the hour, replacing Grenville as Treasurer of the Navy, was none other than the oft-prostituted Bubb Dodington. When he broke the news at Leicester House, 'Her Royal Highness received me very coldly.'[2]

At this point one can seek enlightenment from the memoirs of Earl Waldegrave. Equally devoid of bias, ambition and political genius, he seems to have been that very rare bird, a truthful and objective witness. It was with some reluctance that he had accepted the office of Governor to the Prince of Wales. Recent research has revealed that the boy was neither backward nor unintelligent, but bored, averse from work and indifferent to pleasure – a challenge to any tutor. But Waldegrave had yielded to the royal persuasion, and at Leicester House he was well placed to observe people and events. The Princess, he found, though reputed to be of good sense, was in fact a shallow person, whose deficiencies were disguised by a natural dissimulation, civil address and assenting conversation. She dreaded Cumberland, and feared what he might do if the King died while her son was still too young to rule. The Prince, when Waldegrave first took charge of him, was 'uncommonly full of princely prejudices, contracted in the nursery and improved by the society of bedchamber women and pages of the back stairs'.[3]

The Princess relied for advice on John Stuart, Earl of Bute, Lord of the Bedchamber to the late Prince who had described him as 'a fine showy man, who would be an excellent ambassador in a court where there was no business . . .' But the sagacity of the Princess Dowager had discovered other accomplishments, of which the Prince, her husband, may not perhaps have been the most competent judge.[4]

According to Horace Walpole, Frederick had been complaisant towards his wife's association with Bute. 'When he affected to retire into gloomy *allées* with Lady Middlesex, he used to bid the Princess walk with Lord Bute. As soon as the Prince was dead, they walked more and more, in honour of his memory.' The Scotsman's assiduity at Leicester House was rumoured to be addressed less to the Prince than to his mother; 'His bows grew more theatric, his graces contracted some meaning, and the beauty of his leg was constantly displayed in the eyes of the poor, captivated Princess.'[5] This scandal is now generally discounted: it was not in character of either party, and secrecy in the glass house that was a court would have been difficult to preserve. But it was widely believed at the time and exploited by Opposition politicians for twenty years.

Bute had an 'extraordinary appearance of wisdom, both in his looks and manner of speaking; for whether the subject be serious or trifling, he was equally pompous, slow and sententious'. His ability was, in fact, mediocre, his knowledge of the world superficial.[6] However in the spring and summer of 1755 the Princess not only arranged for him to take over her son's education (though others were officially charged with the task) but accepted his advice to make an approach to Pitt, as the only barrier to Cumberland's supposed despotic ambitions. Thus the pattern of an opposition clustered round the heir to the throne was revived three years after Frederick's death. With a King aged seventy-three, and his grandson attaining his legal majority on his seventeenth birthday on 4 June 1755, the reversionary factor would obviously operate with great force, and Pitt was not above exploiting it. Meanwhile Bute appeared as a new political force of the first importance. For years it was believed that his extraordinary influence at Leicester House was derived from his relations, whatever they may have been, with the Princess. Recent research has proved conclusively that in reality his power was based on the complete, slavish devotion of the Prince of Wales. Whatever Bute's defects, as a tutor he was an undoubted success with a very difficult pupil.[7]

Political differences between St James's and Leicester House were, in keeping with family tradition, aggravated by a family row. It was about time, the King thought, for his grandson to marry, and he selected for a bride Princess Sophia of Brunswick-Wolfenbüttel. She was attractive, aged seventeen, and, as George Augustus confessed to Waldegrave, had he been twenty years younger he would have been happy to marry her himself. But the Princess Dowager saw that this girl would soon dominate her son, destroying all her own influence, and she turned the youth against the match 'until his prejudice against her amounted to aversion itself'.

From this time, on the Prince's side, 'all duty and obedience to his grandfather entirely ceased . . . He was ready to think right whatever was prompted by the mother or the favourite'. They showed in every way their support for Pitt and their aversion to His Majesty's Government. Indeed they rather overdid it, for 'the sober and conscientious part of the world doubted whether it was strictly right that a boy of seventeen should be taught to set his grandfather at defiance; nor were they much edified by rumours of a less serious nature which were now universally credited'.

The King, who before his departure to Hanover had tried hard to be tender and loving towards his bereaved daughter-in-law and her orphan children, returned to England in a very different mood, and summoned the boy for a royal reprimand. 'The discourse was short, the substance kind and affectionate; but the manner not quite gracious. The Prince was flustered and sulky; bowed, but scarce made any answer; so the conference ended very little to the satisfaction of either party.' Waldegrave thought the King should have tackled the Princess and charged her with keeping her son in order: 'He might then have ended his admonition, by whispering a word in her ear, which would have made her tremble, in spite of her spotless innocence.'[8]

While domestic politics resumed a pattern which to George Augustus was painfully familiar, in foreign affairs there took place a diplomatic revolution. The King's treaty with Russia, intended merely to strengthen the old system, in the event destroyed it and brought about the very alliance which George had believed impracticable. The Court of Versailles, seeing Prussia neutralized by the threat of Russian intervention, began to pay more attention to offers from Vienna. After all, the Empire was still a great power, and a Franco–Austrian treaty would break up the system of alliances which had confronted France for the last sixty years. Frederick felt isolated. He had paid little attention to George II's suggestion in the summer that he should undertake not to attack Hanover, but now he began to have second thoughts. With bewildering speed the Convention of Westminster was negotiated and came into force on 16 January 1756. Britain and Prussia agreed not to attack one another's possessions, and to resist any foreign power – including, by implication, France and Russia – who should enter Germany. In May a Franco–Austrian convention was signed providing for Austrian neutrality in a war between Britain and France; and Holland declared its neutrality. The old system was destroyed.

Although he had himself favoured an alliance with Prussia, Pitt disapproved of the Convention of Westminster, which he believed was negotiated purely in Hanoverian interests, a violation indeed of the Act of Settlement. He was in a thoroughly difficult mood. He had previously supported an increase of 15,000 in the standing Army, but coupled this with a fulsome expression of tenderness towards the Sovereign 'in his old age', and his amiable posterity 'born among us'. In April, although the war had not yet begun, a French invasion was apprehended, and Lord George Sackville, a promising soldier of whom Pitt had a good opinion, suggested bringing Hanoverian troops to defend the white cliffs of Dover. Pitt, swathed impressively as an invalid, belaboured this humiliating expedient. However, it was voted and the King was so relieved that he ordered his German cook, 'Get me a very good supper; get me all the rarities; I don't mind expense.'[9]

'We have,' said Pitt in May,

provoked the French before we can defend, and neglected after provocation; we are left inferior to the French in every quarter; the vote of

credit has been misapplied to secure the Electorate ; . . . If I see a child*
driving a go-cart on a precipice, with that precious freight of an old king
and his family, sure I am bound to take the reigns out of his hands. I
pray that His Majesty may not have Minorca written on his heart.[10]

Pitt's pessimism was well founded. Realizing that an invasion
of Britain was beyond their resources, the French early in May
mounted an attack on Minorca, the British garrison of which was
inadequate and unready. Admiral Byng was sent with an under-
manned, ill-found fleet to relieve it, but his conduct was unenterprising and the island, key to control of the Mediterranean, was
lost.

This disaster was followed by the capture of Fort Oswego by the
Marquis de Montcalm, the able new French commander in Canada.
This opened for the French and blocked for the British the way to
the west. In central Europe, the Prussians seemed to be preparing
their military machine. The dismayed George Augustus sent a
personal message begging his nephew to do nothing rash ; but on
30 August, too late in the year for effective Russian intervention,
Frederick invaded Saxony. George Augustus was aghast, but there
was nothing that he could do about it.

It was hardly fair to blame anyone in Westminster for what went
wrong in Bengal, six to twelve months' voyage away. But it did the
Ministry no good when news arrived that the Nawab, Suraj-ud-
Doulah, had captured Fort William in circumstances which reflectd
no credit on the Governor and garrison, and shut up his prisoners
in an ill-ventilated semi-basement cell where, during a stifling
June night, 123 died of thirst, heat-stroke and suffocation.

As though this were not enough, there was more trouble in the
Royal family. Prince George's eighteenth birthday seemed an
appropriate occasion for detaching him from his mother's apron-
strings and from Bute, of whom George Augustus spoke 'with the
greatest contempt'. The Princess and her son were therefore
informed that he would in future have a separate establishment,
his own apartments at Kensington Palace and St James's, and an
allowance of £40,000 a year. In a reply drafted perhaps by Legge,
the Prince desired Lord Waldegrave

* Newcastle.

to lay him at His Majesty's feet, and to assure His Majesty of his being deeply penetrated with his most gracious message. He wants words to express the sense he has of His Majesty's tenderness towards him . . . From these and many former instances of His Majesty's indulgence towards him, the Prince flatters himself that His Majesty will permit him to continue with the Princess his mother.

A second message, equally dutiful in its wording, equally insubordinate in its contents, expressed the 'earnest wish that the Earl of Bute might be placed in some principal situation about my person . . . Nothing can make me happier or fill my mind with warmer gratitude'.[11]

As Hardwicke observed to Newcastle, the assurances of the Prince's duty and devotion were personal to his grandfather: they did not imply any cessation of political activity in Leicester House. Twenty years earlier George Augustus might have stamped, raged at the puppy's insolence and plunged with alacrity into the resultant battle. But at seventy-four, beset by other troubles, he agreed to his grandson's demands, only requiring as a face-saver the boy's promise of dutiful obedience. Although previous solicitations on behalf of Bute had never obtained from His Majesty a serious answer, and the King had laughed whenever Waldegrave had brought up the subject, Bute was now made Groom of the Stole to His Royal Highness, which in fact regularized a situation which had existed for over a year. The King, however, flatly refused to receive the new Groom of the Stole or to give him in person the gold key of office, which the Duke of Grafton quietly slipped into his pocket.[12]

Defeat abroad – humiliation at home. 'In short,' wrote Sir Thomas Robinson,* 'everything looks gloomy. The good old King who is a friend to his kingdom and mankind and would do justice to all is disturbed by private cabals in the decline of his life, which is everyone's duty to make easy and happy for him.'[13]

So the wheel had turned full circle. Young Hanover Brave, Young Rattletrap, His Hanoverian Majesty, the Travelled Hottentot – was now 'the good old King'. He had not really changed. He was still irascible and tactless, he still 'rumped' anyone of whom

* Not the Secretary of State: his namesake.

he disapproved. He still did everything in a hurry. He had his pet aversions, with Pitt heading a rather long list: but in fact he never pressed his personal opinion beyond constitutional propriety. Schooled by Walpole, he knew that in the end the will of the House of Commons must prevail over that of the King. He inveighed against this, he stamped and cursed and kicked the furniture, but in the end he could accept the facts of politics in the mid-eighteenth century.

Lord Waldegrave's opinion of him in 1758 is here worth quoting. It is manifestly that of an objective observer, writing for the sake of truth, not to amuse or titillate the reader.

The King is in his 75th year; but temperance and an excellent constitution have hitherto preserved him from many of the infirmities of old age. He has a good understanding, though not of the first class; and has a clear insight into men and things, within a certain compass. He is accused by his ministers of being hasty and passionate when any measure is proposed which he does not approve of; though, within the compass of my own observation, I have known few persons of high rank who could bear contradiction better, provided the intention was apparently good, and the manner decent.

When anything disagreeable passes in the closet, when any of his ministers happen to displease him, it cannot long remain a secret; for his countenance can never dissemble: but to those servants who attend his person, and do not disturb him with frequent solicitations, he is ever gracious and affable. Even in the early part of life he was fond of business; at present, it is become almost his only amusement. He has more knowledge of foreign affairs than most of his ministers, and has good general notions of the constitution, strength and interest of this country: but being past thirty when the Hanover succession took place, and having since experienced the violence of party, the injustice of popular clamour, the corruption of parliaments, and the selfish motives of pretended patriots, it is not surprising that he would have contracted some prejudices in favour of those governments where the royal authority is under less restraint.

Yet prudence has so far prevailed over these prejudices, that they have never influenced his conduct. On the contrary, many laws have been enacted in favour of public liberty; and in the course of a long reign, there has not been a single attempt to extend the prerogative of the crown beyond its proper limits.

He has as much personal bravery as any man, though his political courage seems somewhat problematical: however, it is a fault on the right side; for had he always been as firm and undaunted in the closet as he shewed himself at Oudenarde and Dettingen, he might not have proved quite so good a king in this limited monarchy.

In the drawing-room, he is gracious and polite to the ladies, and remarkably cheerful and familiar with those who are handsome, or with the few of his old acquaintances who were beauties in his younger days. His conversation is very proper for a *tête-à-tête*: he then talks freely on most subjects, and very much to the purpose; but he cannot discourse with the same ease, nor has he the faculty of laying aside the king, in a larger company; not even in those parties of pleasure which are composed of his most intimate acquaintance.

His servants are never disturbed with any unnecessary waiting; for he is regular in all his motions to the greatest exactness, except on particular occasions, when he outruns his own orders, and expects those who are to attend him before the time of his appointment. This may easily be accounted for: he has a restless mind, which requires constant exercise; his affairs are not sufficient to fill up the day; his amusements are without variety, and have lost their relish; he becomes fretful and uneasy, merely for want of employment; and presses forward to meet the succeeding hour before it arrives.

Too great attention to money seems to be his capital failing; however, he is always just, and sometimes charitable, though seldom generous: but when we consider how rarely the liberality of princes is directed to the proper object, being usually bestowed on a rapacious mistress or an unworthy favourite, want of generosity, though it still continues a blot, ceases, at least, to be a vice of the first magnitude.

Upon the whole, he has some qualities of a great prince, many of a good one, none which are essentially bad; and I am thoroughly convinced that hereafter, when time shall have wore away those specks and blemishes which sully the brightest characters, and from which no man is totally exempt, he will be numbered amongst those patriot kings, under whose government the people have enjoyed the greatest happiness.[14]

The judgement of Lord Waldegrave, who liked the King, does not greatly differ in assessment of the royal intellect from that of Lord Chesterfield, who did not. 'Within certain bounds, and they were indeed narrow ones, his understanding was clear and his conception quick . . . he pronounced sensibly and justly upon single propositions; but to analyse, separate, combine and reduce to a point, complicated ones, was above his faculties.' George II was, in short, a man of a shrewd but rather narrow intelligence, reflecting a narrow range of interests. To this may be added that His Majesty had a sense of humour which, if not highly developed, at least passed the acid test of appreciating a joke against himself. Chesterfield tells a story which illustrates this agreeable trait. He was obliged to recommend for an appointment a peer whom the King much disliked.

'I would rather have the devil,' replied the King.

'With all my heart,' said Chesterfield. 'I only beg leave to put Your Majesty in mind that the commission is entrusted to "our right trusty and well beloved cousin." '

George Augustus laughed heartily. 'My lord, do as you please.'[15]

By the autumn of 1756 the Newcastle administration was suffering that public odium which not infrequently afflicts British governments at the start of a war for which they have neglected to make proper preparation. The urgent need was to strengthen ministerial support in the Commons, and the obvious way to do this was to bring in Pitt, for whom 'an afflicted, despairing nation' was clamouring.[16] But would he agree to serve with Fox and Newcastle? If so, would the King accept him? Primed by Lady Yarmouth, who took a part in all these negotiations, Hardwicke wrote to Newcastle on 13 October,

My poor opinion is that it will be right to talk to the King . . . The King may possibly evade it at first, but something you may discover at the first mention of it. His Majesty will feel the necessity of getting more strength in the House of Commons. I would not advise the shocking of him at first with Mr Pitt.

The best, indeed the only good feature of the situation was that the King was now angry with Fox who, he believed,* had intrigued to get 'that puppy, Bute' made Groom of the Stole. Hardwicke felt relieved by 'the indisposition of the King to Mr Fox . . . [But] the present state of affairs makes it necessary to have the first attention *to the House of Commons.*'[17]

Fox was the weakest link in the chain. He was not the man for the bridge of a sinking ship; he resented having no hand in ministerial patronage; he was irked by Newcastle's fussy interference;

* Newcastle had sneaked on Fox.

and he had the perception to realize that, if it really came to a choice between him and Pitt, Newcastle and even the King would find him expendable. He had, indeed, learned that Newcastle was contemplating an approach to Pitt. 'I am heart and hand for Pitt at present,' wrote Newcastle to Hardwicke. On the 15th Fox, feeling the rug being pulled from under him, begged His Majesty's leave to resign, and on the 18th he had an interview with the King who was in a sour mood but kept his temper and did not ask him to change his mind.[18]

Fox's departure made it necessary for Newcastle to tackle the King about Pitt. The King damned Fox and reflected at some length on his family and antecedents. 'But,' he concluded, 'what is now to be done?'

Newcastle said that he must either gratify Fox or take in Pitt. There was no other course.

'But Mr Pitt won't come,' replied His Majesty peevishly.

'Sir, if that was done, we should have a quiet session.'

'But Mr Pitt won't do my German business.'

Here was the crux of the matter. The King, schooled by Walpole, was a realist: he knew that he must have in the Commons a responsible Minister who would both 'do his German business' and keep the Commons sweet.

'If he comes into your service, Sir, he must be told he must do Your Majesty's business.'

'But I don't like Mr Pitt. He won't do my business.'

'But unfortunately, Sir, he is the only one who has the ability to do the business.'

'Something must be done, my lord. You must consider. I will talk to Fox.'

'He will not talk to you, Sir. If it was now made up, it would break out again in a month or six weeks.'

'We should, however, gain time, *if* he would stay this session only.'[19]

Newcastle told Hardwicke that Lady Yarmouth was for Fox: 'she is peevish with me'. His own opinion was that

His Majesty wishes to avoid Pitt and would go a great way to gratify Fox. At the same time, could the King be assured that Pitt would *do his business*, he might be brought to take him in . . . I know his demands will

272

be very high. He will come in as a conqueror. I always dreaded it. But I had rather be conquered by an enemy who can do our business than by one in conjunction with us who has deserted us [i.e. Fox].[20]

It took the King very little time to see the logic of the situation. 'I know a person of consequence,' he genially informed Newcastle on the 15 October, 'who said there were but three things. To take in Pitt, to make up with my own family – and, my lord, I have forgot the third. Pitt, says this person, is a man who, when once he has taken a part, will go through with it speedily, honourably and more ably than Fox.'

'That, Sir, is what everybody says.' Newcastle showed His Majesty Hardwicke's letter of the 13th, and the King

immediately gave me leave to have Mr Pitt sounded whether he would come and support the King's affairs and be Secretary of State . . . What is more, if he would, he would have a good reception. These were the King's own words and great use must be made of them . . . Lord Grenville told me that the King was so angry with Fox that he had rather have anybody but him. The King . . . told Grenville that he has done too much for Fox.

'Suppose,' the King asked shrewdly, 'Mr Pitt will not serve with you?'

'Then, Sir,' replied Newcastle, 'I must go.'

'My lord,' replied the King graciously, 'I know your faults, but I know also your integrity and zeal for me.' In short, Newcastle reported, he was in excessive good humour. Lady Yarmouth, too, had 'quite altered, saying good things of Pitt. She said, that if Mr Pitt did come, then there was the possibility that things would go well with the King; but with the other, never.'[21]

Pitt did indeed pitch his demands high. The first was that Newcastle should go; the second, that Fox should not return. His strength was not in Parliament, where he had few friends among the front rank of politicians, nor in the country, where his admirers were noisy but ineffective. The strength of his position lay in the support given by Leicester House which, with the King's reign obviously drawing to a close, grew more and more powerful. The despised Bute was now a great man, and addressed Pitt as 'My worthy Friend'. No aspiring politician could afford to offend

Leicester House and Bute took a leading hand in the Ministry-making. No one was more odious to Leicester House than Cumberland's henchman, Henry Fox.[22]

On the 19th Hardwicke invited Pitt to join Newcastle's Ministry. 'His answer was an absolute, final negative.' 'Mr Pitt', wrote Newcastle, 'absolutely refused to come into the administration whilst I had a share in it . . . The conduct of the war by sea and land was the thing he found fault with.'

So Newcastle, after thirty-two years in great office, offered his resignation, 'finding one of these gentlemen [Fox] would not stay with me, and the other [Pitt] would not come to me, and that one of them was necessary to conduct the House of Commons.'[23]

Pitt wanted office, provided he could get it on his own terms. These he set out in an interview with Lady Yarmouth, the most serviceable channel of communication with the King. His presumption – he had even given the lady a list of his selections – enraged the King, partly because he did not like people to think he was influenced by her. 'Mr Pitt,' he raged, 'shall not go to that channel any more. She does not meddle and shall not meddle.'[24]

The King's plan was for the Duke of Devonshire, a close friend of Fox and a Whig grandee of blameless character, spotless repute and minimal understanding, to form a Ministry built round Pitt and, if possible, Fox. Pitt, realizing the weakness of his own Parliamentary support, consented to serve under – or rather with – him.

He knew that the independent country gentlemen would vote for him but were not potential Ministers, and that for the rest he had no friends but the Grenvilles and their hangers-on. Pitt agreed to take for himself the Southern Department, all-important in a war against France. Lords Holdernesse and Barrington, friends of Newcastle, could have the Northern Department and War Office respectively, so long as Legge took the Exchequer, Temple the Admiralty and George Grenville became Treasurer of the Navy. The King told Fox to see Pitt personally about a place for himself: meeting his rival fortuitously at Leicester House, Fox raised the subject and got snubbed. George Augustus, making the best of a bad job, received Pitt himself quite graciously, but took it out on Pitt's friends who, on kissing hands, were received in the least gracious manner possible. Legge was flatly refused admission to the Closet.

Pitt's terms included the right of full access to the Closet; the formation of an efficient militia which, with the Navy, could defend the kingdom, freeing the regular troops, Hanoverians and Hessians for service abroad; and an inquiry into the discipline and legal position of the Hanoverians. They were so unpopular in England that they were everywhere refused billets for the winter, and a Hanoverian soldier, convicted on somewhat flimsy grounds of stealing two handkerchiefs, was sentenced to three hundred lashes.

These views were reflected in the King's Speech from the Throne at the opening of the session. The militia, which His Majesty (recalling its performance in Monmouth's rebellion, the '15 and the '45) had always ridiculed, was now extolled. The Hanoverians and Hessians would be sent back to Germany. Two battalions of Highlanders would be raised, though the King thought this was very risky. The success and preservation of the American colonies would be the main object of the 'royal attention and solicitude'.[1]

His Majesty's private opinion was that the words he uttered were 'stuff and nonsense'. A spurious copy of the speech was circulated. The King said he hoped the printer would not be severely punished, for he had read both the genuine and spurious speech, and so far as he understood either, he preferred the latter. Pitt, he complained, 'made him long speeches which possibly might be very fine, but were greatly beyond his comprehension'. In fact Pitt had a bad attack of gout, did most of his business from his bed and in the next four months entered the Closet only half a dozen times, when His Majesty gave him a patient hearing.[2]

The new Ministry's first problem was the hideously embarrassing one of Admiral Byng, who was held to be responsible for the naval disaster which resulted in the loss of Minorca. Pitt and Temple wished Byng to be spared. Their motives were mixed, common humanity and political expediency. They did not believe that Byng had displayed cowardice or disaffection, two of the charges for which he was to be tried. For Byng to be executed would relieve Newcastle, Anson and Fox of the blame for the loss of Minorca: but if Byng were acquitted or pardoned, the finger of blame would point to his political masters, Pitt's political rivals. On the other hand, Byng had been burnt in effigy in every town in England, and public opinion called loudly for his blood. So while they wanted Byng to be spared, they wished to avoid the odium of protecting him.[3]

On 27 January 1757, the Court Martial, after a month's trial, found Byng guilty, and duly passed sentence of death. They acquitted him of cowardice or disaffection, attributed merely to an error of judgement his failure to do his utmost to destroy the enemy, and added that their verdict was against their conscience but mandatory under the terms of Article 12. This annoyed the King, who was 'horrid angry with the Court Martial who have shoved the odium of Byng's death, if he is to suffer, in some measure off their own shoulders'. The King's view of this very difficult case, like other people's, seems to have varied: sometimes he was 'inclined to mercy', but on at least one occasion he declared that he thought Byng guilty of cowardice. In general he thought that, as Parliament had made this very harsh law, he must abide by it, and not reprieve the first prominent offender or, as was suggested in some quarters, allow Byng to escape from prison. To gain time and in the hope that they would relieve him of the dreadful burden, he referred the sentence to the Judges for an opinion on its legality: they replied that it was perfectly legal.[4]

It was unfortunate for Byng that his most prominent advocates were Pitt and Temple, neither exactly *persona grata* to His Majesty.

The King [wrote Waldegrave], who had a quick conception, and did not like to be kept long in suspence, expected that those who talked to him on business should use no superfluous arguments, but should come at once to the point: whilst Pitt and Lord Temple, who were orators even in familiar conversation, endeavoured to guide His Majesty's passions, and to convince his judgment according to the rules of rhetoric.

He had a particular aversion to Temple who had 'pert familiarity', was totally ignorant of his office, and *à propos* Byng, had used some 'insolent expressions' reflecting on His Majesty's personal courage. When, therefore, Temple pressed the King for a pardon, it did poor Byng no good. When Pitt told the King that the House of Commons hoped for a pardon, His Majesty replied tartly, 'Sir, *you* have taught me to look for the sense of my subjects in another place than the House of Commons', that is, to public opinion, which still clamoured for Byng's execution.[5]

On 25 February the King made a last attempt to spare Byng's life without compromising the law or naval discipline.

H.M. agreeable to his Royal Word, for the sake of Justice, and by way of example for the discipline of the Navy and the safety and Honour of the Nation was determined to have the Law take its course with relation to Mr Byng as on the Monday next and resisted all Solicitations to the contrary. But having to his great surprise been informed that some Members of the Court Martial are desirous to discover that the Sentence was given upon motions which will shew it to be unjust; H.M. has thought fit to respite the sd Mr Byng, that there may be an opportunity of knowing by the separate examination of the Members of the sd Ct. upon Oath (in such manner as H.M. shall direct) what ground there is, for so extraordinary a Suggestion as that they could unanimously concur in a capital condemnation of a Man, unless he was guilty. H.M. is determined still to let sentence be carried into execution, unless the said suggestion should be fully proved, so as to shew that he has not had a fair Trial.[6]

The King granted the fortnight's respite in order that Parliament might have time to pass a Bill absolving members of the court martial from their oath of secrecy: they could then explain their doubts. But there was no escape, for admiral or King. The House of Lords, actually on the advice of members of the court martial, threw out the Bill. According to the law as it stood, the law which could be changed only by Act of Parliament, Byng must die.

The man who had not shown much resolution in the heat of action met his fate with the utmost *sang froid*. On the eve of his execution one of his friends, deputed for this unpleasant task, said in an elaborately casual manner, 'Which of us is tallest?'

'Why this ceremony?' asked Byng. 'Let the man come in and measure me for my coffin.'

Next morning, on his own quarterdeck, he was persuaded to be blindfold lest his eyes, uncovered, upset the Marine firing squad. 'Very well,' he replied unconcernedly, 'if it will frighten *them*, let it be done: they would not frighten me.'

Then, calmly sitting on a chair, he was shot to death.[7]

Voltaire quipped that it was done '*pour encourager les autres*'. That indeed was the essence of the twelfth Article of War under which Byng was tried, of the Court's sentence and of the King's refusal to intervene. The extraordinary aggressiveness, against any odds, of British naval officers in the wars which filled the next half-century may have been due in part to the fate of this unfortunate officer.

Pitt made to Devonshire the arrogant claim: 'I know I can save this country and that no one else can.' But there was, in fact, in the dismal winter of 1756-7 very little he could do. His interests lay in the American war, but the colonists were reluctant to exert themselves in their own cause, and demanded always regular British troops to counter the French regulars. He lost popularity through his efforts to save Byng, and the King barely tolerated his occasional presence in the Closet.

Of Pitt and his colleagues George Augustus admitted to Waldegrave: 'I do not look upon myself as King, when I am in the hands of these scoundrels: I am determined to get rid of them . . .'

The occasion to get rid of them arose from the continental war. Now that Pitt was in office he saw the logic of supporting Prussia and Hanover in order to keep the French busy in Europe and thus relieve the British forces in America. It was decided to send to north Germany an army of observation which would both defend Hanover and cover Frederick of Prussia's right flank. The obvious commander was Cumberland; but he, prompted probably by his friend Fox, refused to take command so long as Pitt was Secretary of State. So, on 4 April, after 'an unkindly audience in which His Majesty did by no means yield', the odious Temple was dismissed, in the hope that Pitt would then resign. He did not react as expected, so on 6 April he was dismissed. George Grenville and Legge then went too.[8]

Pitt's popularity had been dented by his efforts to save Byng and his failure to provide instant victory, but with his dismissal, his reputation recovered: people felt that if anyone could win the war, it was he; and it positively 'rained gold boxes' as city after city bestowed Freedoms on their hero. The King found that it was one thing to sack Pitt, quite another to replace him. Few were willing to brave Pitt in the Commons, a people angry with defeat, and the wrath of Leicester House.[9] The fact was that a strong and stable Ministry could only be built round a Newcastle–Pitt coalition, with Newcastle providing the division fodder in the House to get supplies and subsidies through, while Pitt supplied the popularity, the fire, the dynamic will to victory. This was very clear at Leicester House and Bute and Hardwicke persisted in their attempts to bring about this alliance.

Newcastle was as usual torn between an obsessive lust for the bustle and importance of office and his nervous apprehensions. His indecision was pathetic. George Augustus, too, kept changing his mind. With a war on his hands and with all the difficulties and delays in forming an alternative Ministry, he turned in despair to his old and faithful friend, Lord Waldegrave.

'What must be done,' he had asked a few days earlier after complaining how ill he had been used, 'if after all this delay, the Duke of Newcastle at last shall fail me?'

Waldegrave suggested that Devonshire hold the fort for a while.

'This will never do. I have promised that he be at full liberty at the end of the session, and I must keep my word. If the Duke of Newcastle should disappoint me, I know but one person I could trust at the head of the Treasury. Can you guess who I mean? Why, it is yourself.'

When Newcastle did at last fail the King, Waldegrave with infinite reluctance accepted the dreadful responsibility. His royal master and friend shook him warmly by the hand. 'I heartily thank you. You have now given me your word and cannot go back.' It was understood that Fox would support him.[10]

But this arrangement could not possibly last. It was not long however before both men had to tell the King that their task was impossible, though they would still attempt it if he insisted. The King, however, replied that he

did not desire his friends should suffer for him: he found he was to be prisoner for the rest of his life; he hoped, whatever he might be made to do, his friends would not impute to him, for he should not be a free agent: he had not thought that he had so many of Newcastle's *Footmen* about him: soon, he supposed, he should be able to make a Page of the Back-stairs. For Hanover, he must give it up, it cost an hundred and twenty thousand pounds a month for forage alone: he found he must lose his Electoral dominions for an English quarrel: while at the same time he lost all authority over England.[11]

Waldegrave, presuming on old friendship, took upon himself to give the King a good talking-to about the absolute necessity both of taking in Pitt and treating him civilly. If His Majesty would

give way to the necessity of the times: and if he would graciously over-look some past offences, and would gratify Pitt's vanity with a moderate share of that affability and courteousness, which he so liberally bestowed on so many of his servants, I was convinced he would find him no intractable minister.

That I was not ignorant that Pitt could be guilty of the worse of actions, whenever his ambition, his pride, or his resentment were to be gratified; but that he could also be sensible of good treatment; was bold and resolute, above doing things by halves; and if he once engaged, would go farther than any man in this country. Nor would his former violence against Hanover be any kind of obstacle, as he had given frequent proofs that he could change sides, whenever he found it necessary, and could deny his own words with an unembarrassed countenance . . .

His Majesty heard everything I said with great patience; and answered with some cheerfulness, that according to my description, his situation was not much to be envied; but he could assure me it was infinitely more disagreeable than I represented it. That he believed few princes had been exposed to such treatment; that we were angry because he was

25. 'The English Lion Dismember'd Or the Voice of the Public for an enquiry into the loss of Minorca' 1756: on the left Admiral Byng before the Council points to a battle plan; on the right a French cock tramples the English flag

26. George III as Prince of Wales
by Sir Joshua Reynolds

27. William Pitt, 1st Earl of Chatham
by William Hoare c. 1754

partial to his electorate, though he desired nothing more to be done for Hanover than what we were bound in honour and justice to do for any country whatsoever, when it was exposed to danger entirely on our account.

That we were, indeed, a very extraordinary people, continually talking of our constitution, laws, and liberty. That as to our constitution, he allowed it to be a good one, and defied any man to produce a single instance wherein he had exceeded his proper limits. That he never meant to screen or protect any servant who had done amiss; but still he had a right to choose those who were to serve him, though, at present, so far from having an option, he was not even allowed a negative.

That as to our laws, we passed near a hundred every session, which seemed made for no other purpose, but to afford us the pleasure of breaking them; and as to our zeal for liberty, it was in itself highly commendable; but our notions must be somewhat singular, when the chief of the nobility chose rather to be the dependants and followers of a Duke of Newcastle than to be the friends and counsellors of their sovereign.[12]

His Majesty, in fact, was in excellent form and the outburst did him good. But he paid attention to Waldegrave's admonition and appealed again to Hardwicke to 'hasten some Administration that would not be changed in five months'. The audience was, Hardwicke told Newcastle, 'very unpleasant in the manner of it, but I suppose some good may come of it'.[13]

Some good did come of it – the most glorious and successful Ministry that has ever led Britain to unimagined triumphs. It was a Ministry which was produced under very unfavourable auspices, and it was built round Newcastle as First Lord of the Treasury, Pitt and Holdernesse as Secretaries of State, and George Legge as Chancellor of the Exchequer. The King agreed to Temple being Lord Privy Seal, so long as he saw as little of him as possible. Fox in the Pay Office applied himself to accumulating an enormous fortune, and promised to offend neither in thought, word nor deed.[14]

The new Ministry worked better than anyone expected. Within a few days Newcastle was writing, 'We go on well beyond expectation. Mr Pitt and I are equally pleased with each other . . . The Closet is tolerably well, but extremely low for the situation abroad.' Ten days later Newcastle told Hardwicke: 'Pitt talked to the King much as he has done to me and His Majesty was much pleased by it'. On 27 August: 'We go on very well together and the King and Mr Pitt act towards each other extremely properly and right. I must do them both justice, they do their parts well.' Pitt had a long audience with the King in mid-January, extremely to His Majesty's satisfaction.[15]

It all came, Hardwicke commented, of the King putting Pitt into a good humour rather than vexing him. That extraordinary man, who had baited the King for most of his political career, having stormed the Closet, now exerted his considerable charm to gain the royal confidence. The fact was that the Tribune of the People, for all his radicalism and demagogy, was something of a snob and had a great reverence for kingship – so long, *bien entendu*, as the King took his advice. As Burke was afterwards acidly to remark, he was 'intoxicated by the least peep into the royal Closet'.

What really impressed and surprised the King was that Pitt was now prepared to do his German business. This was in sad disarray. Cumberland, commanding the Army of Observation in north Germany, could hardly complain that he had been starved of advice. Beginning with detailed preliminary instructions on 30 March, he had been bombarded with counsel on his plan of encampment, a bridge of boats, the horse his father had lent him for the campaign, the raising of a special corps of Jägers, the moves of battalions and even squadrons. Cumberland, it seems, was far from satisfied with some of his senior officers and with the troops under his command. His father commiserated with him on 'the negligence of those old fools by whose stupidity you are distressed', and promised that 'all, without distinction, who were not obedient to your orders, whether through cowardice or otherwise, shall be strictly tried by Court Martial'.

He was warned against any action that would draw him away from his prime duty of protecting Hanover; but all was left to his discretion 'to act defensively – to attack the enemy if you think it can be effected with any moral certainty of success, and without waiving the main point which is covering my German dominions'. But despite this plenitude of parental counsel, on 16 July Cumberland managed to be badly defeated at Hastenbeck, whereupon Hesse-Cassel and half Hanover were overrun by the French, lost (as Newcastle admitted) '*singly* on account of our English quarrels'.[16]

The King took these disasters well. Calm but determined and even civil, he said that his son 'must get out of it as well as he could'. 'How,' he asked Cumberland, 'can my troops be saved? And what if the French push demands too far and insist on disarming my troops and making them prisoners of war?' He would do his best to help in their distress the Landgrave of Hesse-Cassel and the Dukes of Wolfenbüttel and Gotha, but as for Frederick of Prussia, 'I can do no more for him. I will acquaint him with what I am necessitated to do.'[17]

What he was necessitated to do was, in his electoral capacity, to make a separate peace for Hanover, a move which his English Ministers deplored but could not prevent. 'His Majesty,' Holdernesse told Newcastle on 12 August, 'seems to think nothing else would save the debris of his German army and territories . . . I see the utmost hazard in a separate peace, and I hope and believe the King of Prussia will have timely notice.'[18] On 9 August, the King wrote privately in his own hand:

Dear William,

I just now received your letter of the 2nd August by which I see the distracted condition of my affairs in Germany. I am convinced of your sense and capacity and zeal for my service. Therefore you will receive powers to get me and my country out of these difficulties at the best rate you can by a separate peace as Elector, including my allies the Duke of Wolfenbüttel, and the Landgrave [of Hesse-Cassel] . . . Nobody attributes your bad [illegible] either to you or the troops under your command, to any cowardice or want of precaution. But it seems fate is everywhere against us. I trust my affairs entirely to your conduct . . . As in the case of war I depend upon your courage and skill, so I now depend on your affection, zeal and capacity to extricate yourself, me, my brave army and my dearly beloved subjects out of the misery and slavery they groan under.

I am, dear William, your loving father,

George, R

I hear with great concern your leg is not well, and your health not of the best. Pray take care of a life that is both so dear and so necessary to me, and when you have settled everything, come to a father who esteems and loves you dearly.

Take care in your negotiations about cavils and that there be no tricks played, either to my army or to the troops of my allies.[19]

Two days later these private instructions were amplified by official authorization to Cumberland to treat for a separate peace 'for me as Elector, that the several dominions may be relieved and the troops saved'. He was to make it clear that 'as Elector I am not at war with the Court of France or the Empress Queen . . . If peace be not procurable, endeavour to save my army in the best manner possible'. George Augustus, however, 'absolutely would not submit to terms including the disarming of troops'.

Perhaps Cumberland was not a very good negotiator, but it is not easy to strike a hard bargain when you have just been heavily defeated and are both outnumbered and outgeneralled. The Convention of Klosterzeven, signed on 8 September, immobilized the Hanover troops and sent home those of Hesse-Cassel and Brunswick, thus exposing Frederick's flank. Hanover and the allied states were not guaranteed, but were opened to occupation and plunder.[20]

George Augustus was equally angry and ashamed: it was, perhaps, the bitterest moment in his life, when his beloved William signed a convention which disgraced him and let down his much disliked nephew of Prussia. On 21 September he wrote Cumberland a furious letter.

You have seen fit to make a convention . . . by which not the least thing has been stipulated in favour of my states and those of my allies, but which soon gives the enemy possession of the posts and countries . . . my troops like prisoners of war . . . All this was done without writing for my ratification . . . a convention shameful and pernicious . . . Come back at once by a warship and explain.[21]

To Newcastle the King

was pleased to say that his honour and interest were sacrificed by it, that he had been by it given up, tied hand and foot, to the French. That he did not know how to look anybody in the face: that he had lost his honour and was absolutely undone. That he thought the Duke's head was turned or he had lost his courage. That he did not know what to make of it, but that he would not have it lay upon him. That if any other man in the world had done it, he would conclude he had been bought by France.

If, he added, the 'army had been cut half to pieces, this convention would still have been scandalous'. 'In short', wrote Newcastle, 'I never saw such a scene in my life, so moving and so unhappy a man I never beheld – after saying that Providence had abandoned him, he hoped the nation would not forsake him.' Never one to conceal his emotions, George Augustus frequently wept for shame.[22]

The English Ministers disapproved of the Convention, congratulated themselves that it had nothing whatsoever to do with them and lamented 'the tarnishing of the King's honour at the close of a reign not yet sullied by anything of that nature'.[23] But Newcastle and Pitt did their best to comfort him.

Every circumstance of the Convention increased the King's distress. It was his beloved son who was responsible, his dear William, of whose valour he was so proud. Now he spoke of 'his rascally son' whose blood was 'tainted'. When Newcastle suggested that he might at least give the Duke a chance to justify his action, His Majesty replied, 'A scoundrel in England *one day* may be thought a good man *another*. In Germany it is otherwise. I think like a German.'[24]

Not only was it his beloved son who had let him down: it was his beloved Hanover that William had exposed to the ravages of a French army. It was his abhorred nephew, Frederick of Prussia, who loudly and constantly complained of English decadence and lack of spirit, and now really had something to complain about. To him, the King felt obliged to send a personal letter of apology, writing in his own hand to lament the harm done by '*la conduite molle et pusillanime de la dernière campagne et la convention*'.

Finally, he could hardly avoid a sense of guilt himself. True, he had not authorized such shameful terms, but he had given full authority to a singularly inexperienced negotiator to undertake a singularly difficult negotiation. Pitt detested and distrusted Cumberland, but in fairness made this point when His Majesty said he had given no order for such a convention. 'But *full powers*, Sir; *very full powers*.'[25]

The English Ministers, sorry as they were for their good old King, knew very well that he was not altogether blameless. 'I am afraid,' wrote Newcastle, 'the Great Person who signed it had authority to go further than we, the English Ministers, could have advised. But His Majesty is firmly persuaded that his orders and authorities have been mistaken and exceeded.'[26]

The worst damage was to the British name abroad. Colonel Yorke reported to Newcastle from the Hague: 'The reflections on it are not such as can be inscribed in any office letter. It is not possible to represent to Your Grace in colours strong enough the reproaches to which the authors of that measure are exposed. Friends, foes and neutrals all hold the same language, and their remarks cut me to the heart.' Sir Andrew Mitchell, the British Minister to the Court of Berlin, wrote: 'No man will trust us. I know not how to look the King of Prussia in the face.'[27]

Cumberland appeared in London with a strong sense of injured innocence. He had, he told Fox, written orders in his pocket for everything he did, and set about summarizing papers to prove it. But the King would have none of his excuses. When Cumberland presented himself at Court, he was very coldly received, and George Augustus remarked loudly to his card-table: 'Here is my son, who has ruined me and disgraced himself.'[28]

That evening Cumberland asked Lady Yarmouth to inform His Majesty that he wished to resign his regiment, his post as Captain General, all his military offices. In his disgrace he behaved with a certain dignity, but his father was implacable and Lady Yarmouth (wrote Newcastle) was 'outrageous'.

The King told me that when he talked with the Duke about the French coming here and taking measures to oppose them, the Duke was always for securing his retreat. The King used to say, 'We must think of attacking them. You are always talking about retreat.' I hope your lordship does not think that I imagine the blame is singly there.

That was the general opinion, even among those (like Pitt) who distrusted Cumberland. The King's shame and anger, which was entirely genuine for he was incapable of dissimulation, deceived only himself.[29]

One good thing came of this affair. In place of Cumberland the King appointed as Commander-in-Chief (not Captain General) the valiant and capable Huguenot, Lord Ligonier, making it clear that Ligonier was only his deputy. Cumberland, he conceded, whatever his faults (which, he now declared, included cowardice) 'knew the officers well and made proper recommendations. Ligonier must find out the best officers'. As for the Convention of Kloster-zeven, the Elector of Hanover was able on 28 November to repudiate it, because the French had been guilty of some minor infringements of its terms.

20

The man on whom George II so reluctantly bestowed the Seals of the Southern Department was confident that he, and only he, could lead the country to victory, provided his colleagues refrained from any interference. Pitt had the imperial vision. He saw the war as a worldwide struggle, fought in five theatres – Europe, North America, the West Indies, the West Coast of Africa and the East Indies. In each theatre of war the local object was individual: in North America, the removal of the French threat and the consequent opening of the continent for the settlement by Britons; in the West Indies, the acquisition of rich sugar islands; in West Africa, the seizure of a lion's share of the trade in slaves and other local products; in the East Indies, the removal of Britain's only trading competitor. To the necessity of a major British effort in Germany, he was a late convert, arguing that so long as the French were heavily engaged there, their efforts in America must languish. His addiction to descents on the French coast, too large for raids but not large enough for invasions, he justified on similar grounds – that they tied up French forces which would otherwise have been employed elsewhere. Sea power he saw as linking these diverse campaigns, ensuring that none was fought in isolation, and starving detached French garrisons of supplies and reinforcements. Armies, navies and subsidies to continental allies were all welded together in a master design, the end of which was the downfall of France and the establishment of Britain as the world's greatest imperial power.

Pitt brought to his office a daemonic energy, a singleness of purpose which communicated itself to his country and made men feel that so long as Pitt was Minister, although some campaigns might go awry, the end was sure. He imposed his will on every department of state, but would not suffer the smallest interference or the mildest advice from any of his colleagues. So autocratic was he that he would allow no junior Minister to sit in his presence, and he required Anson to sign without reading his orders to naval commanders.

He was convinced that Britain's resources for war were prodigious, and by convincing others of this, he made them so. Flourishing trade, industry and agriculture bore without undue strain the prodigal expenses of his campaigns and his subsidies; and a fortuitous increase in population provided the soldiers, sailors and shipwrights he demanded. He found the Army and Navy, particularly the former, depressed by failure and destitute of commanders who inspired confidence. Pitt axed the failures and appointed younger men of unorthodox brilliance, with minds sufficiently flexible to apply the rules of war to unfamiliar conditions. Having chosen the men to lead the expeditions he launched, he supported them generously, prodigally, sparing neither lives nor guineas, and meticulously ensuring that the strategic effort did not fail for lack of shipping, land transport and administrative backing.

He was not without flaw in assessing either men or measures. He thought highly, for instance, of Lord George Sackville, who, whatever the reason for his conduct at Minden, proved himself twenty years later to be a man of singular incompetence. Like many amateur strategists, he seemed unable to grasp, or at any rate to apply, the cardinal military principle of concentration: the amphibious operations he launched against Rochefort, St Malo and Cherbourg achieved very little at very high cost, and were compared by their intended victims as the strategy of breaking windows with guineas. He drew magnificent plans, and left Newcastle and Legge to find the magnificent means, giving them little credit for doing so.

Nevertheless, when all else is said, the last word rests with Frederick of Prussia, to whom praise of an ally did not come easily.

'*Il faut avouer que l'Angleterre a été longtemps en travail, et qu'elle a beaucoup souffert pour produire Monsieur Pitt, mais à la fin elle est accouchée d'un homme.*'[1]

On the whole Pitt and the irascible little King rubbed along better than expected, largely because Pitt in office saw clearly what Pitt in Opposition would never admit – the necessity in any war against France for engaging the main French armies on the mainland of Europe. He endeavoured to rationalize his *volte face* by claiming that he was conquering Canada on the banks of the Elbe. This characteristically grandiose boast hardly holds water: it was naval control of the Atlantic, not military diversions in Germany, which prevented the French Government from reinforcing Canada. The real purposes of subsidies to Frederick of Prussia, and eventually a sizeable British contingent in Prince Ferdinand's Army of Observation, was to prevent the French from launching an invasion of Britain from the Austrian Netherlands; and to safeguard Hanover, which if overrun again, might have been played by the French at the peace conference as a bargaining counter for the return of Canada.

Pitt's differences with the King were mainly over the appointment of military commanders. It was a matter in which the King had always held strong views, and resented the interference of politicians;[2] but it was not possible to deny Pitt a say in the appointment of commanders for expeditions planned in the Southern Department, that is to say for all expeditions against France in North America, the West Indies, West Africa and the coasts of France herself. The trouble was that he and the King seldom saw eye to eye in these matters, Pitt looking for commanders blessed with a streak of genius and more than a streak of luck, while the King, like any other man of his age and military background, set more store on experience, orthodoxy and seniority.

The Ministry functioned better than one would expect from the circumstances of its formation. Anson as First Lord of the Admiralty and George Grenville as Treasurer of the Navy brought the senior service to the highest pitch of efficiency, and were well served by a brilliant team of admirals, many of them Anson's old pupils. Holdernesse, Secretary of State for the Northern Department, did what he was told. Newcastle suffered, of course, from jealousy of

Pitt, and constantly besought Hardwicke to 'talk to him'.[3] But on the whole, with his encyclopaedic knowledge of the seamy side of politics and his unrivalled command of patronage he saw to it that Pitt could concentrate on winning the war, without worrying about the security of his political base. He and Legge somehow produced the vast sums needed for Pitt's armies, ships and subsidies. Temple, adept at intrigue and subversion, arch-enemy of almost every government, was neutralized as Lord Privy Seal, and Fox as Paymaster minded his own lucrative business. Only the Bedfords and Cumberland were in Opposition: even Leicester House could at first be counted as friendly, so Pitt need not be distracted by apprehensions for his future. Nor should the influence, wholly beneficial, of Lady Yarmouth be ignored. She was the principal channel between the King and his Ministers, advising them on how and when to approach him, protecting His Majesty from personal importunities and from the irritations inevitable in day-to-day contact with such an abrasive personality as Pitt's.[4]

In his plans for 1758 Pitt thought first of Canada. Louisburg was the key to the St Lawrence and must be taken; a force would advance from New York up the Hudson valley and capture Crown Point and Ticonderoga, whence the way would be open to Montreal; a southern force, based on Philadelphia, would take out the menacing French stronghold, Fort Duquesne, thus gaining control of the Ohio valley. It was the sort of campaign which is easily envisaged on a small-scale map. On the ground, spread over a front of a thousand miles, the three expeditions would be uncoordinated, with long, fragile lines of communication, and operating against an enemy who had the benefit of far better lateral communications – the St Lawrence River and the lakes.

After being invested for six weeks Louisburg was taken with due deliberation and by orthodox siege tactics on 26 July but it was too late in the year for further operations against Quebec. Another British force approached Fort Duquesne slowly and methodically, reaching it on 20 November, only to find it abandoned. A frontal attack against prepared positions at Ticonderoga was bloodily repulsed. The year's campaign had not fulfilled all Pitt's hopes, but on balance it was decidedly in Britain's favour. The way was now open to Quebec, the threat from Fort Duquesne was removed and the Indian tribes, always quick to spot a winner, began to transfer their allegiance and their formidable war bands from the French to the British side.

In Germany it was at first Pitt's policy to subsidise Prussia and Prince Ferdinand's Army of Observation rather than engage British troops. He induced the Commons to grant £670,000 for King Frederick and £1,200,000 for Prince Ferdinand, as a result of which the French were driven from north Germany back over the Rhine. In the late summer, indicating his wholehearted commitment 'to this glorious school of war' he reinforced the Army of Observation with a British contingent, five regiments of horse and four of foot. The good old King, failing now in his sight and hearing, was overjoyed at Prince Ferdinand's success, 'though he has no ears to hear it and but one eye to read it, having totally lost the sight of the other'.[5]

These successes transformed the whole aspect of the war, quite overshadowing the countrywide riots against the ballot for home-service in the militia. The King was as pleased as anyone, though this did not prevent him occasionally expressing his dislike of Pitt and his strong preference for Fox, who 'could never be Minister, but was a brave fellow'. He told Lady Yarmouth he could get on perfectly well without Pitt, who was hated by everybody. The lady 'talked with great honesty and resolution to him and told him . . . that if Pitt went out, His Majesty would be in the same case he was last year when he thought everybody would come in and when he found in three days no one would accept employments'. 'He was very angry with her,' commented Newcastle, 'to a degree that stopped her mouth, but I hope I have opened it again.'[6]

What is less surprising is, that Pitt fell into disrepute at Leicester House. While in Opposition he was their man, but as soon as he took office he became the King's Minister, which Princess Augusta and her son could never be. Leicester House was always anti-Hanover and opposed to any involvement in Germany. Pointing to the changed views of a man who a year ago had said he 'would not send a drop of our blood to the Elbe to be lost in that ocean of gore', Prince George wrote to his dearest Bute: 'I am certain he has given himself up to the King or the Duke of Newcastle, or he would not act the infamous and ungrateful part he does now.' It was a curious comment to make on the relations between His Majesty's Secretary of State, His Majesty himself and the First Lord of the Treasury.[7]

George Augustus was always a believer in the therapeutic qualities of plenty of fresh air, the colder the better. Newcastle was not, and complained, 'the Closet is all window, and His Majesty keeps all sashes up ... so that there is no avoiding the draught'. In November 1758 the King paid the penalty for his dangerous habits, catching a severe cold coming up to London with his coach windows open. For a while, hopes at Leicester House ran high, but eventually Prince George had sadly to admit that 'My intelligence of the King's health is, that he begins to gain strength and is likely to last till summer'.[8] The old King must have felt very lonely when in January his favourite daughter, Anne, died. His idiosyncrasies had not weakened with age. His levée room still had the atmosphere of a lion's den as the sovereign stood in one spot, eyes fixed royally on the ground, dropping bits of German news. He still, when he met people of whom he disapproved, did them the honour of rumping them without saying a word or even looking civil; and they still joked about it. But with his friends, particularly military men like Lord Granby, he could be almost gracious if they caught him in a good mood.[9]

By the end of 1758 Pitt had weathered the bad years and had the Navy, the Army and the country as a whole eager for battle and confident of victory. The advance into Canada was to be pressed, with the northern thrust, aimed up the St Lawrence at Quebec, led by one of Pitt's bright young men, Major General James Wolfe, aged thirty-two. It was one of Pitt's appointments of which His Majesty approved. When someone warned him that Wolfe was reputed to be mad, George Augustus replied, 'Oh? He is mad, is he? Then I wish he would bite some of my other generals.'[10]

Martinique, a rich sugar island with a fine harbour at Port Royal, was the objective of a combined operation in the West Indies. Even Pitt could hardly expect complete success for all his plans, but in the astounding 'year of victories' he very nearly achieved it. Martinique proved too strong to be taken by a *coup de main*, but Guadeloupe, almost as rich, was captured. Amherst in his steady, methodical advance on Montreal took the French outposts of Niagara, Ticonderoga and Crown Point, which gave control of Lake Champlain, most useful for the transport of supplies and equipment. Wolfe, as every schoolboy knows, rowed up the St Lawrence at night with muffled oars, scaled the Heights of Abraham and was killed in the moment of victory. Quebec fell a month later.

Meanwhile at home there was serious danger of a French invasion, launched from the Austrian Netherlands, with little but the amateurish militia to withstand the French veterans. It was important to display, even if he did not feel, confidence in these bucolic part-time soldiers, so His Majesty reviewed the Norfolk militia which marched past behind Lord Orford, grandson of his great Minister, 'with the port of Mars himself and really the genteelest figure under arms'. With the regiment's discipline, turnout and bearing the veteran of two wars expressed the greatest satisfaction.[11]

The French invasion plan was for the Toulon fleet to evade the blockading squadron, join the Brest fleet and together gain the naval control of the Channel which would enable forces to be landed in south-east England, Ireland and the Clyde. The crisis occasioned another passage with Leicester House, Prince George writing to his grandfather on 20 June:

Sir,
I beg leave to lay myself at Your Majesty's feet, humbly to offer up a petition in the success of which I feel extremely interested. While this country remains in tranquility, I thought my time best employed in acquiring a thorough knowledge of all matters peculiarly suited to my situation but now that every part of the Nation is arming for its defence, I cannot bear the thoughts of continuing in this inactive state.

When Your Majesty's kingdoms are threatened, a quiet retreat ill becomes my birth or station.

Permit me therefore humbly to request of Your Majesty to give me an opportunity of convincing the World that I am neither unworthy of my high situation, nor of the blood that fills my veins. Your Majesty's known valour will diffuse its influence on my head, to make the presence of your grandson an encouragement to your people, a terror to the enemy, and joined to his own resolution may in some measure supply his want of experience in military affairs, and enable him to support with dignity the post of danger, which he esteems the post of honour. I earnestly beseech of Your Majesty to receive this humble request with your accustom'd goodness. I intended to have made it in person on Tuesday, but too great anxiety kept me silent, and the fear of that returning reduces me to the necessity of having resource in this manner to Your Majesty's favour and indulgence.

I remain, Sir,

Your Majesty's most dutiful, most humble and most obedient grandson, subject and servant[12]

It was understood that the Prince, now aged nineteen, would be content with command of the home forces. The King, remembering a similar application by Frederick in 1745, did not take it seriously, but as an attempt to embarrass the Ministry. 'He wants to be rising, *monter un pas*,' he said to Newcastle. Lady Yarmouth believed that the underlying motive was fear of Cumberland regaining supreme command. So a douche of cold water was poured over the proposal. The King expressed the 'highest satisfaction of his grandson's spirit and zeal', but thought it 'improbable that the enemy would execute so rash and hazardous attempt'. In that unlikely event, 'I shall not fail to remember your application' and 'on the proper occasion' would give the lad a chance to prove himself. So the Prince was left, he complained, kicking his heels, immured like a girl, and Bute advised that 'the proper occasion' was a put-off. The King's intention was only that the Prince should 'review troops, visit Portsmouth etc.' and 'ask on return how he found things'. According to Lady Yarmouth, it was the King's intention, if the French landed, to go and fight himself, and take the Prince of Wales with him, as he had taken Cumberland to Dettingen. It was a spirited proposal for a man of his age, deaf and half-blind; and fortunately it was not put to the test.[13]

Pitt's reliance was less on the militia than on the highly professional Navy. It was entirely justified. The Toulon fleet, taking its chance when the blockading squadron had to return to Gibraltar for refitting and supplies, got clear through the Straits by night, but was then mauled by Boscawen, losing four ships, in the battle of Lagos Bay. The Brest fleet suffered a catastrophic defeat by Hawke among the treacherous rocks, shoals and breakers of Quiberon Bay. The danger of invasion, and of the Prince exercising his military talent, was over.

The storms of Quiberon Bay were nothing to the storms at Westminster over the affair of Lord Temple's Garter. In September 1758 Temple, 'though not insensible of the many marks I have had the misfortune to receive of His Majesty's displeasure', had the effrontery to apply to Newcastle for the Garter – an honour very much in the King's personal gift. Newcastle gave him a smooth, practised rebuff. But the following year Pitt took up his brother-in-law's case, positively threatening to resign if the King refused to grant this outrageous demand.[14]

Poor Newcastle had to approach George Augustus, who flew into a royal temper. His Ministers, he said, did as they pleased: he was *nothing* here: he wished he had stayed in Hanover in 1735: he wished even now he could take a bark and go to Hanover. Newcastle began to argue that Pitt was indispensable. 'I know,' retorted His Majesty, 'you have been tormenting Lady Yarmouth about it. Why do you plague her? What has she to do with these things? The only comfortable two hours I have in the whole day are those I pass there, and you are always teasing her with these things.'

The wretched Newcastle explained that Pitt would probably resign unless he had his way.

'Well, if Mr Pitt comes to Court seldom, so much the better. I don't like to see him.' He was, in fact, shrewd enough to know that Pitt, when it came to the point, would not resign. 'Pitt will not oppose his own measures.'

'No, but his friends will oppose everything else.'

But the King was adamant. If Temple, the most odious man, was rewarded for his insolence with the Garter, 'I will be forced,' he said, 'the world shall see how I am used. I will have it known.'

Newcastle hurried off to Pitt with word of the royal refusal and Pitt very properly disclaimed any intention of forcing the King by threats of resignation. So back to St James's, to try again.

It was of no avail. 'Well, now, I see I am to be *wheedled, forced*
sometimes, *wheedled* to bring about what you want. I see it very
plainly. I am nothing and wish to be gone. I will not be bullied into
it. I will not give it to him.'

So that was that.

'Now, my dear lord,' Newcastle appealed in despair to Hardwicke, 'what is to be done?'

The King insisted that Pitt was bluffing. 'Oh, he won't quit his
own schemes and measures.' Pitt insisted that if Temple were not
honoured, although Pitt would not resign, he would boycott the
Court and make no secret of his disapprobation. 'No man,' argued
Newcastle, 'will set his face against Pitt in the House of Commons.'

Eventually, as usual, the King's prejudices surrendered to reason.
'If I am confined and bound, I must do it.'[15]

Newcastle found the affair desperate, especially when Temple
resigned. But at last Temple apologized for offending and was
promised the Garter. It was bestowed with the worst possible grace.
The King, instead of placing the ribbon decorously over the new
Knight's shoulder, 'averting his head and muttering indistinctly
some expressions of dissatisfaction, threw it across at him', as a
bone is thrown to a dog, and promptly rumped him. When Temple
went to kiss hands on resuming the Privy Seal, 'My reception', he
wrote ironically, 'was of the most *distinguished* kind. You know,
rumpatur quisquis rumpitur invidia.'* But the Garter made Temple
'the happiest man in the world' and he wore the ribbon on every
possible occasion.[16]

Although George Augustus threatened to leave them all and go
to Hanover, the storm blew over, and soon he was congratulating
Pitt, publicly though not perhaps very graciously. 'So, Sir, all your
plans have succeeded.'[17]

They reached the summit of success in 1760 with the surrender of
Montreal and the cessation of the war in Canada. 'No end of glory
and exultation!' wrote Temple to Pitt. 'The close of the King's
reign is strikingly distinguished by lustre of every sort. May he

---

* This pun on the King's habit of rumping his pet aversions is almost impossible to translate. Roughly, 'He who is bursting with hatred, let him break
wind.'

feel it as he ought, and long enjoying the comfort of it without forgetting who has wrought the wonderful change.'[18]

No King of England had more passionately longed for martial glory, and it was ironical that he received it in full measure only at the close of his long reign, at the hands of the man whom he could not like. (In this misfortune George Augustus was not alone: few in daily official contact with Pitt actually liked him.) Half blind now, too deaf to hear a word that foreign ambassadors uttered,[19] he could still bask in the triumphs of British and Hanoverian arms, such as that of Minden in June 1760. Before the battle Ferdinand felt himself to be in a tight corner, and asked that ships be sent to Emden ready for a possible evacuation. The old King's reply showed him at his finest and best: if Ferdinand hazarded a battle, he could count on His Majesty's complete confidence and support, whatever the outcome. The outcome was a resounding victory, in which six incomparable British battalions covered themselves with glory.

In the summer of 1760, with the King manifestly nearing his end, it was thought prudent at Leicester House that Bute, destined to be principal Minister in the new reign, should gain some acquaintance with his duties. Pitt was approached to bring Bute into the Cabinet, and in his most lofty, arrogant style, poured cold water on the scheme. The young Prince of Wales was furious, writing almost hysterically to his Dearest Friend:

He [Pitt] has shown himself the most ungrateful and in my mind the most dishonourable of men, I can never bear to see him in a future Ministry . . . All men will find the only method of succeeding in their desires will be by first acquainting you with what they mean to request before they address themselves to me. Whilst my Dearest is near me, I care not who are the tools he may think necessary to be in the Ministry, provided the blackest of hearts [Pitt] is not one of them.[20]

When this boy could apply such a term to the greatest living statesman, the King's end must clearly be near. Death came to George Augustus on 25 October 1760, wearing the cap and bells of low comedy: for this, like other crises in the King's life, was coloured by farce. He rose at his normal hour of six in the morning, called as usual for his chocolate and repaired as usual to the close-stool. The German *valet de chambre*, hearing 'a noise louder than the royal wind', and then a groan, ran in and found him lying on the floor, having cut his face in falling. He was laid on his bed and blooded, but not a drop flowed: 'The ventricle of his heart had burst.'[21]

'What an enviable death!' wrote his old enemy, Horace Walpole. 'In the greatest period of the glory of his country and of his reign, in perfect tranquillity at home, at seventy-seven, growing blind and deaf, to die without a pang.'

He died, wrote Hardwicke's son, 'in the height of his glory, loved, honoured and respected by all Europe'. Newcastle, who had so often flinched under the lash of his irascibility, now lamented losing 'the best King, the best Master and the best Friend that ever subject had'.[22]

Well, that perhaps was laying it on a trifle thick, but the considered judgement of most of those who worked with him, particularly those who later had to work with his grandson, was a great deal better than the cursory treatment accorded him by historians. Pitt, for instance, had little cause to love him, but declared, 'The late good old King had something of humanity and, among many other royal and manly virtues, he possessed justice, truth and sincerity in an eminent degree.'[23]

Justice, truth and sincerity – these were hardly qualities which Lord Hervey or Horace Walpole would discern, or on which they would set a high value; admirers of Frederick the Great or Napoleon might indeed deprecate them in a King. But most of George II's subjects liked him the better for being incapable of dissimulation. 'He was always what he appeared to be: he might offend, but he never deceived.'[24] This and his well-attested courage were his most obvious virtues, both as man and monarch.

His most obvious defect as King of England was his devotion to Hanover. But this, though sometimes unfortunate, could hardly be cited as a defect in character.

As a man his most obvious faults were his abominable temper, parsimony amounting sometimes to avarice, vanity and a somewhat unseemly sexual promiscuity. They hardly detracted from his performance as King. Much as he detested, say, Temple and Pitt, when it came to the point he was shrewd enough to distinguish between the one who was merely objectionable, and the one who, though objectionable, was nevertheless a great man. Much as he railed at Newcastle, he never underrated his importance. Of the many women in his life, only Caroline and Lady Yarmouth were allowed any political power, and both used it generally for the good. He was not a King ruled by favourites. His parsimony, like his lusts, might have made him ridiculous, but it is a far better quality in a King than extravagance.

He was a shrewd rather than a clever man, and his intellectual limitations, had he been a private man, would have stopped him short of the summit in any career. But within his somewhat limited interests, he was at least as knowledgeable as any of his Ministers.

The paradox of his reign is that his real virtue as a King was one which he would have derided and denied. He would have liked to go down to history not merely as the hero of Oudenarde and Dettingen, which he was, but as a King noted for firmness, of resistance to ignorant popular clamour, which he was not. Instead, he will go down to history as the first King of England who, schooled by Walpole, really understood the limitations on a constitutional monarch. He resented these limitations, he complained bitterly of being in toils, but he accepted them. He was a good judge of men: his favourite statesmen, Walpole and Carteret, were both very able men; but he realized that one could control the contumacious Commons and the other could not, and he treated them accordingly.

The legend that he took no interest in his adopted country and allowed the royal powers to lapse is devoid of foundation. He took an intense interest in politics, and used his constitutional powers to the full, though without overstretching them. If his reign had been one of failure, he would have been blamed, and rightly. But during his reign the nation was united as it had not been since the days of Elizabeth; the Union with Scotland was made a reality; the nation made spectacular gains in health, wealth and stability; liberty under the law and religious tolerance became well established; the dangerous predominance of France was ended; colonial territories of immense potential were acquired. Doubtless this was mainly the work of his Ministers, Walpole, the Pelhams and Pitt; but as he would have been blamed for failure, so he should not be denied some credit for success.

Let us leave the last word with two of his contemporaries, Elizabeth Montague and Lord Hardwicke: 'His character would not afford subject for epic poetry, but will look well in the sober page of history.'[25] 'He died in the height of his glory, loved, honoured and respected by all Europe.'[26]

REFERENCES

Details of printed sources where not given in the notes are supplied in the Bibliography which follows.

CHAPTER ONE (pp. 1–19)

1. Quoted by Wilkins, *Love of an Uncrowned Queen*, 59.
2. A. W. Ward, *The Electress Sophia and the Hanover Succession* (1903), 214–15.
3. *Ibid*, 239.
4. *Ibid*, 254–5.
5. *Ibid*, 512.
6. Walpole, *Memoirs*, iii, App. 313–15.
7. Wilkins, *Love of an Uncrowned Queen*, quoting proceedings of the Consistoral Court of Hanover, 28 Dec. 1694.
8. Walpole, *Letters*, i, 7.
9. *Ibid*, i, 8.
10. *Ibid*, i, 9.
11. Wilkins, *Caroline*, i, 59–61.
12. Cowper, 13.
13. Wortley Montagu, i, xcvii.
14. Michael, i, 6.
15. Chesterfield, *Miscellaneous Works* (1777), i, 59.
16. Chesterfield, *Characters* (1778), 4–7.
17. Wilkins, *Caroline*, i, 13–16, 41.
18. *Ibid*, i, 42, quoting Poley's despatches.
19. *Ibid*, i, 43.
20. *Ibid*, i, 44–51, quoting Elector's letter of 17 June 1705.
21. *Letters from Liselotte*, 121.
22. Michael, i, 86.
23. Wilkins, *Caroline*, 88–9.
24. *Ibid*, 90.

25. Yorke, *Hardwicke*, i, 179.
26. Young, *Poor Fred*, 7–11.
27. The account of the battle is compiled from Sir John Fortescue, *History of the British Army*, i (1899), 493–9, and W. S. Churchill, *Marlborough* (4 vols, 1933–8), ii, 356–80.
28. 'Jack Frenchman's Lamentation', included as attributed to Jonathan Swift in Swift's *Poems*, ed. Harold Williams (3 vols, 1937), iii, 1079 ff.
29. Hervey, 40–1.
30. Wilkins, *Caroline*, i, 93–7.

CHAPTER TWO (pp. 20–37)

1. *Works of Henry Fielding* (12 vols, 1903).
2. L'Abbé Jean Bernard Le Blanc, *Letters on the English and French Nations* (1747), 279.
3. G.M. Trevelyan, *England Under Queen Anne*, vol. iii, *The Peace* (1934), 317.
4. HMC, *Ancaster MSS*, 437.
5. Plumb, *Walpole*, i, 50–2.
6. Sidney and Beatrice Webb, *The History of Liquor Licensing* (1903), 17–18.
7. Michael, i, 8 ; Plumb, *Political Stability*, 71–4.
8. Michael, i, 8.
9. Plumb, *Political Stability*, 94–5.
10. *Ibid*, 153, quoting Shaftesbury MSS.
11. N. Tindal, *Mr Rapin's History of England* (21 vols, 1757–63, vols 14–21 being entitled *The Continuation of . . .*), xvii, 499, 543–61; J.Milner, *Journals of the Marches* (1723), 356; *Letters and Correspondence of Lord Bolingbroke* (4 vols, 1798) ii, 274, 320–1.
12. Trevelyan, *England under Queen Anne*, vol. iii, *The Peace*, 216–20, quoting French Foreign Office archives.
13. Michael, I, 8, 328; Wilkins, *Caroline*, i, 111–12, 117; Young, *Poor Fred*, 19.
14. Wilkins, *Caroline*, i, 117.
15. Ibid, 114–15.
16. *Ibid*, 119–21.
17. *Ibid*, 128.
18. Add. MSS 35837, f. 509 ; Coxe, *Walpole*, ii, 78.
19. Laprade, 160–1.
20. Wilkins, *Caroline*, i, 178.
21. *Ibid*, 132.

CHAPTER THREE (pp. 38–62)

1. Michael, i, 77.
2. Tindal, *Mr Rapin's History* . . . xviii, 312

3. Wortley Montagu, i, 12–13.

4. *Ibid*, xciv.

5. *Ibid*, 12–13.

6. Michael, i, 86.

7. Wilkins, *Caroline*, i, 151.

8. Cowper, 4–5, 7, 22.

9. *Ibid*, 11.

10. *Ibid*, 7 ; Michael, i, 91.

11. Michael, i, 91.

12. *Ibid*, i, 92.

13. Wortley Montagu, i, 92.

14. Berwick, *Memoires*, lxvii, 226.

15. Laprade, 166.

16. Plumb, *Political Stability*, 190–1, quoting Worsley MSS in Lincoln Record
    Office ; Sedgwick, *House of Commons, 1715–54*, 20.

17. HMC xv, pt. 2 ; Hodgkin 224.

18. HMC xv, 2; Hodgkin, 227 ; HMC, *Stuart Papers*, i, 343.

19. Sir Charles Petrie, *The Jacobite Movement* (Eyre & Spottiswoode, 1959),
    280.

20. HMC xv, pt 6, 14–15.

21. Wilkins, *Caroline*, i, 233.

22. Wilkins, *Caroline*, i, 229 ; *A True Account of the Proceedings at Perth,
    by a Rebel* (1716).

23. Berwick, *Memoires*, lxvi, 262 ; Wilkins, *Caroline*, i, 235.

24. Cowper, 61–2.

25. Wortley Montagu, i, 6–7.

26. Michael, i, 380. Wortley Montagu, i, xcv, 6–7.

27. Wilkins, *Caroline*, i, 207.

28. Walpole, *Reminiscences*, ed. Paget Toynbee (1924), 29–30.

29. Michael, i, 377.

30. Cowper, 10.

31. Ibid, 11.

32. Hervey, 488–9.

33. Michael, ii, 65.

34. Hervey, 261–2.

35. Alan Yorke-Lang, 'George II and Handel', *History Today*, October
    1951

36. Cowper, 46–7.

37. Michael, i, 376–9 ; Coxe, *Walpole*, ii, 205.

38. Cowper, 99–100.

39. *Ibid*, 99–100.

40. *Ibid*, 87, 78–9.

41. *Ibid*, 102.

42. *Ibid*, 68–9.

43. Plumb, *Political Stability*, 106, quoting unpublished passage from Lady Cowper's Diary.
44. Wilkins, *Caroline*, i, 166–7; Michael, i, 53.
45. Hervey, 40–1.
46. Suffolk, i, 56–8, 105.
47. Walpole, *Memoirs*, i, 170; Suffolk, i, 62.
48. Wilkins, *Caroline*, i, 168.
49. *Ibid*, 172–3.
50. *Letters from Liselotte*, 171–2.
51. Michael, i, 88.
52. Cowper, i, 21, 65.
53. Michael, i, 378.
54. Cowper, 79.
55. Plumb, *Political Stability*, 174.

CHAPTER FOUR (pp. 63–73)

1. Michael, i, 376–8.
2. *Ibid*, i, 107, iii, 559 *et seq.*; Plumb, *Political Stability*, 106, quoting unpublished passage from Lady Cowper's Diary.
3. Michael, i, 22; Plumb, *Walpole*, i, 225; Cowper, 108.
4. Cowper, 108–9.
5. Wilkins, *Caroline*, i, 262; Cowper, 108–9.
6. Wilkins, *Caroline*, i, 262; Michael, i, 223, ii, 24; Cowper, 111.
7. Cowper, 117; Michael, i, 222.
8. Wilkins, *Caroline*, i, 263; Cowper, 117.
9. Wilkins, *Caroline*, i, 255; Cowper, 114.
10. Cowper, 123–4.
11. Wilkins, *Caroline*, i, 262.
12. Plumb, *Walpole*, i, 228–9.
13. In general, for information on Robert Walpole, see Plumb, *Walpole*.
14. Hervey, 17.
15. Plumb, *Walpole*, i, 208–9.
16. Hervey, 80–1.
17. Wortley Montagu, i, cxiii.
18. Cowper, 114 and note.
19. Newman, *Stanhopes*, 60.
20. Ibid, 63.
21. Cowper, 124–5.
22. Plumb, *Walpole*, i, 237–8.
23. Stair, i, 42.

CHAPTER FIVE (pp. 74–96)

1. Cowper, 126–7.
2. Stair, ii, 25–6, 94; HMC xv, pt 6, 42, 21.

3. The account of this quarrel is compiled from: Cowper, 171; Michael, ii, 25–6, App. 310 ; Wilkins, *Caroline*, i, 276–81; HMC, *Stuart Papers*, v, 274–5; Hervey, 884; Newman, *Stanhopes*, 26; *Letters of Liselotet*, 191.

4. Hervey, 844.

5. HMC, *Stuart Papers*, v, 274, 337, 356, 158–9.

6. Marchmont, ii, 84. HMC, *Stuart Papers*, v, 277, 285, 381; Wilkins, *Caroline*, i, 287.

7. Michael, ii, 27–8.

8. Plumb, *Walpole*, i, 260; Wortley Montagu, i, 393–4, note.

9. Marchmont, ii, 409. Michael, ii, 28.

10. Wilkins, *Caroline*, i, 283 ; *Letters from Liselotte*, 193.

11. Wilkins, *Caroline*, i, 282.

12. Wilkins, *Caroline*, i, 311–12.

13. *Ibid*, 313–14.

14. Wortley Montagu, i, 311.

15. RA, Geo. Add. 28, 48.

16. Wilkins, *Caroline*, i, 290–1.

17. *Memoirs of Charles Mordaunt* (1853), ii, 209.

18. *Ibid*, 209.

19. RA Add. 28/52; Michael, ii, 284–6.

20. RA Add. 28/49.

21. *Ibid*, 28/53; Sedgwick, *The House of Commons, 1715–1754*, ii, 444.

22. Coxe, *Walpole*, ii, 12–13; Michael, ii, 278. Dr Richard Drögereit, 'The Testament of George I and the problem of personal union of England and Hanover', in *Research and Progress*, v, March/April, 1939, 83–6.

23. Hervey, 241.

24. Cowper, 134. Professor Plumb notes that 'lye with' in the original ms has been bowdlerized into 'intrigue with' in the printed edition.

25. Wilkins, *Caroline*, i, 322.

26. Cowper, 161.

27. Wilkins, *Caroline*, i, 335; Cowper, 136–7, 145.

28. Cowper, 129, 133–4, 145.

29. *Ibid*, 129–32.

30. *Ibid*, 131.

31. Wilkins, *Caroline*, ii, 5–6.

32. Cowper, 135–9.

33. *Ibid*, 137.

34. *Ibid*, 141–4.

35. *Ibid*, 145.

36. *Ibid*, 147–8.

37. Suffolk, i, 53–4.

38. Cowper, 146.

39. *Ibid*, 149–50.
40. *Ibid*, 158, 152.
41. *Ibid*, 124–5.
42. Hervey, 702.
43. Cowper, 139–40.

CHAPTER SIX (pp. 97–115)

1. Defoe, quoted by Laprade, 232.
2. Suffolk, i, 155.
3. Coxe, *Walpole*, ii, 2–3.
4. *Ibid*, ii, 7–11; Marshall, *Eighteenth-century England*, 118–21.
5. Coxe, *Walpole*, ii, 16.
6. Laprade, 237.
7. *Ibid*, 232.
8. Suffolk, i, 52; Cowper, 158.
9. RA, 52538, f. 40; Stair, ii, 151; Sedgwick, *The House of Commons, 1715–54*, i, 542.
10. Plumb, *Walpole*, i, 309.
11. Coxe, *Walpole*, ii, 18.
12. Isaac Kramnick, *Bolingbroke and his Circle* (Harvard University Press, 1968); Coxe, *Walpole*, ii, 18.
13. RA, 52838, f. 40.
14. Laprade, 236.
15. *Ibid*, 238.
16. HMC, xv, 6, 26–7.
17. Coxe, *Walpole*, ii, 22; Plumb, *Walpole*, i, 344, 353–4.
18. Coxe, *Walpole*, ii, 25.
19. *Ibid*, 27–8.
20. Plumb, *Walpole*, i, 339.
21. Lord John Campbell, *Lives of the Chancellors* (1845–69) iv, 428–9; Plumb, *Political Stability*, 190.
22. Edmund Burke, *Works and Correspondence* (1852), iii, 152–3. Williams, *The Whig Supremacy* (1962), 17.
23. Sedgwick, *House of Commons, 1715–54*, i, 64.
24. Sedgwick, *House of Commons*, i, 136–55.
25. *Ibid*, 20; Burke, *Correspondence*, ii, 166.
26. Plumb, *Political Stability*, p. 94; Namier, pp. 181–9.
27. Namier, 99.
28. Marshall, *Eighteenth-century England*, 57.
29. Plumb, *Walpole*, ii, 99–100.
30. Chesterfield, Letters, ed. Bonamy Debree, v, 2058; Sedgwick, *House of Commons, 1715–54*, i, 444.
31. *Ibid* i, 107, 34; Namier, 262; Add. MSS 38334, ff. 269–70.

32. Marshall, *Eighteenth-century England*, 52; Williams, *Whig Supremacy*, 81; Hervey, 499.

33. Egmont, i, 225.

34. Plumb, *Political Stability*, 178.

35. *Ibid*, 86, 96.

36. Sedgwick, *House of Commons*, i, 115-24.

CHAPTER SEVEN (pp. 116-128)

1. Sedgwick, *House of Commons*, i, 65.

2. Plumb, *Walpole*, ii, 44-5; Coxe, *Walpole*, ii.

3. Sedgwick, ii, 115.

4. Namier, 75-6; Bedford, xxvii; Walpole, *Memoirs*, ii, 184, 225.

5. Coxe, *Walpole*, ii, 106-8; Hervey, 86-8; *The Craftsman*, collected edition (1727 and 1731), ii, 33 *et seq*; iii, 69 *et seq*.

6. Suffolk, ii, 46-7; *Ibid*, ii, 49.

7. A. L. Newman, 'The political patronage of Frederick Lewis, Prince of Wales', *Historical Journal*, i, no. 1 (1958) 68 *et seq*.

8. Laprade, 248.

9. H. R. Fox-Bourne, *English Newspapers* (1887) i, 105-6.

10. Hervey, 29-30.

11. Chesterfield, *Miscellaneous Works*, (1778), iii, 194.

12. Suffolk, i, 175-6.

13. Wortley Montagu, i, 367-9.

14. RA 74057.

15. Wilkins, *Caroline*, i, 93.

16. RA Add. 28/2-18.

17. *Letters from Liselotte*, 240-1.

18. Sedgwick, *House of Commons*, ii, 53.

19. Wortley Montagu, i, 393-4.

20. *Ibid*, i, 135-6.

21. Wilkins, *Caroline*, i, 360; ii, 86.

22. *Ibid* i, 362.

CHAPTER EIGHT (pp. 129-148)

1. Coxe, *Walpole*, ii, 228; Hervey, p. 22.

2. Walpole, *Memoirs*, iii, App. 315.

3. Dr Richard Drögereit, 'The Testament of George II and the problem of the personal union of England and Hanover', in *Research and Progress*, v (March/April, 1939), 83-6; Lord John Campbell, *Lives of the Chancellors*, iv, 318.

4. Wilkins, *Caroline*, ii, 25; Glover, 55-6.

5. Add. MSS 32751 ff. 121-2.

6. Add. MSS 39751 ff. 24, 26.

7. Add. MSS 32750, f. 534: 32751 ff. 153–4, 185.
8. Egmont, i, 272, Drögereit, as n. 3 above.
9. Hervey, 23.
10. HMC xiv, pt 9, 5–6; Hervey, 25.
11. Hervey, 35–6.
12. Egmont, ii, 157; Wilkins, *Caroline*, ii, 12–13; Coxe, *Walpole*, ii, 290.
13. *Ibid*, 294, 372; Hervey, 39, 45, 36.
14. Wilkins, *Caroline*, ii, 20; *The Craftsman*, collected edition (1731) iii, 41 *et seq*, 51, 70, 187 *et seq*.
   Chesterfield, *Miscellaneous Works* (1777), i, 276.
15. Hervey, 44–5.
16. *Ibid*, 69.
17. *Ibid*.
18. Egmont, i, 41.
19. Wilkins, *Caroline*, ii, 29, 30, 37 and a letter of Lady Mary Wortley Montagu dated 11. 10. 1727.
20. HMC xv, 6, p. 52; Wilkins, *Caroline*, ii, 56–7, 61–2.
21. Hervey, 444.
22. *Ibid*, 221.
23. Wilkins, *Caroline*, ii, 84.
24. Hervey, 94–5.
25. Young, *Poor Fred*, 77; Egmont, iii, 327.
26. Walpole, *Memoirs*, i, 76; HMC xv, 6, 55; Hervey, 95, 50–1; Lyttelton, i, 49; Add MSS 37836, f. 97.
27. Hervey, 96–7.
28. HMC xv, 6, 55; Egmont,ii, 35.
29. Egmont, i, 92; ii, 35, 205; Hervey, 98.
30. Wilkins, *Caroline*, ii, 103; Egmont, i, 16.
31. Egmont, i, 127, 343, 176.
32. *Ibid*, 152–3, 356.
33. Wilkins, *Caroline*, ii, 123.
34. *Ibid*, ii, 131.
35. *Ibid*, ii, 126–8.
36. *Ibid*, ii, 121–2.
37. Hervey, 98–100.
38. *Ibid*, 83; Coxe, *Walpole*, ii, 390.
39. Hervey, 85–6.
40. Coxe, *Walpole*, ii, 384–5.
41. Hervey, 85–6; Coxe, *Walpole*, ii, 422–6.

CHAPTER NINE (pp. 149–158)

1. Hervey, 217.
2. *Ibid* 257; Egmont, i, 40–1.

3. HMC xv, 6, 79.

4. Egmont, i, 41; Hervey, 250–1.

5. Hervey, 501–2.

6. Egmont, i, 196–7, 228–9.

7. Wilkins, *Caroline*, ii, 109–10.

8. *Ibid*, 220–1; HMC, xv, 6, p. 81.

9. Egmont, i, 41, ii, 34.

10. *Ibid*, ii, 35.

11. Hervey, 67–8; Egmont, i, 41.

12. Hervey, 305, 261.

13. Hervey, 261–2.

14. *Ibid*, 488–9.

15. Egmont, i, 304; Hervey, 535.

16. *Ibid*, 449.

17. *Ibid*, 69; Wortley Montagu, ii, 71.

18. Hervey, 587–8.

19. Egmont, ii, 133–4.

20. Hervey, 93–4, 493–4.

21. *Ibid*, 105–6.

22. Laprade, 331.

CHAPTER TEN (pp. 159–180)

1. HMC xv, 76.

2. Egmont, i, 205, 216.

3. *Ibid*, i, 160.

4. *Ibid*, i, 207–8.

5. *Ibid*, i. 290, 390.

6. *Ibid*, i, 235–6, 264–5; Hervey xl, 290–1.

7. HMC xv, 6, 158.

8. Hervey, xlvi.

9. HMC, xv, 6, 158.

10. Egmont, i, 375, 42; HMC, xv, 6, 11–12.

11. Neville Williams, *Contraband Cargoes* (1954), 93 *et seq.*; Plumb, *Walpole*, i, 121; Marshall, *Eighteenth-century England*, 148–50; Williams *Whig Supremacy*, 189–91.

12. Hervey, 133.

13. Milton Percival, *Political Ballads* (1916), viii, 614.

14. Plumb, *Walpole*, ii, 252–3; Egmont, i, 357.

15. Plumb, *Walpole*, ii, 247–8; Hervey, 132, 153.

16. *Ibid*, p. 426, 387; Hervey 796.

17. Egmont, i, 357, 387.

18. Hervey, 140–1.

19. Young, *Poor Fred*, 65; Hervey, 224.

20. Add. MSS 32688 f. 113; Coxe, *Walpole*, i; Hervey, 162.

21. Sedgwick, *House of Commons, 1715–54*, i, 115–24; Add. MSS 32688 f. 420; Plumb, *Walpole*, ii, 314–16.
22. Young, *Poor Fred*, 58; Hervey, 273; Alan Yorke-Lang, 'George II and Handel', *History Today*, October 1951.
23. HMC, xv, 6, 143; Egmont, ii, 138; Wilkins, *Caroline*, ii, 275–6; Hervey, 501.
24. Hervey, 233, 206, 371.
25. *Ibid*, 277–8.
26. *Ibid*, 305–6.
27. *Ibid*, 554.
28. *Ibid*, 206–8.
29. *Ibid*, 234.
30. *Ibid*, 194–5, 231–2; Sundon, 288; Egmont, i, 427.
31. Hervey, 271–2.
32. Hervey, 280–1.
33. *Ibid*, 381–2; Walpole, *Memoirs*, i, 445.
34. Wilkins, *Caroline*, ii, 259–68; Hervey, 600.
35. Hervey, 388–9; Lyttelton, i, 51, 58, 77.
36. Hervey, 421.
37. *Ibid*, 340, 361; HMC, xv, 6, 139, 142 Lyttelton, i, 70; Egmont, ii, 429.
38. *Ibid*, 121; Hervey, 298–9, 474.
40. *Ibid*, 457–8; Walpole, *Memoirs*, i, 446.
41. Hervey, 484–6.
42. *Ibid*, 485–7.
43. *Ibid*, 480–7, 539.
44. *Ibid*, 497.
45. *Ibid*, 293.
46. Lyttelton, i, 52.
47. Hervey, 490–1.
48. Hervey, 492.
49. HMC xv, 6, 159; Hervey, 503–4.
50. Hervey, 506, 529.
51. Egmont, ii, 264; HMC, xv, 6, 170.
52. *The Gentleman's Magazine*, April 1736; Hervey, 459; HMC xv, 6, 167.
53. Hervey, 552–3.
54. *Ibid*, 553–4; Egmont, ii, 264–7; A. L. Newman, 'The political patronage of Frederick Louis, Prince of Wales', *Historical Journal*, i, no. 1 (1958), 70.
55. Lyttelton, i, 72.

CHAPTER ELEVEN (pp. 181–197)

1. Egmont, ii, 265.

2. Hervey, 560.

3. *Ibid*, 564–5.

4. *Ibid*, 597–9, 732 ; Egmont, ii, 307, 319.

5. *Ibid*, 604–5.

6. *Ibid*, 609–10.

7. Egmont, ii, 304–7, 325.

8. *Ibid*, 308–10, 302, 325.

9. *Ibid*, 302, 308.

10. *Ibid*, 321.

11. Hervey, xxxiii, 795–7 ; Egmont, ii, 436.

12. Egmont, ii, 177, 290 ; Hervey, 610 ; Walpole, *Memoirs*, i, 446.

13. Hervey, 614–18.

14. *Ibid*, 625–6.

15. *Ibid*, 628–9.

16. *Ibid*, 633.

17. *Ibid*, 637, 912 ; Add. MSS 32690 ff. 216, 218 ; Egmont, ii, 330.

18. Hervey, 638–9 ; HMC xv, 6, 176.

19. Egmont, ii, 325.

20. Hervey, 641.

21. *Ibid*, 646–50.

22. *Ibid*, 651–2.

23. *Ibid*, 656.

24. *Ibid*, 656–7, 372 ; Egmont ii, 336–9, 427.

25. Hervey, 658, 662–3, 670 ; Egmont, ii, 346.

26. Hervey, 671, 674–5 ; Yorke, *Hardwicke*, i, 371 ; Coxe, *Walpole*, ii, 342 ; Egmont, ii, 354 ; Lyttelton, i, 80.

27. Hervey, 677, 681.

28. *Ibid*, 692, 673 ; Egmont, ii, 353.

29. Hervey, 674–5.

30. *Ibid*, 744–7.

31. *Ibid*, 748.

32. Hervey, 749–52.

33. *Ibid*, 756.

34. *Ibid*, 757–8 ; *Reflexions on the Character, Life and Death of Frederick, Prince of Wales* (by Parson Etoffe [1862]), 14–17.

35. Hervey, 757 ; Egmont, ii, 425–6.

36. Young, *Poor Fred*, 114–15.

37. Marchmont, ii, 89 ; Egmont, ii, 426 ; Lyttelton, i, 82.

38. Hervey, 758–61.

39. *Ibid*, 762–3.

40. *Ibid*, 793.

41. Egmont, ii, 489 ; RA 54025 ; Hervey, 791.

42. *Ibid*, 802–7.

43. *Ibid*, 812–14.

44. RA 54026, 54043; Hervey, 814–15.
45. *Ibid*, 817, 820, 833–9; Egmont, ii, 432, 459–61.
46. Egmont, ii, 432–6.
47. Hervey, 843–4.
48. *Ibid*, 837.

CHAPTER TWELVE (pp. 198–203)

1. Hervey, 891, 877–80; Egmont, ii, 443; HMC, xv, 6, 6; Add. MSS
    32684, ff. 16, 18.
2. Hervey, 884–6, 888.
3. *Ibid*, 892; Egmont, ii, 443.
4. Hervey, 896.
5. *Ibid*, 897–9.
6. *Ibid*, 904–6.
7. *Ibid*, 906; Coxe, *Walpole*, ii, 382; Egmont, ii, 445–6.
8. Hervey, 907; Egmont, ii, 442.
9. Hervey, 910.
10. *Ibid*, 911.
11. *Ibid*, 913.
12. *Ibid*, 914; RA 52824.
13. Egmont, ii, 454, 462; HMC, xv, 6, 190–1; RA 52824; Hervey, 917;
    Wilkins, *Caroline*, ii, 365; Coxe, *Walpole*, ii, 389.
14. Hervey, 917; HMC xv, 6, 191.
15. Hervey, 919.
16. Marchmont, ii, 91–2; Lyttelton, i, 87–90; Egmont, ii, 459.
17. Egmont, ii, 471, 458, 503.
18. *Ibid*, ii, 459; Lyttelton, i, 103.

CHAPTER THIRTEEN (pp. 204–214)

1. Coxe, *Walpole*, i, 575.
2. Lyttelton, i, 107.
3. Rosebery, *Chatham*, 284.
4. *Parliamentary History*, x, 1291.
5. Add. MSS 32801, ff. 38–9, 67–9, 98–9, 117–27, 187, and 32692, ff. 75,
    79, 225, 226–7; Stair, 256.
6. Lyttelton, i, 133–4.
7. Rosebery, *Chatham*, 164–5.
8. Williams, *Whig Supremacy*, 213–22.
9. Stair, 201.
10. Lyttelton, i, 141.
11. Williams, *Whig Supremacy*, 234; Egmont, iii, 280.
12. Coxe, *Walpole*, i, 638.
13. Marchmont, i, 238.
14. Coxe, *Pelham Administration*, i, 19.

15. Egmont, iii, 238–40.
16. H. Walpole, *Letters*, i, 166–8; Egmont, ii, 240, 243.
17. Sedgwick, *House of Commons, 1715–54*, i, 484; Walpole, *Letters*, i, 171.
18. Williams, *Whig Supremacy*, p. 238; Marshall, *Eighteenth-century England*, 187–90; Rosebery, *Chatham*, 177–9, 189; Hervey, 946.
19. Egmont, iii, 254; Walpole, *Letters*, i, 180.
20. Egmont, iii, 257.
21. Walpole, *Memoirs*, i, 169–70.

CHAPTER FOURTEEEN (pp. 215–223)

1. H. Walpole, *Letters*, iii, 312.
2. H. Walpole, *Letters*, i, 239.
3. *Parliamentary History*, xii, 1033.
4. *Ibid*.
5. Fortescue, *History of the British Army*, ii, 86–7.
6. *Ibid*, ii, 88.
7. Add. MSS 32700, f. 154; Walpole, *Letters*, i, 288.
8. Add. MSS 32700, ff. 201–3.
9. The account of the battle is taken from Fortescue, *History of the British Army*, ii, 88–101; *Gentleman's Magazine*, xiii, 386–7; Mitchell, i, 122; HMC, *Frankland-Russell-Astley* MSS, 253–4, quoted in *English Historical Documents*, x, 853–4.
10. Wortley Montagu, 73.
11. Add. MSS 37000, f. 223.
12. *Ibid*, f. 245.
13. *Ibid*, ff. 246–9, 264; Lyttelton, i, 225.
14. Stair, 454–5; Egmont, ii, 274–5; Add. MSS 37000. ff. 264–6.
15. Pamphlet published London, 1743; BM 103 K 27.
16. *Ballads and Broadsides*, 1743, ii, 129.
17. Add. MSS 32701, ff. 5, 8.
18. RA 54120; Add. MSS 32700, f. 283.
19. Egmont, ii, 276; Walpole, *Letters*, i, 391.

CHAPTER FIFTEEN (pp. 224–239)

1. *Parliamentary History*, xiii, 136; Rosebery, *Chatham*, 222.
2. Marchmont, i, 76–7.
3. Coxe, *Pelham Administration*, i, 185; Marchmont, i, 77, 82; Bedford, xxxiv.
4. Williams, *Whig Supremacy*, 249–50; Coxe, *Pelham Administration*, i, 189.
5. Marchmont, i, 84.
6. Rosebery, *Chatham*, 240.
7. Rosebery, *Chatham*, 238–9; Coxe, *Pelham Administration*, i, 201.

8. *Ibid*, ff. 210–15.
9. *Ibid*, ff. 226–32.
10. *Ibid*, ff. 226–32.
11. *Ibid*, ff. 373–8.
12. *Ibid*, ff. 243–4.
13. *Ibid*, f. 239.
14. Add. MSS 32704, ff. 24–5.
15. Rosebery, *Chatham*, 241.
16. Add. MSS 32904, ff. 279–82.
17. Coxe, *Pelham Administration*, i, 259, 263; Walpole, *Memoirs*, i, 277; Marchmont, i, 98 *et seq.*; Walpole, *Letters*, ii, 130.
18. *Ibid*, 131.
19. Add. MSS 32705, ff. 137–42.
20. Coxe, *Pelham Administration*, i, 264–5; Walpole, *Letters*, ii, 130; Stair, 322; Marchmont, i, 99, 160–1.
21. Walpole, *Memoirs*, i, 72; Add. MSS 32766, ff. 17–20.
22. Walpole, *Letters*, ii, 160–1.
23. *Ibid*, p. 149; HMC x, 1, 287.
24. Add. MSS 32705, ff. 411, 483, 389; Marchmont, i, 160–5.
25. Walpole, *Letters*, ii, 155.
26. *Ibid*, ii, 153; Rosebery, *Chatham*, 246.
27. *Ibid*, 249; Coxe, *Pelham Administration*, i, 289–90, 292–5; Private Correspondence of Chesterfield and Newcastle, 1744–6, Edited by Sir R. Lodge (Royal Historical Society, 1930), 108–11.
28. Williams, *Whig Supremacy*, 259; Glover, 40; Coxe, *Pelham Administration*, i, 291.
29. Lyttelton, i, 252; Rosebery, *Chatham*, 254.
30. Add. MSS 32706, ff. 247–50, 221–4.
31. Coxe, *Pelham Administration*, i, 301.
32. Walpole, *Letters*, ii, p. 222; Marchmont, i, 194–7.
33. Walpole, *Letters*, ii, 217, 225.
34. *Ibid*, ii, 222, 232; Add. MSS 32707, f. 492.
35. Walpole, *Letters*, ii, 237–8.
36. Add. MSS 32708, f. 120.
37. Coxe, *Pelham Administration*, i, 355.

CHAPTER SIXTEEN (pp. 240–251)

1. Coxe, *Pelham Administration*, i, 284, 397–400; Add. MSS 32708, ff. 64, 278–9; Bedford, i, 336.
2. Walpole, *Memoirs*, i, 184–5; Coxe, *Pelham Administration*, i, 431, 454.
3. *Ibid*, ii, 313–14; Bedford, i, 484–5.
4. Coxe, *Pelham Administration*, ii, 310–11; Suffolk, ii, 251–2.
5. *Ibid*, ii, 214.
6. RA 54058, 54056; Bedford, i, 320–2, ii, 25; Lyttelton, ii, 425.

7. Young, *Poor Fred*, 172–5.
8. Dodington, 1, 4–6; HMC, xv, 20.
9. Dodington, 14–15.
10. Coxe, *Pelham Administration*, ii, 365, 371, 373; Hardwicke, ii, 87.
11. Walpole, *Memoirs*, i, 21.
12. Coxe, *Pelham Administration*, ii, 359.
13. Add. MSS 32722, ff. 157, 373–4; Coxe, *Pelham Administration*, 384–5.
14. Walpole, *Memoirs*, i, 71–2; Dodington, 96–7.
15. Coxe, *Pelham Administration*, ii, 165–6; Walpole, *Memoirs*, i, 83; Dodington, 102–4.
16. Lyttelton, i, 440.
17. Walpole, *Letters*, iii, 43; *Memoirs*, i, 79.
18. Sedgwick, *George III to Bute*, xx; Dodington, 100, 103, 111; Waldegrave, 22; Walpole, *Memoirs*, i, 38, 428–9.
19. Add. MSS 32860, f. 16.
20. Lyttelton, i, 442–3.
21. Walpole, *Memoirs*, i, 157–8.
22. Hervey, 227, 331; Walpole, *Memoirs*, i, 227–8.
23. Dodington, 168.
24. Dodington, 198; Williams, *Whig Supremacy*, p. 341.
25. Walpole, *Memoirs*, i, 378.

CHAPTER SEVENTEEN (pp. 252–261)

1. Walpole, *Memoirs*, i, 93; John Wilkes, *Letters*, i, Introduction, 57–62. *Grenville Papers*, ii, 219; Brougham, *Statesmen of George III* (1839–1843) 1st series, i, 24. Lord Edmond Fitzmaurice, *Life of Lord Shelburne* (1912) i, 77. *The North Briton*, No. 31.
2. Rosebery, *Chatham*, p. 316; Lyttelton, ii, 448; *Grenville Papers*, i, 110.
3. Lord Ilchester, *Henry Fox, 1st Lord Holland* (1920) i, 231; Hardwicke, ii, 71.
4. *Grenville Papers*, i, 113, 100; Rosebery, *Chatham*, 317–18, 321.
5. Lyttelton, ii, 449–52.
6. Lord Macaulay, *Critical and Historical Essays*, iii (1860) 532, 561–2.
7. *Grenville Papers*, i, 112–13.
8. Rosebery, *Chatham*, 325.
9. Hardwicke, ii, 206, 208, 211, 223; Walpole, *Letters*, iii, 219.
10. Ilchester, *Henry Fox*, i, 194; Rosebery, *Chatham*, 343.
11. Add. MSS 32734, f. 322.
12. Add. MSS 32735, f. 21; Yorke, *Hardwicke*, iii 8; Lyttleton, ii, 466, 472–3.
13. Walpole, *Memoirs*, i, 386–7.
14. Walpole, *Letters*, iii, 78; Bedford, ii, 231; Dodington, 290.
15. *Grenville Papers*, i, 309.
16. Yorke, *Hardwicke*, ii, 107, 70; Walpole, *Memoirs*, iii, 303.
17. Yorke, *Hardwicke*, ii, 116, 122–3.

18. Yorke, *Hardwicke*, ii, 285; Walpole, *Memoirs*, ii, 229.
19. Dodington, 317.
20. *Table Talk of Samuel Rogers*, 100; Charles Butler, *Reminiscences* (1822), ii, 144.
21. Walpole, *Letters*, iii, 268.
22. Walpole, *Memoirs*, i, 417.
23. *Ibid*, ii, 37–8; *Grenville Papers*, i, 142–3.

CHAPTER EIGHTEEN (pp. 262–274)

1. Walpole, *Memoirs*, ii, 20.
2. Dodington, 374.
3. Waldegrave, 29–31, 63.
4. *Ibid*, 38–9.
5. Walpole, *Memoirs*, ii, 204–5.
6. Waldegrave, 38.
7. *Chatham Correspondence*, i, 134; Sedgwick, *Letters*, xlvii, lvi.
8. Waldegrave, 39–41, 50–4; Rosebery, *Chatham*, 433–4, 424; Walpole, *Letters*, 425.
9. Walpole, *Memoirs*, ii, 194.
10. *Grenville Papers*, i, 163–5; *Chatham Correspondence*, i, 163.
11. Add. MSS 32868, ff. 120–3.
12. Waldegrave, 77, 79.
13. HMC xv, 6, 210.
14. Waldegrave, 4–7.
15. Chesterfield, *Characters* (1778), 4–7; Chesterfield, *Miscellaneous Works* (1777), i, 324; Glover, 84–5.
16. Add. MSS 32868, ff. 249–50; Walpole, *Memoirs*, ii, 256.
17. Add. MSS 32868, f. 251; Walpole, *Memoirs*, ii, 256.
18. Add. MSS 32868, ff. 286–7.
19. *Ibid*, f. 289.
20. *Ibid*, ff. 306–7.
21. Rosebery, *Chatham*, 454.
22. Glover, 94–5; Walpole, *Memoirs*, ii, 263–4; Add. MSS 32868, ff. 360, 380, 431, 480.
23. Walpole, *Memoirs*, ii, 256–9, 263; Rosebery, *Chatham*, 467; Walpole, *Letters*, iv, 8–9; Bedford, ii, 206–7.
24. Walpole, *Letters*, iv, 12–13; Glover, 108; *Grenville Papers*, i, 186; Add. MSS 32869, f. 49; Walpole, *Memoirs*, ii, 262; i, 381.

CHAPTER NINETEEN (pp. 275–287)

1. Walpole, *Letters*, iv, 9; *Memoirs*, ii, 248–9.
2. *Grenville Papers*, i, 186; Waldegrave, 89; Glover, 108; Brian Tunstall, *William Pitt, Earl of Chatham* (1938), 166–7,178–9.
3. Walpole, *Memoirs*, ii, 210, 311–12; Waldegrave, 91.

4. Augustus Hervey, 232–6; Bedford, ii, 229, 233; Lyttelton, ii, 288.

5. Augustus Hervey, 238; Waldegrave, 90–95; Bedford, ii, 239; Walpole, *Memoirs*, ii, 198, 331.

6. RA Add. 49/64.

7. Walpole, *Letters*, iv, 38–9; Augustus Hervey, 241; Walpole, *Memoirs*, ii, 369–70.

8. *Ibid*, ii, 273, iii, 5; Waldegrave, 95–6; HMC xv, 6, 37; Add. MSS 32870, ff. 264, 232, 287.

9. HMC xv, 6, 38; Walpole, *Memoirs*, iii, 5; Add. MSS 32870, ff. 376, 395.

10. Waldegrave, 99.

11. Walpole, *Memoirs*, iii, 30.

12. Waldegrave, 131.

13. Walpole, *Memoirs*, iii, 31; Add. MSS 32871, f 309.

14. *Grenville Papers*, i, 279; Walpole, *Memoirs*, iii, 31.

15. Add. MSS 32872, ff. 358, 492; 32873, ff. 305, 16, 19, 24.

16. RA Add. 54/16, 50/72, 50/73, 54/90, 54/20, 52/967, 54/317; RA 52967; Add. MSS 32872, ff. 445, 358.

17. Yorke, *Hardwicke*, ii, 389, 426–7.

18. Add. MSS 32872, ff. 426–7; 32873, f. 42; RA Add. 55/11.

19. RA 52970.

20. RA Add. 55/111, 55/114, 55/116, 55/176; Bedford, ii, 278.

21. Add. MSS 32874, ff. 195–7.

22. *Ibid*, f. 148; Yorke, *Hardwicke*, iii, 170.

23. Add. MSS 32874, f. 148.

24. Yorke, *Hardwicke*, iii, 186–7.

25. Mitchell, i, 145; Add.MSS 32876, f. 128; Walpole, *Memoirs*, iii, 60.

26. Add. MSS 32874, f. 418.

27. *Ibid*, f. 167; Add.MSS 32873, f. 323.

28. Walpole, *Memoirs*, iii, 61; RA Add. 57/19.

29. Walpole, *Memoirs*, iii, 61; RA Add. 57/19; Bedford, ii, 276–7; Add. MSS 32874, f. 151.

CHAPTER TWENTY (pp. 288–301)

1. Mitchell, i, 171.

2. Add. MSS 32889, f. 223.

3. Yorke, Hardwicke, iii, 39.

4. *Grenville Papers*, i, 291.

5. *Ibid*, 244; HMC xv, 6, 211.

6. Add. MSS 38880, f. 99.

7. Sedgwick, *George III to Bute*, 19; Yorke, *Hardwicke*, iii, 155.

8. Sedgwick, *Letters*, 17.

9. Add. MSS 32877, ff. 291, 310; Walpole, *Letters*, iv, 455; Augustus Hervey, 294.

10. F. Thackeray, *History of William Pitt*, i, (1777), 425.

11. *Chatham Correspondence*, ii, 5.
12. RA 15701–2.
13. Add. MSS 32893, f. 173; Sedgwick, *George III to Bute*, 27–8; Add. MSS 32893, f. 1173.
14. *Grenville Papers*, i, 267–8, 272–3.
15. Yorke, *Hardwicke*, iii, 60 *et seq.*
16. N. Wraxall, *Historical Memoirs*, 1884, i, 89; Yorke, *Hardwicke*, iii, 91.
17. Augustus Hervey, 308.
18. *Chatham Correspondence*, ii, 67.
19. *Ibid*, 47.
20. Sedgwick, *Letters*, 45.
21. Walpole, *Letters*, iv, 439.
22. *Ibid*, 440; Yorke, *Hardwicke*, iii, 156, 254.
23. *Parliamentary History*, xvi, 849.
24. HMC, *Charlemont*, i, 13.
25. *Correspondence of Mrs Elizabeth Montague*, ed. E. J. Climenson (2 vols, 1906) ii, 210.
26. Yorke, *Hardwicke*, iii, 156.

BIBLIOGRAPHY

MANUSCRIPT SOURCES

Documents in the Royal Archives at Windsor Castle [RA; RA Add.]
British Museum Additional Manuscripts [Add. MSS]

PRINTED SOURCES

Bedford	BEDFORD, John Russell, 4th DUKE OF. *Correspondence*, 3 vols, 1843.
Chatham Correspondence	CHATHAM, William Pitt, EARL OF. *Correspondence*, ed. W. S. Taylor and E. W. Pringle, 4 vols, 1830–40.
Chesterfield, *Characters*	CHESTERFIELD, Philip Dormer Stanhope, 3rd EARL. *Characters of Eminent Personages*, 1778. *Miscellaneous Works*, 3 vols, 1777.
Chesterfield, *Letters*	*Letters of Lord Chesterfield*, ed. Bonamy Dobree, 6 vols, 1932.
Coxe, *Walpole*	COXE, WILLIAM, Archdeacon. *Memoirs of Sir Robert Walpole*, 3 vols, 1816.
Coxe, *Pelham Administration*	*Memoirs of the Administration of . . . Henry Pelham*, 2 vols, 1829.
Craftsman	*The Craftsman*, Collected edition, 2 vols, 1731.
Cowper	COWPER, MARY, COUNTESS. *The Diary of Mary, Countess Cowper, 1714–20*, 1864.
Dodington	DODINGTON, GEORGE BUBB. *The Diary of the late George Bubb Dodington*, 1784.
Egmont	EGMONT, EARL OF. *Manuscripts of the Earl of Egmont*, 3 vols, Historical Manuscripts Commission (hereafter cited as HMC), 1920.

Letters from Liselotte	ELIZABETH CHARLOTTE, Princess Palatine and Duchess of Orleans, *Letters from Liselotte*, ed. Maria Kroll, 1970.
E.H.R.	*English Historical Review.*
Glover	GLOVER, RICHARD. *Memoirs of a Celebrated Literary Character*, 1813.
Grenville Papers	GRENVILLE, GEORGE, *The Grenville Papers*, ed. W. J. Smith, 1852.
Augustus Hervey	HERVEY, AUGUSTUS. *Augustus Hervey's Journal*, 1953.
Hervey	HERVEY, JOHN, Baron Hervey of Ickworth. *Some Materials towards Memoirs of the Reign of George II*, ed. Romney Sedgwick, 3 vols, 1931.
HMC	HISTORICAL MANUSCRIPTS COMMISSION. *Report of the Royal Commission on Historical Manuscripts.*
Laprade	LAPRADE, W. T. *Public Opinion and Politics in Eighteenth-century England*, 1936.
Lyttelton	LYTTELTON, GEORGE, 1st BARON LYTTELTON. *Memoirs and Correspondence of George, 1st Lord Lyttelton*, 2 vols, 1845.
Marchmont	MARCHMONT, EARLS OF. *A Selection from the Papers of the Earls of Marchmont*, 3 vols, 1831.
Marshall, *Eighteenth-century England*	MARSHALL, DOROTHY. *Eighteenth-century England*, 1962.
Michael	MICHAEL, WOLFGANG. *Beginnings of the Hanoverian Dynasty*, 1936.
Mitchell	MITCHELL, A. *Memoirs and Papers of Sir A. Mitchell*, 2 vols, 1850.
Namier	NAMIER, SIR LEWIS. *The Structure of Politics at the Accession of George III*, 1957.
Newman, *Stanhopes*	NEWMAN, AUBREY. *The Stanhopes of Chevening*, 1969.
Plumb, *Walpole*	PLUMB, J. H. *Sir Robert Walpole*, 2 vols, 1956, 1961.
Plumb, *Political Stability*	*The Growth of Political Stability in England, 1675–1725*, 1967.
Rosebery, *Chatham*	ROSEBERY, LORD. *Chatham, His Early Life and Connections*, 1910.
Sedgwick, *House of Commons*	SEDGWICK, ROMNEY. *The House of Commons, 1715–54*, 2 vols, 1970.
Sedgwick, *George III to Bute*	*Letters of George III to Lord Bute*, 1939.
Stair	STAIR, EARLS OF. *Annals of the 1st and 2nd Earls of Stair*, 2 vols, 1865.

Suffolk	SUFFOLK, COUNTESS OF. *Letters of Henrietta Howard, Countess of Suffolk*, 1824.
Walpole, *Letters*	WALPOLE, HORACE. *Letters of Horace Walpole*, ed. Mrs Paget Toynbee, 16 vols, 1903–5.
Walpole, *Memoirs*	*Memoirs of the Reign of George II*, ed. Lord Holland, 3 vols, 1947.
Walpole *Reminiscences*	*Reminiscences written by Mr Horace Walpole in 1788*, with notes by Paget Toynbee, 1924.
Waldegrave	WALDEGRAVE, LORD. *Lord Waldegrave's Memoirs from 1754 to 1758*, 1821.
Wilkins, *Caroline*	WILKINS, W. H. *Caroline the Illustrious*, 1901.
Wilkins, *Love of an Uncrowned Queen*	WILKINS, W. H. *The Love of an Uncrowned Queen*, 1901.
Williams, *Whig Supremacy*	WILLIAMS, BASIL. *The Whig Supremacy*, 1965.
Wortley Montagu	WORTLEY MONTAGU, LADY MARY. *The Letters and Works of Lady Mary Wortley Montagu*, 2 vols, 1887.
Yorke, *Hardwicke*	YORKE, P. C. *The Life and Correspondence of Philip Yorke, Lord Chancellor Hardwicke*, 2 vols, 1913.
Young, *Poor Fred*	YOUNG, SIR GEORGE. *Poor Fred, the People's Prince*, 1937.

INDEX